Strategic Fashion Manage

Strategic Fashion Management: Concepts, Models and Strategies for Competitive Advantage is a highly accessible book providing a unique look into the strategic drivers of the dynamic and ever-growing fashion industry. Derived from the knowledge gap in quality strategic fashion management literature, this book blends theory with a variety of examples and uses 18 case studies to help bring to life contemporary topics faced by senior executives.

The analysis is highly global in nature and aims to accelerate the strategic skills required to navigate the industry and contribute to a firm's growth. Using copious examples from across the world, this book provides in-depth discourse and progressive theoretical concepts and strategies which readers will be able to apply to their studies or practices.

The book is particularly suitable for final-year undergraduate and postgraduate students studying fashion management or marketing, as well as those on MBA and international business courses who wish to understand more about the fashion ecosystem. It is also designed to serve as an important reference for executives who are interested in conceptualising strategic issues that are pertinent to the industry.

Ranjit Thind has nearly 20 years' global experience in the fashion industry and has worked for a variety of iconic brands, such as Nike, Asprey and Ralph Lauren. He is an alumnus of the London College of Fashion, United Kingdom and Harvard Business School, United States.

Strategic Fashion Management
Concepts, Models and Strategies for Competitive Advantage

Ranjit Thind

LONDON AND NEW YORK

First published 2018
by Routledge
2 Park Square, Milton Park, Abingdon, Oxon OX14 4RN

and by Routledge
711 Third Avenue, New York, NY 10017

Routledge is an imprint of the Taylor & Francis Group, an informa business

© 2018 Ranjit Thind

The right of Ranjit Thind to be identified as author of this work has been asserted by him in accordance with sections 77 and 78 of the Copyright, Designs and Patents Act 1988.

All rights reserved. No part of this book may be reprinted or reproduced or utilised in any form or by any electronic, mechanical, or other means, now known or hereafter invented, including photocopying and recording, or in any information storage or retrieval system, without permission in writing from the publishers.

Trademark notice: Product or corporate names may be trademarks or registered trademarks, and are used only for identification and explanation without intent to infringe.

British Library Cataloguing-in-Publication Data
A catalogue record for this book is available from the British Library

Library of Congress Cataloging-in-Publication Data
Names: Thind, Ranjit, 1977– author.
Title: Strategic fashion management : concepts, models and strategies for competitive advantage / Ranjit Thind.
Description: Abingdon, Oxon ; New York, NY : Routledge, 2018. | Includes bibliographical references and index.
Identifiers: LCCN 2017014241 (print) | LCCN 2017030942 (ebook) | ISBN 9781315160344 (eBook) | ISBN 9781138064546 (hardback : alk. paper) | ISBN 9781138064553 (pbk. : alk. paper)
Subjects: LCSH: Fashion merchandising–Management. | Clothing trade–Management. | Strategic planning.
Classification: LCC HD9940.A2 (ebook) | LCC HD9940.A2 T45 2018 (print) | DDC 746.9/20684–dc23
LC record available at https://lccn.loc.gov/2017014241

ISBN: 978-1-138-06454-6 (hbk)
ISBN: 978-1-138-06455-3 (pbk)
ISBN: 978-1-315-16034-4 (ebk)

Typeset in Times New Roman
by Out of House Publishing

This book is dedicated to all those who have unconditionally shared their knowledge and experience with me

I am forever grateful

Contents

List of figures ix
List of tables x
List of case studies xi
Foreword xii
Acknowledgements xiii

Introduction: why did this book come about? 1

1 The business environment: industry dynamics and value drivers 4

2 Emerging markets: a new paradigm 19

3 Strategy: creating and capturing a competitive advantage 28

4 Creating winning business models: past, present and future 43

5 Brand management: leveraging the fundamentals 62

6 Innovation-driven growth: the formula for success 75

7 Mergers and acquisitions: deal strategy, execution and integration 90

8 Management and leadership: approaches, styles and activities 113

9	Culture and inclusion: capabilities, diversity and action	123
10	Work-life harmony: strategies for successful assimilation	139
11	The future of fashion: a new reality	148
	Index	164

Figures

1.1	The ELIPSE macro business environment	6
1.2	The global fashion industry 2012–2025	14
3.1	The value net	31
3.2	The Balanced Scorecard framework	38
4.1	Cost leadership and the Five Forces	49
4.2	The value linkage model	59
5.1	Brand purpose	64
5.2	The positioning statement	70
6.1	Innovation and value matrix	77
6.2	Rules of engagement for successful innovation	81
6.3	Managing innovation streams	85
6.4	Attribute mapping	87
7.1	The facilitation of mergers and acquisitions	92
7.2	Business process re-engineering levers	105
9.1	The cultural continuum	125
9.2	The global pay differential between men and women	135
11.1	Workplace skills for the future	156
11.2	The creative and design thinking process	158

Tables

2.1	Projected top 20 global economies	20
4.1	Taxonomy of business models	46
4.2	Social impact through shared value	54
4.3	The ephemeral firm	57
5.1	Social media developments in 2016	66
7.1	Acquisitions in the fashion industry by value	94
8.1	Taxonomy of leadership styles	118
8.2	Differences between competitive advantage and operational strategies	121
9.1	Models of colour on the front cover of American fashion magazines	129

Case studies

1.	W.L. Gore & Associates	40
2.	Rent The Runway	47
3.	TOMS	56
4.	Moynat	67
5.	Modanisa	71
6.	The Dandy Lab	76
7.	Adidas	80
8.	Coach	93
9.	Kate Spade	96
10.	LVMH versus Hermès	102
11.	Roberto Cavalli	107
12.	Zappos	115
13.	Nike	125
14.	Patagonia	136
15.	Lee Alexander McQueen	140
16.	Soma Analytics	146
17.	Sewbo	150
18.	Hearst Magazines and Blippar	155

Foreword

Strategic Fashion Management: Concepts, Models and Strategies for Competitive Advantage features a wide range of strategic theory and concepts, which are explained and applied to contemporary fashion cases and scenarios. In doing so, the book provides an excellent balance between academic concepts and industry insights. Many fashion business books concentrate on one at the expense of the other. However, in this text Ranjit Thind does both, having applied many years of international management experience to provide thoughtful analysis and practical direction for readers. It is ideal for final-year undergraduate and postgraduate students, together with anyone working in the fashion industry who wants an understanding of winning strategic thinking.

The business of fashion is at an inflection point as rapidly evolving technologies, geopolitical stresses and changing consumers are all disrupting traditional business models and adding great complexity to decision-making. Simultaneously, the Millennial generation is reshaping business practices through their attitudes, values and behaviours. Consequently, managers need to think in new ways and fully leverage the talent in their organisations to respond effectively. *Strategic Fashion Management: Concepts, Models and Strategies for Competitive Advantage* acknowledges these issues and addresses many of the contributing macro drivers, which are at the heart of the changes. There are new models and updated applications of existing concepts and frameworks that help the reader develop strategies to succeed in the modern fashion world. The book is a must-read for anyone studying or involved in the strategic management of fashion.

Tim Jackson
Fashion Writer and Programme Director,
MBA Luxury Brand Management
British School of Fashion
Glasgow Caledonian University, London

Acknowledgements

I am indebted to the following people and institutions who helped contribute to this book:

Amy Laurens
Editor, Routledge UK

Laura Hussey
Editorial Assistant, Routledge UK

Sanaul Mallick
Education Consultant

Tim Jackson
Course Director, MBA Luxury Management & MSc Luxury Marketing
Glasgow Caledonian University

Harvard Business School
Harvard University

London College of Fashion
University of the Arts, London

Introduction
Why did this book come about?

Many young people graduate from university with the aim of being in a management position or having some management dimension to their work. *Strategic Fashion Management: Concepts, Models and Strategies for Competitive Advantage* aims to accelerate the journey by covering 11 key perspectives that have never been captured before in a single text. Being active in the industry, the author focuses on key contemporary themes and thinking that is central to today's management agenda and that is often taught in a fragmented nature or not fully developed into teaching material. This book blends theoretical models and strategic frameworks with industry-specific examples and seeks to fill the void in the availability of quality strategic fashion management literature.

The content is highly global in nature and particularly suitable for final-year undergraduate and postgraduate students studying fashion marketing and management or those on MBA and international business courses who wish to understand more about the fashion ecosystem. It is also designed to serve as an important reference for executives and researchers who are interested in conceptualising strategic issues that are pertinent to the industry.

Chapter overview

Depending on your level of knowledge, each chapter can be read as a standalone body of work. However, because of the strategic nature of the subjects and their inter-relatedness, it is best each chapter is read sequentially. To help maximise the content of this book, each chapter contains the following:

Chapter goals

Each chapter begins with a set of goals. The aim is to help you understand what the section will cover and by the end of it, you should have a good grasp of the key points of discourse.

Key terms

Key terms have been highlighted in bold and will help you identify some of the terminologies commonly used in academia and in the workplace.

Review questions

At the end of each chapter are thought-provoking review questions which aim to build on the topic and stimulate a lively conversation for debate.

Further reading

A list of referenced work acts as a platform for further recommended reading should you wish to conduct your own research and delve deeper into the selected topics.

Case studies

Throughout the book, multiple case studies are embedded to support and amplify the various perspectives. These cases are a great way to understand how the various strategies, theories and frameworks are being deployed in the industry.

Chapter outlines

Chapter 1, 'The business environment: industry dynamics and value drivers', explains how the firm can utilise the ELIPSE framework to navigate the macro business environment and the forces that shape it. This chapter also covers some of the key drivers that form the engine of growth in the industry.

Chapter 2, 'Emerging markets: a new paradigm', discusses the rise of the BRIC countries and the next cluster of 11 emerging markets that are becoming globally competitive and their paths to advancement.

Chapter 3, 'Strategy: creating and capturing a competitive advantage', defines the role of strategy and explores several constructs on how the firm can create a continued competitive advantage.
   Case study: W.L. Gore & Associates

Chapter 4, 'Creating winning business models: past, present and future', examines the importance of the firm's business model and the underling architecture needed to create and maintain value through the value linkage model, plus it explores what types of business models may exist in the future.
   Case studies: Rent The Runway, TOMS

Introduction 3

Chapter 5, 'Brand management: leveraging the fundamentals', analyses the six key characteristics that define successful brands and under the lens of consumer-orientated marketing, how the firm can create a marketing strategy that delivers prolonged value.
Case studies: Moynat, Modanisa

Chapter 6, 'Innovation-driven growth: the formula for success', identifies the foundation for creating, capturing and sustaining innovation along with the principal rules of engagement for successful innovation.
Case studies: The Dandy Lab, Adidas

Chapter 7, 'Mergers and acquisitions: deal strategy, execution and integration', explains from a historical context the rise of mergers and acquisitions, the current forces driving it and the deal-making process from conducting due diligence to exit options.
Case studies: Coach, Kate Spade, LVMH versus Hermès, Roberto Cavalli

Chapter 8, 'Management and leadership: approaches, styles and activities', outlines how management is distinct from leadership, but why it is equally important. The role of senior leadership teams is covered along with an overview of the key topics that gravitate to the top of their agenda.
Case study: Zappos

Chapter 9, 'Culture and inclusion: capabilities, diversity and action', covers the different cultural contexts in which the firm operates in and the importance of culture in creating a competitive advantage. Diversity and inclusion is discussed with a focus on gaining an equal platform for women in the workplace.
Case studies: Nike, Patagonia

Chapter 10, 'Work-life harmony: strategies for successful assimilation', explores why work is important and discusses strategies to identify, integrate and maintain a healthy work-life balance in the fast-paced fashion industry.
Case studies: Lee Alexander McQueen, Soma Analytics

Chapter 11, 'The future of fashion: a new reality', presents a selection of key trends that are affecting the industry and have the potential to significantly change the way we work, live and interact. It also identifies four key skills that employees will need to be successful in tomorrow's workplace.
Case studies: Sewbo, Hearst Magazines and Blippar

1 The business environment
Industry dynamics and value drivers

> **Chapter goals**
>
> This chapter explains how the firm can utilise the ELIPSE framework to navigate the macro business environment and the forces that shape it. This chapter also covers some of the key drivers that form the engine of growth in the industry. The key areas covered are:
>
> - Contextualising the role of fashion
> - Introduction to the macro business environment
> - Industry value drivers

Contextualising the role of fashion

> Fashion must be amusing, modern and fun. (Yves Saint Laurent, fashion designer).[1]

Clothing is one of humanity's basic needs and its primary function has been to protect the body from the elements. As the centuries progressed, this rapidly evolved into material artefacts used to present human beings as clothed, adorned and gendered individuals. Accordingly, in the nineteenth century clothing took on a new meaning and through gender, appearance and the circumstances of different lifestyles and cultural influences, it symbolised membership to a certain stratum of society.[2] As this movement became ever more popular, the term **fashion** was embodied as a means of self-expression, emotion, identity and ethnicity. Deriving its origins from the Latin word 'fasoun', which translates as the 'physical make-up' of artefacts, and in French 'façon', which means 'appearance' and 'construction', fashion can be defined as a phenomenon that is identifiable by the wearer or viewer when being consumed. Consequently, fashion has become incredibly diverse and is a global industry which is influenced by the world around us. Trends often generated by celebrities, media, art, religion, culture and science have become the industry's currency and continue to nourish each other. The customary Spring-Summer (S/S) and Autumn-Winter (A/W) collections have been rethought to incorporate constant deliveries of 'seasonless' merchandise on a weekly and monthly basis. Coupled with the rise of fashion immediacy and the merging of men's and women's catwalk shows, a newly emerging fashion system continues to counterweight the traditional S/S and A/W platform and calendar. Subsequently, fashion requires constant reinvention through a restless rotation of patterns, colours, logos, fabrics, textures and shapes. This has led consumers to seek products, sometimes regardless of quality and price, that are cool, fresh and relevant, and those that match their own unique tastes and lifestyles. Because of this, firms endeavour to create trends that seize the moment, whether they are conspicuous in nature or obscure in sensibility. Therefore, to capture maximum value, the link with consumption has become strategic. The effects of these trends are further exacerbated as fashion never tires of being observed, scrutinised, exaggerated, applauded or abused. Attraction and repulsion. Passion and indifference. Sensual and abrasive. Expensive and cheap. Visible and discerning. Traditional and modern. These are just a few of the dichotomies that the world of fashion infuses into the everyday lives of consumers as the battle for the hearts, minds and wallets of shoppers intensifies.

According to the management consultancy McKinsey & Company, in 2014 100 billion items of clothing were manufactured for the first time, more than double what was produced in the year 2000. This equates to nearly 14 items for every person on earth, of which 60 per cent ended up in a landfill site within the same 12 months.[3] As a result, the fashion industry can be classified as a creative and high velocity environment where fashion is rapidly adopted, diffused and discarded. This causes ramifications in terms of supply and demand, and equates to the industry being characterised as highly resource-intensive, having short life cycles, high volatility and low predictability. The industry continues to be under pressure as increasing consumer choice diverts expenditure away from traditional fashion (clothing, footwear and accessories) to other consumer durables. Smartphones and leisure activities such as fine dining, adventure holidays and well-being, which fall under the rubric of 'experience', 'entertainment', 'indulgences' and 'self-discovery', are increasingly major threats to the industry. That said, in today's context fashion encompasses a wider sociological and cultural significance beyond the economic and technical relationship between producer and consumer. From trendy clothes, fast cars and chic hotels to luxurious travel, hip food and stylish technology, the term 'fashion' in its broadest sense touches everyone's life in some form or another. Subsequently, fashion has become a form of cultural entertainment, spectacle and even hysteria. Astute firms maintain the consumer's desire for more diverse experiences and immersive-based pursuits. Consequently, never before have we had more people interested in fashion and style than we do today.

6 *The business environment*

Introduction to the macro business environment

Though history can be a prologue to the future, its usefulness is becoming progressively limited as today's world is increasingly unpredictable and advancing at a faster rate than most firms can adapt. The oscillation of the **macro business environment** has increased in turbulence since the beginning of the Industrial Revolution and continues to disrupt markets. According to the 2017 Global Risks Report by the World Economic Forum (WEF), factors including governance failure, rising urbanisation and geographical mobility, a degrading environment, shifting consumer attitudes, and advances in science and technology are just some of the pressing forces that all firms must rapidly navigate to remain relevant, regardless of their size or stage of growth.[4] Keeping pace with these drivers ensures that the firm operates in a tumultuous and complex environment. This has led to increasing market rivalry as tectonic changes in products, processes and business technologies have an impact on the firm's costs, prices and profits. The general trend is towards dynamic, diverse, complex and hyper inter-connected environments. This is leading to virtually every firm having to come to terms with sharply changing market conditions, as their scope, structure and relationships are radically redefined.[5]

In a similar manner to checking a radar screen, firms that scan the business environment to detect patterns of change and form trend lines are better equipped to take action against the competition. Importantly, this aids executives in developing a capacity for systemic thinking so that they 'connect the dots' by separating the noise and everyday activities from the fundamental shifts that are taking place in the industry. Figure 1.1 depicts the **ELIPSE**

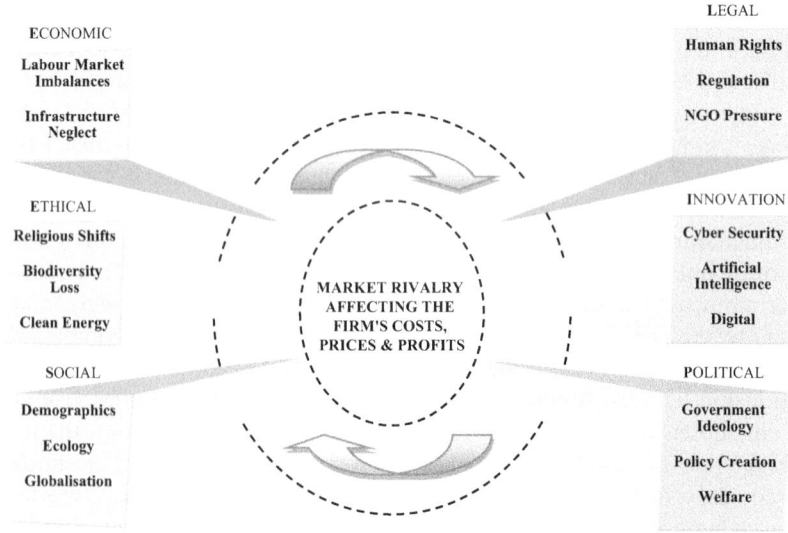

Figure 1.1 The ELIPSE macro business environment

framework and is a mnemonic to the changing reality of the business environment and the conditions that senior executives and stakeholders must understand and respond to in their formulation of strategic choices for the firm. This is a crucial skill for executives to develop, as being able to determine how quickly changes in the environment are going to impact and which movements require an immediate response versus those that require a less urgent response can mean the difference between survival and death. Subsequently, with the luxury of time, understanding the scope, significance and speed of these shifts can help executives prioritise the resource allocation process and become comfortable with these moves so that opportunities are not missed or the firm is not paralysed by inaction.

The **economic** environment has become ever more unpredictable. The early 1990s to mid-2000 saw a prolonged period of global economic growth with low inflation. Progress faltered with the start of the global financial crisis of 2007–2008, which originated as a credit risk problem, and low confidence led to the meltdown in the sub-prime mortgage market in the United States. This caused shockwaves throughout the world and was the tipping point for several trends that led to profound changes in both the competitive landscape and consumer behaviour. This crisis particularly affected international firms operating in multiple geographical locations and product categories, as executives faced a slowdown in cross-border capital flows, a sharp drop in consumer confidence and a decrease in national productivity. Disruption caused to global supply chains by a reduction in reliable suppliers, increases in raw material costs and changes in the price of borrowing, along with intense fluctuations in exchange rates, piled pressure on disposable income, sales and the cost of goods, which provided fresh discourse on the ability of firms to compete. Other macro economic challenges that further heighten the complexity of navigating the environment include volatility in energy prices, severe income disparity and infrastructural neglect. Therefore, the focus remains on economic stability and creating a sustainable growth platform to ensure that firms are not over-exposed.

Legal issues vary nationally and understanding this plays an integral part of a firm's forward-looking global strategy. This is because legal technicalities frequently gravitate to the top of the management agenda, but are often an afterthought and a costly response to structural change in the industry. Lobbying pressure from non-governmental organisations (NGOs) such the Fair Wear Foundation or the Better Cotton Initiative can also wield strong influence in shaping legislation and regulation. These responses affect the entire spectrum of the firm's operations, from functions such as production and marketing to sales and human resources. Prominent topics span regulatory issues such as taxation challenges in dealing with the digital economy as firms lobby for tax reform, false advertising and protecting intellectual property (IP) rights, and introducing new minimum wage levels. Other examples include how legislation can be used to combat parallel trade, including importing goods into free trade zones like those in Dubai and South Africa, and conducting due diligence on business partners and suppliers to increased compliance, such as the Sarbanes-Oxley Act of 2002, which stipulates expanded financial reporting and audit requirements to protect investors from the possibility of fraudulent accounting activities. Moreover, good progress has been made in countries such as Brazil and Chile, which have made major strides in reforming the law, although others such as Africa, Colombia and Russia still have a long way to go. However, legal issues usually take time to implement and because of the dynamic business environment, the employed reforms are often outdated and backward-looking.[6] Therefore, firms should ensure they not only stay close to changes in legislation but also help shape it through active participation with governments, NGOs and industry bodies.

Breakthroughs in **innovation** in terms of research and development have been profound and continue to influence the entire spectrum of a firm's operations and business strategy. Innovation in **Information Communications Technology (ICT)** has progressed rapidly since the primitive punched card system used in the early nineteenth century to control textile looms. Today, new technology and methodologies including nanotechnology, electronic wallets, stem-cell leather as produced by the biomimicry firm Modern Meadow and silk proteins from Bolt Threads continue to evolve the industry. The price to store, process, retrieve and distribute information has decreased dramatically and this has made ICT widely available to the masses. This has rendered existing tasks more efficient and is also revolutionising the way business is conducted. For example, mobile communications have moved on from the simple phone call or text message to touch-screen smart devices and using near-field communication (NFC) is capable of scanning a quick response (QR) code and instantly putting the consumer in touch with a firm's portfolio of products and services. Video messaging, voice and facial recognition, instant notification and the thousands of available apps has meant that ICT has further added another layer of interaction. Spurred on mainly by Generation Y, also known as Millennials (those aged approximately 18–34), and particularly Generation Z (those approximately aged 19 and under), social media platforms such as WeChat, Snapchat, Pinterest and Instagram have put the consumer in direct control 24/7 and with a global audience. As the digital consumer is ubiquitously connected, the traditional channels and methods of marketing communication are being transformed into a new paradigm of connected business and a proliferation of interested parties, each with its own set of opportunities and challenges. This implies that consumers are changing the value equation through the way they shop, how they are informed and how they seek to be entertained. A case in point: in 2012 there were 2.7 billion people connected to the Internet. By 2018, that number is expected to be 3.8 billion, a growth of nearly 40 per cent.[7] This has caused firms to drastically re-allocate their budgets and how much they spend across online marketing, like search advertising, which was barely invented 10 years ago, from traditional media such as print, radio or television.

With the rise in online inter-connectivity, masses of data is being generated, captured and analysed for business use, which is creating new methods of data analysis. The application of data to business management has moved firmly on from market research to data analytics and risk management as a more scientific dimension is being applied. For example, real-time dynamic pricing, where mathematical algorithms and predictive formulas rather than human beings turn large amounts of data sets into rules and decisions, is being conceived. Firms like Amazon with its millions of customers hold a deluge of 'big data' on the type of products viewed and bought. This can be analysed to inform factors such as the likelihood of purchasing, cross-selling opportunities, price sensitivity, communication preferences, behavioural changes and to assess customer lifetime value. Nonetheless, they are yet to fully extrapolate the power of this vast data to help them further analyse and predict future sales through, for example, personalised pricing. This is partially due to the legal framework, security issues and the cost of mining the data. Moreover, it is important to note that data is based and limited to the customers you have, but not to whom you do not have and is not a substitute for deep understanding, experience and intuition, which only humans can provide.

Political perspectives include keeping abreast of changes in government and public policy. This requires effective due diligence by firms at the local, regional and transnational levels. Geopolitical uncertainty has meant that the best firms regularly undertake risk management scenario planning (e.g. Identify, Manage, Accept, Debrief) to fully assess potential threats and consequences. Looking at the world, major shifts continue to occur. For example, China, a major global power, continues to reassert its dominance and has focused on strengthening its investment and trade with Africa. This has caused tensions with India's government as it tries to catch up in fostering closer ties with Africa and also with the United States, as they try to decipher Africa's foreign policy intentions. China is also taking provocative measures to assert its territorial claims in the East and South China Seas. By flexing its military power, it has heightened concerns about access to natural resources such as oil and gas and control over trade routes where trillions of dollars pass through. This has strained relationships with its neighbours like Japan, Vietnam and the Philippines, and has put regional powers such as India, Australia and the United States under intense political pressure to act. On a local level, the recent crackdown by Xi Jinping, China's President, on ostentatious gift-giving has weighed heavily on industry sales of menswear and particularly luxury goods as the artificial consumption by corrupt government officials and firms ceases. This is causing many international brands to reduce their operations or close their stores in the region. For instance, at the end of 2016 in Hong Kong, Prada closed its boutique, which has been a part of the Peninsula Hotel since 1986, and Ralph Lauren closed its 20,000-square foot store in Causeway Bay, whilst Burberry is to reduce the size of its flagship store in Pacific Place by 50 per cent in 2017.[8]

Like China, Russia with its unpredictable behaviour continues to defy international sanctions and insists on testing the international community with its own territorial ambitions such as in Ukraine and its continued support for Iraq in fighting Syria. In Europe, the United Kingdom is the second-largest economy by gross domestic product (GDP) and the most powerful in terms of military firepower.[9] Britain's exit or 'Brexit' from the European Union (EU) and its impact on the economy, its relationships and strategic decisions for firms and neighbouring governments is yet to be fully understood. This is causing many firms and employees to rethink their position if Britain is the right country for them to invest, live and work in as concerns regarding standard regulations, customs, trade and tariffs, talent retention and freedom of movement come to the fore. Another major theme is how to deal with governments enforcing restrictions on firms doing business with a repressive region such as North Korea or Zimbabwe and how to act on political pressure in response to controversial politician ideologies such as Donald Trump, America's forty-fifth President, whose disparaging comments on Mexican immigrants caused Macy's to drop his merchandise from its stores after carrying it exclusively for nearly 10 years.[10] More disturbing is that we are living in a world where social needs are going up and the ability of governments to meet them is coming down. Political turmoil through protests, strikes and negative media coverage can cripple a firm's business by halting production, such as in Cambodia, where demands for higher wages from factory workers are causing severe tension in the supply chain. This can lead to a wider supplier fallout and can cause a political headache for a nation which is a garment-intensive producer.

Other political factors range from matters including privatisation, money laundering and attracting foreign direct investment to the creation and relaxation of trade embargoes. Moreover, in mature markets like the United Kingdom, the industry has seen a drastic decline in domestic manufacturing and government lobbying has been high on the agenda to preserve dying skills through training and apprenticeships. As an illustration of this, the eponymous firms on Savile Row formed the Savile Row Bespoke Association in order to protect and promote the craft of bespoke tailoring.[11] Overall, it would be a mistake to think that managing geopolitical volatility is easy, as the really complex issues are not black or white, but grey. This requires corporate diplomacy, a thorough analysis on the impact of future investment decisions and a keen sense of how firms can protect their reputation whilst being resilient in the context of a transnational setting. This is because the firm's greatest partner can also very easily become its greatest competitor.

It is essential that executives understand the competitive consequences of **social** issues. One such force that has been a major factor is the rise and effect of globalisation. In December 1978 Deng Xiaoping, the communist leader of the People's Republic of China, reformed China's political, economic and social laws by abandoning many Marxist doctrines. Deng stressed individual responsibility in making economic decisions and material incentives as a reward for industry and initiative. He started by establishing free trade zones and easing restrictions on start-ups. Soon after, the 1980s became an inflection point and globalisation started to gain pace across the world through events such as the creation of the EU Single Market and the North American Free Trade Agreement. Similarly, at a press conference on Thursday 9th November 1989, the fall of the Berlin Wall commenced. This allowed East Germany officially known as the German Democratic Republic and a communist nation established by the Soviets at the end of the Second World War to embrace capitalism and join the Western world. In 1991 India embraced liberal economic reforms and ushered in an era of entrepreneurial freedom as set out by the Cambridge and Oxford University-educated Dr Manmohan Singh, then a little-known finance minister who would go on to become Prime Minister. In 1995 the World Trade Organization (WTO) was also formed to provide a framework for the rapidly expanding global trade system. These are just a few of the historical events that were a logical step towards liberalising world trade. The march of globalisation has been partially facilitated by a number of factors: for example, advancements in ICT, the rise of English as a global language, rapid improvements in infrastructure, liberalisation of trade and finance, plus the freer cross-border movement of people seeking better education and employment. Globalisation has reshaped supply chains and has created a huge increase in prosperity, especially in developing markets like China, which is often dubbed the 'workshop of the world'. Conversely, the efficiency of the open market economy can be a risky strategy, especially for export-orientated and inwards investment-dependent countries like China, where if the growth of its major trading partners like Japan or Germany slows down, it could face dire consequences. In the early days of globalisation, many firms thought they would be on to a winner with going global, but this is changing and the balance of power is shifting towards a trend of regionalism or 'guarded globalisation'.[12] Increased political hostility, enhanced regulatory frameworks and an uptake in defending nationalistic cultures is driving globalisation at a slower pace, and with this comes new costs and risks for the firm.

Other social factors high on the agenda include urbanisation, the expansion of education, democracy, ecological change, shifts in consumer demographics and lifestyles, and the eradication of social poverty. Even though basic education and literacy is on the rise, extreme poverty still exists. Unlike some players in the fast-moving consumer goods sector, the fashion industry is yet to develop products and services to serve the needs of the four billion consumers who live on less than $2.50 per day as part of the solution to extreme inequality. This has stirred up much debate on whether market-based solutions such as profiting from the poor are ethical.[13] Whether firms in the fashion industry will enter this domain remains to be seen, as the economics of doing business remains an ideological sphere for many. In particular, changing consumer behaviour and rethinking the way in which products are manufactured, delivered and marketed are major obstacles when serving those at the bottom of the pyramid. In parallel, social ambitions of this nature must be matched by a realistic assessment of the firm's capabilities and resources, along with the overall profitability of the venture to ensure its long-term success. Spill-over effects of this type of venture include uncovering opportunities for innovation in new markets, increased employee motivation and enhanced firm reputation, which can lead to increased demand for a firm's products and services.

Strangely, as firms begin to act more **ethically**, the more they get blamed for society's failure. Cynical consumers and press distortion have allowed firms to be seen as a major cause of social, environmental and economic problems. Firms are widely perceived to pursue profit making at the expense of the environment and their community. This has resulted in many firms being caught in a vicious circle that undermines competitiveness and economic growth, at a time when consumers are becoming increasingly interested and knowledgeable in the backstory of how a firm's products are manufactured. Currently, two main approaches have been adopted by the industry. First, philanthropy activities such as those of Tod's, the luxury leather goods manufacturer, which contributed €25 million to help restore Rome's Colosseum in Italy, can be considered as a noble effort to protect a key heritage site.[14] However, these donations are more of a personal gesture of goodwill and are aimed at building a legacy rather than creating true long-term value. Second, in the 1990s and 2000s, issues surrounding corporate ethics were often bought to the attention of senior management by consumers and NGOs such as People for the Ethical Treatment of Animals (PETA). Firms aimed to be good corporate citizens by launching sustainability and compliance initiatives in order to ultimately improve their reputation in the community and to mitigate risk and harm. This enabled the perceived creation of utopia by putting the fragmented needs of firms, customers and society into a united group. Termed corporate social responsibility (CSR), prominent topics that executives face include conserving resources and a commitment to procuring a stable and sustainable source of supply. In particular, as in today's low-price and fast-fashion culture, the supply chain is facing heavy cost pressures and is even becoming unsustainable and unprofitable for some.[15] Furthermore, a transparent environmental footprint and protecting animal rights as advocated by the luxury conglomerate Kering, whose brands include Alexander McQueen and Christopher Kane, has become increasingly important to consumers who want to know the origin and processes used to make their products. For example, Kering-owned Stella McCartney has made an exemplary commitment to sustainability by using materials such as eco-friendly Viscose, regenerated cashmere, organic cotton and low-impact dyes, and shuns the use of leather and fur. Instead, the firm produces shoes and bags from bio-plastic coated in a vegetable oil derivative. Additionally, in 2014 Levi Strauss & Co launched its lower-cost working capital scheme to 550 suppliers that met its environmental, labour and safety standards. In conjunction with the International Finance Corporation, the private arm of the World Bank, suppliers who improve their measures on a sliding scale are rewarded with lower interest rates on working capital.[16] For some firms during the economic downturn, acting ethically slipped down the corporate agenda as they focused on survival rather than costly environmental and social schemes, some of which could be seen as purely marketing projects. Unfortunately, the good intentions of many firms still leaves them exposed to the scrutiny of the media, as was experienced by Ralph Lauren. As outfitter of the national team for the 2012 London Olympics, there was strong criticism by American politicians who felt that as a key sponsor, the apparel worn by the athletes should be manufactured in the United States rather than in China. This was an issue which exposed holes in the firm's CSR strategy and forced it to later publicly announce that all apparel for future Olympic events would be domestically produced.

Overall, philanthropy and CSR has clearly gained momentum as more than 70 per cent of the world's 500 largest firms by market value now report information on their environmental impact and advocate working ethically.[17] This commitment is also reflected through the publication of voluntary citizenship reports by firms such as Yoox, Gap and PVH. Likewise, launched in 1999, the Dow Jones Sustainability Index evaluates the sustainability performance for investors by benchmarking and tracking the stock performance of the world's leading firms in terms of long-term economic, environmental and social criteria by assessing issues like corporate governance, risk management, branding, climate change mitigation, supply chain standards and labour practices.

Ultimately, when analysing the ELIPSE framework, it is important to note that the intensity of these industry dynamics will change over time and that they are not mutually exclusive, but inter-related and help set the strategic framework and context in which the firm will operate and compete. As the tension of some of these forces shifts much quicker than others, managing the future of the firm will require executives to plot an agile course of action as increased market rivalry and the need to remain competitive rise to the top of the corporate agenda. This is further augmented by the presence of chance factors, including natural disasters, outbreaks of a human pandemic disease and tier-1 threats, such as terrorism and cyber-crime, which have become ever more prevalent. The end result for the firm is to mitigate a fragmented supply base and to find sustainable growth in the global business environment. This is causing 'business as usual' to become a rapidly moving target.

Industry value drivers

The fashion industry as an entity remains hugely important and is one of the largest and most value-creating industries in the world. As the fashion sector is present in almost every country across the globe, it contributes a significant amount to growth, provides crucial employment opportunities and is the largest employer of all the creative industries, particularly the retail

14 *The business environment*

sector.[18] Tracking the industry remains largely fragmented as much of the data is not reported systematically across product categories, operating models or regions, and tends to centre on the more quantifiable textile-garment sector. According to Key Note the market intelligence agency, the global clothing market grew by 8.4 per cent from 2008 to 2012 and sales were estimated to be worth £835 billion at retail value in 2012. Europe is regarded as having the most economic weight in terms of sales and constitutes 37.7 per cent of the total global market. Nevertheless, as a mature market, Europe has only grown 5 per cent from £300 billion in 2008 to £315 billion in 2012. The United States is the second-largest market at 22.2 per cent and grew 9.5 per cent from £169 billion in 2008 to £185 billion in 2012. The rest of the world and other developed countries amount to 40.1 per cent of the market or £335 billion in 2012, compared to £301 billion in 2008. Importantly, developing countries contributed growth of 11.3 per cent over the period and are expected to drive future growth, particularly in China and India.[19] This is partly due to a large, young and aspirational population and the increased investment in economic development that is helping to fuel the vast buying potential of these countries. Statista provides an alternative view on the size of the industry from 2012 to 2025. As shown in Figure 1.2, the total value of the industry is forecasted to go from $1,105 trillion in 2012 to $2,110 trillion in 2025. Europe will go from $350 billion in 2012 to $440 billion in 2025 and the United States from $225 to $285 billion. China is targeted to grow $390 billion from $150 billion in 2012 to $540 billion in 2025 and overtake Europe to become the largest market. India will overtake Japan to become the fourth-largest market in 2025 and will be worth $200 billion, compared to $45 billion in 2012.[20]

However, whilst the industry is growing, there are many opportunities and challenges. When examining factor inputs such as land, capital, information, labour and entrepreneurship, the latter two can be considered as the main focus. **Productivity** is probably the most important measure of economic health. It centres on the amount a worker produces per hour and is the fundamental determinant of people's standard of living. A decline in productivity

Figure 1.2 The global fashion industry 2012–2025
Source: adapted from Statista (2017).

for many countries is due to a shortage of technical and managerial skills and insufficient employee engagement because of a lack of training and education. In addition, inadequate funding and over-complicated regulatory measures have stifled the development and growth of many small and medium-sized enterprises (SMEs). This has forced firms to seek alternative strategies and business models as the classic mechanisms from the industrial era have become superfluous. For example, many firms have turned to offshoring to remain competitive as domestic costs rise. This is because many countries are considered to have a wage disadvantage against many other competing countries. For instance, in 2014 the average monthly minimum wage for a clothing factory worker in Cambodia was approximately $100 compared to $800 in Hong Kong and $300 in Morocco.[21] This is extremely influential as productivity is both the engine of economic growth and national competitiveness. Second, low barriers to entry have made the industry more attractive and consequently demand for products and services is intense. A proliferation into new territories by overseas retailers such as Uniqlo and Forever 21 has increased choice and rivalry. This has been aggravated by increasing presence from non-traditional players such as supermarkets, discounters and duty-free outlets. Third, successful **entrepreneurial activities** have been deficient as few names come to mind when thinking of successful entrepreneurs. This can be attributed to both the lack of entrepreneurial spirit and a low risk-taking culture in many countries. This is due to the sector being unattractive in terms of being historically low in profitability and having been held back by the lack of capital expenditure required to remain competitive.

Many countries have tried to leverage their strengths to forge a **comparative advantage**, such as Germany, which is seen as efficient and technically excellent, Italy, which is regarded as the home of superb designers, and Japan, which is seen as containing prolific innovators. Still, the industry continues to struggle in terms of attracting and retaining domestic design and management talent as many are lured to work abroad by the leading design houses. The long-term future of the industry is also threatened by other industries such as aeronautics, hi-tech goods and digital services, which are taking priority for many governments. With this in mind, the industry has reacted by searching for new value-laden opportunities such as producing products like industrial apparel, medical textiles and protective clothing. In addition, marketing measures such as labels stating 'Made in England' or 'Made in Italy' remains an integral and unique selling point for many firms. This is because it offers a perceived higher value in the eyes of consumers such as the Chinese and Japanese, who often make up a large proportion of the client base and appreciate the creative and cultural heritage associated with these products. An example of the 'Made in Italy' strategy is the Brioni factory in Penne in the mid-southern region of Abruzzo. Using the finest fabrics, apprentices spend 38 hours a week learning how to hand-make a suit that requires 220 steps, between 5,000 and 7,000 stiches and more than 22 hours of effective workmanship. Each item is created by workers who have trained for four years in Brioni's own tailoring school and provides the firm with the expertise it requires.[22]

What seemed like an unlikely topic of conversation a few years ago has become an unexpected turnaround for the industry as many firms are **nearshoring** their production activities. For example, in the United States firms such as Walmart, Rag & Bone and Brooks Brothers are investing more of their production in this direction and support the 'Made in America' (MIA) campaign. The MIA renaissance has become a prominent factor in places such as San Francisco, where in the 1970s more than 1,000 factories contracted for firms like Gap and Esprit. In fact, until the 1960s, the United States manufactured 95 per cent of its own clothing, but this dropped to 75 per cent in the 1970s. In the 1980s and 1990s cheaper labour costs, lax labour laws and free trade agreements made outsourcing to countries like Bangladesh and China attractive. Consequently, an outflow of orders occurred, which led to the drastic demise of domestic manufacturing – so much so that in 2012, only 2.5 per cent of apparel was produced in the United States and 97.5 per cent was outsourced abroad.[23] Today, headwinds for factories in Asia such as rising labour and transportation costs, increasing rents, insecure supply chains, untimely shipments and extensive amounts of time spent on communication have meant that firms are looking beyond the cost price and margin targets, and instead at the total value equation. This has meant an increase in domestic manufacturing, and today in San Francisco operators focus on high-end pieces in small batches for local brands. Many workers are paid hourly rather than per piece, which encourages a more detailed level of output and better quality. Furthermore, producing and buying domestically has spread to other places, such as the East Coast, where Cone Denim, the oldest mill in the United States, has installed additional American Draper X3 looms to meet demand and boost output by 25 per cent.[24] Additionally, in 2013 under Barack Obama, the former presidential administration launched the 'Select USA' initiative to further highlight the benefits of investing in MIA. Yet, in the short to medium term, many firms realise that as the manufacturing process has become increasingly automated, the heart of the MIA comeback has centred on manufacturing that leverages technology such as yarn spinning and knitting rather than the labour-intensive operations of weaving and cut-and-sew. Despite this resurgence, multiple challenges remain, including chronic shortages in finding a skilled and affordable workforce to operate and service the machinery. In addition, long lead times for machinery components and high duties on imported fabrics along with high business rates pose a substantial barrier for domestic manufacturing, especially those operating in the mainstream fashion market. This leads to the central question of whether it is less about 'made in' and more about 'made how', and whether this resurgence in nearshoring will move the consumers' willingness to pay or force firms to take a margin hit as a part of the wider brand and sustainability agenda.[25] In sum, the growth of the industry will be propelled by the key value drivers of enhanced productivity, the nurturing of entrepreneurial activities and those firms that can leverage the supply chain to gain a competitive advantage.

Review questions

Questions for debate regarding navigating the dynamics of the fashion industry and its value drivers are as follows:

- Using the ELIPSE framework, which forces do you think are the most and least important?
- How can industry leaders come together to influence government policy?
- What can the industry do to create more entrepreneurs?
- What advantage does your country have that can help its fashion industry grow?
- How will the globalisation of labour markets affect a firm's labour strategy?
- What products do you think can be reshored to be manufactured in your country?

Further reading

1 Koski, L. (2014) 'Words and Meaning: Quotes on Modernism', *WWD*, 14 April.
2 Veblen, T. (1994) *The Theory of the Leisure Class: An Economic Study in the Evolution of Institutions*. New York: Penguin Books.
3 Remy, N., Speelman, E. and Swartz, S. (2016) 'Style That's Sustainable: A New Fast-Fashion Formula', McKinsey & Company, www.mckinsey.com/business-functions/sustainability-and-resource-productivity/our-insights/style-thats-sustainable-a-new-fast-fashion-formula?cid=sustainability-eml-alt-mip-mck-oth-1610 (accessed 4 May 2017).
4 World Economic Forum. (2017) *The Global Risks Report 2017*, 12th edn. Geneva: World Economic Forum.
5 Mallick, S. and Thind, R. (2002) 'Dynamics of ICT-Based Supply Chain', International Foundation of Fashion Technology Institutes Conference, Hong Kong Polytechnic University.
6 World Bank (2016) 'Doing Business: Measuring Business Regulations', www.doingbusiness.org/rankings (accessed 4 May 2017).
7 Facebook (2016) 'Going Global with Facebook', www.facebook.com/business/a/going-global (accessed 4 May 2017).
8 Sun, N. (2016) 'Prada to Close Boutique at Peninsula Hotel as Hong Kong's Retail Slump Bites', www.scmp.com/news/hong-kong/economy/article/2054569/prada-close-boutique-peninsula-hotel-hong-kongs-retail-slump (accessed 4 May 2017).
9 World Bank (2016) 'Gross Domestic Product 2015', http://databank.worldbank.org/data/download/GDP.pdf (accessed 4 May 2017).
Allison, G. (2016) 'Study Finds UK is Second Most Powerful Country in the World', *UK Defence Journal*, https://ukdefencejournal.org.uk/study-finds-uk-is-second-most-powerful-country-in-the-world (accessed 4 May 2017).

10 Lee, M.J. (2015) 'First on CNN: Macy's Dumps Donald Trump', *CNN*, http://edition.cnn.com/2015/07/01/politics/donald-trump-macys/index.html (accessed 4 May 2017).
11 Savile Row Bespoke Association (2016) 'Savile Row Bespoke Championing Half a Century of Sartorial Excellence', www.savilerowbespoke.com/about-us (accessed 4 May 2017).
12 Bremmer, I. (2012) *Every Nation for Itself: Winners and Losers in a G-Zero World*. London: Portfolio Penguin.
13 Prahalad, C.K. (2005) *The Fortune at the Bottom of the Pyramid*. Upper Saddle River, NJ: Prentice Hall.
14 Tod's Group (2016) 'Collaboration Agreements', www.todsgroup.com/en/sostenibilita/partnerships (accessed 4 May 2017).
15 Hines, A. (2013) *Supply Chain Strategies: Demand Driven and Customer Focused*, 2nd edn. New York: Routledge.
16 Mirmotahari, F. (2014) 'Shared Prosperity: IFC and LS&Co. Team up to Reward Suppliers for Doing the Right Thing', http://levistrauss.com/unzipped-blog/tag/global-trade-supplier-finance-program (accessed 4 May 2017).
17 CDP (2014) 'CDP S&P 500 Climate Change Report 2014', www.cdp.net/CDPResults/CDP-SP500-leaders-report-2014.pdf (accessed 4 May 2017).
18 Amed, I., Berg, A., Brantberg, L. and Hedrich, S. (2016) 'The State of Fashion', McKinsey & Company, www.mckinsey.com/industries/retail/our-insights/the-state-of-fashion (accessed 4 May 2017).
19 Key Note (2013) *Clothing Retailing Market Report 2013*, 10th edn. London: Key Note.
20 Statista (2017) 'Global Apparel Market Size Projections from 2012 to 2025', www.statista.com/statistics/279757/apparel-market-size-projections-by-region (accessed 4 May 2017).
21 International Labour Organization (2015) 'Global Dialogue Forum on Wages and Working Hours in the Textiles, Clothing, Leather and Footwear Industries', www.ilo.org/gb/GBSessions/GB322/pol/WCMS_345739/lang–en/index.htm (accessed 4 May 2017).
22 Ilari, A. (2012) 'Made in Italy Tag Lures Emerging-Market Consumers', *Financial Times*, 20 September.
23 American Apparel & Footwear Association (2014) 'We Wear the Facts', www.wewear.org/thefacts (accessed 4 May 2017).
24 Pavarini, M.C. (2013) 'Cone Denim Expands Selvage Denim Capacity', *Sportswear International*, www.conedenim.com/press_files/SI072613.pdf (accessed 4 May 2017).
25 Smil, V. (2013) *Made in the USA: The Rise and Retreat of American Manufacturing*. Cambridge, MA: MIT Press.

2 Emerging markets
A new paradigm

Chapter goals

This chapter discusses the rise of the BRIC countries and the next cluster of emerging markets that are becoming globally competitive and their paths to advancement. The key areas covered are:

- BRIC: historical challenges and future growth strategies
- Beyond BRIC: the new world

BRIC: historical challenges and future growth strategies

According to the professional services firm PwC (PricewaterhouseCoopers), the world's economy will double in size by 2042, with an average growth rate of just over 2.6 per cent per year between 2016 and 2050. Brazil, China, India, Indonesia, Mexico, Russia and Turkey are poised to grow at an annual average rate of approximately 3.5 per cent compared to 1.6 per cent a year for Canada, France, Germany, Italy, Japan, the United Kingdom and the United States. In 2016 China overtook the United States to become the world's largest economy based on GDP in purchasing power parity terms (PPP), a title the United States has held since the late nineteenth century. As shown in Table 2.1, India is destined to move from third place in 2016 and become the second-largest economy by 2050, followed by the United States, Indonesia, Brazil and Russia. Emerging markets like Mexico are forecasted to become larger than Japan, Germany, the United Kingdom and France, whilst Turkey, Nigeria and Egypt are projected to become bigger than Italy, Spain and Canada in 2050.[1] However, without a strong recovery in America or Japan or an uptake in Europe (especially in Germany), the global economy is unlikely to grow any faster. It is therefore foreseeable that executives will continue to see a two-speed global economy for some years, especially as in the past, the boom in newly industrialising markets has tended to be followed by busts, which explain why so few poor countries have become developed nations.

20 *Emerging markets*

Table 2.1 Projected top 20 global economies

GDP PPP rank	Country	2016 (Est) US$ billions	Country	2050 (proj.) US$ billions
1	China	21,269	China	58,499
2	United States	18,562	India	44,128
3	India	8,721	United States	34,102
4	Japan	4,932	Indonesia	10,502
5	Germany	3,979	Brazil	7,540
6	Russia	3,745	Russia	7,131
7	Brazil	3,135	Mexico	6,863
8	Indonesia	3,028	Japan	6,779
9	United Kingdom	2,788	Germany	6,138
10	France	2,737	United Kingdom	5,369
11	Mexico	2,307	Turkey	5,184
12	Italy	2,221	France	4,705
13	South Korea	1,929	Saudi Arabia	4,694
14	Turkey	1,906	Nigeria	4,348
15	Saudi Arabia	1,731	Egypt	4,333
16	Spain	1,690	Pakistan	4,236
17	Canada	1,674	Iran	3,900
18	Iran	1,459	South Korea	3,539
19	Australia	1,189	Philippines	3,334
20	Thailand	1,161	Vietnam	3,176

Source: adapted from Audino and Hawksworth (2017).

The term **BRIC** was coined in 2001 by economist Jim O'Neill of Goldman Sachs. His report entitled 'Global Economics Paper No. 66: Building Better Global Economic BRICs' described the contrasting and rapidly emerging economies of Brazil, Russia, India and China. This 16-page report forced executives to rethink their manufacturing strategies, marketing techniques and investment appraisals. Having redrawn the map of global business, today the BRIC countries are four of the largest 10 national economies in the world and have each experienced rapid growth and challenges for different reasons.

Back in 2001, **China** was a $1.3 trillion economy and was the world's sixth largest after the United States, Japan, Germany, the United Kingdom and France. In 2015 it was the second-largest economy and moved into first place in 2016 and has the world's largest population at 1.38 billion, or 18.7 per cent of the total globe.[2] Long praised for its extraordinary annual growth of over 9 per cent for the past three decades, China's growth has been fuelled by the unprecedented migration of low-paid labour from the unproductive rural farmlands to work in factories and construction. This has lifted hundreds of millions of people out of abject poverty and has created more billionaires in China than exist in the United States. However, widespread corruption has mainly benefited China's elite, its private firms and high-ranking politicians. The results have caused severe inequality in terms of income and standards of living. Today, growth has dimmed to mid-single-digit figures if official data is to be believed. Moreover, China has incurred plenty of bad debts due to its earlier turbo-charged investment and export-based growth model, and many rating agencies have cut their outlook on China from stable to negative. This model is now coming under threat due to a number of reasons, such as a rapidly ageing population, increasing rents in major cities like Shanghai and Tianjin and an over-supply of housing in second and third-tier cities like Chengdu. Rising labour costs have also dampened growth and are expected to increase double digit per annum. The erosion in manufacturing and export competitiveness is also increasing the cost of production in China to the same level as some Eastern European markets. This is causing 'qūyù piāoyí' or 'regional drift', as many firms relocate their production activities from the more expensive coastal areas of Guangdong, Fujian and Zhejiang further inland to Hunan, Chongqing and Sichuan, where productive labour is more abundant, stable and cheaper. Even here the flow of labour is reducing as workers demand higher pay, which is putting pressure on low-cost manufacturers and restraining export growth. Called the **Lewis Turning Point** after the Nobel-Prize winning economist Sir William Arthur Lewis, it carries important implications for China's economy.[3] Even though cracks have started to appear in the China-based production model, many higher-end brands such as KENZO and Billionaire Boys Club continue to produce in China as they can charge a higher price point, so can pass on some of this cost to their customers. Others, especially mass-market or fast-fashion firms, are taking stronger measures and moving their production to lower-cost economies such as Vietnam, known for its cut-and-sew operations and now investing heavily in spinning and weaving, and Cambodia, known for its knitted goods and casualwear, whilst also producing swimwear and lingerie. Yet, most of these new beneficiaries still lack the required infrastructure and production competencies to deliver similar volumes and high-quality production. Because of this, China is now moving towards a more balanced consumption-driven and service-orientated model competing on the axis of quality rather than price. This is being supported by investment in indigenous innovation and land reforms, whilst also addressing over capacity challenges. Green issues and loosening controls on capital flows is also being pursued to drive competitiveness. Though growth has slowed, the government still has considerable fiscal strength due to its huge trade surplus to absorb most losses and stimulate the economy. China is also strengthening its global footprint with emerging economies by providing cheap labour and financing. For example, it has now become Africa's largest trade partner (a position until recently held by the United States) and Latin America's second-largest trade partner. Overall, China's economic transition faces severe demographic headwinds along with productivity and competitiveness challenges that require implementing near-term structural reforms. This includes finding ways to develop internal consumer consumption and reducing the tension between state-owned and private firms, as raising capital is currently controlled by the state, which favours its own firms and this puts private SMEs at a disadvantage. In addition, China's government dislikes disruption or challenges to its authority, so innovation, creativity and entrepreneurship are always carefully observed by the state, which can hamper growth. Externally, China could profit from balancing its relationship with the world through a more peaceful and collaborative manner to ensure long-term economic success.

Spanning eleven time zones and as the planet's most sprawling nation, **Russia's** growth has been fuelled by a surge in energy prices and commodities driven by China's growth. As the world's largest energy exporter, Russia has a growing middle-class population that has doubled in size since 2000.[4] Despite this, a declining population from a peak of nearly 149 million in the early 1990s to around 142 million in 2016 is causing labour shortages and pushing up wages.[5] Even though Russia joined the WTO in 2012, it is still a region that is difficult to do business with. Sharing its position with Azerbaijan, Guyana and Sierra Leone, it is placed 119 out of 168 on the 2015 Transparency International Corruption Perception Index and is well known for widespread venality. Renewed tension is fuelling geopolitical instability and causing gyrations in the value of the rouble, and is this is particularly pernicious for a country that imports more than half its consumer goods.[6] The effects are a lack of business confidence and restricted access to important dollar and euro capital markets and new foreign direct investment. Tumbling oil prices, weak tourism and sanctions over its invasion of the Ukrainian peninsula of Crimea have affected not only Russia but also its trading partners, such as Belarus, Armenia and Uzbekistan. Structural economic problems like managing debt and developing domestic consumption also threaten to push the country into further recession as it faces a long journey to restore foreign investment and overall business confidence. In the short to medium term, the rouble has continued to weaken against currencies such as the dollar, where it has gone from 30 roubles to the dollar at the beginning of 2013 to 59 at the start of 2017.[7] This weakening has meant reduced demand for goods as purchases have become domestically less affordable than before. Nonetheless, as cross-border trade drops and the currency devaluation eats into disposable income, many foreign vendors have started to raise prices as consumers try to stick to the brands they prefer, but buy less. Moreover, with its vast geographical landscape Russia's wealth continues to be centred on its capital Moscow and overall the country seems to be focused on restraining rising inflation rather than easing monetary policy. Therefore, Russia's goals to become the fifth-largest economy in the world by 2020 and to raise living standards to the current level experienced in Europe will require an untangling of the turbulence it has created and more than a phase of very modest economic growth.[8]

As one of the world's most stratified societies and for most of its 500-year-plus history, **Brazil's** connection to the global economy was fundamentally that of a provider of raw materials. Back in 2001, Brazil had a population of 177 million people and a land mass nearly the size of Europe, but with an economy that was smaller than that of Spain.[9] It propelled itself via a deep macro economic transformation, which included the increased availability of domestic credit and a boom in the consumption of commodities such as iron ore, Brent crude oil, rubber, coffee and copper. Blessed with abundant natural resources, a 200-million-strong consumer market and with 15 cities housing populations in excess of one million people, Brazil remains Latin America's largest economy, ahead of Mexico.[10] The north and the northeast have traditionally been the poorer parts of the country due to the vast expanse of the Amazon rainforest and is dominated by states such as Bahia and Ceará. However, in the south and the south-east, logistics, infrastructure and education are much better and this has led to prosperity and a better quality of life. Brazil can therefore be considered as a series of markets and not just one national market. Developed regions such as Rio de Janeiro and São Paulo have sizeable pockets of wealth and consumers with a refined taste level. For example, JK Iguatemi mall in São Paulo drew 70,000 people on its first opening weekend and houses over 150 stores, including Hugo Boss, Diane Von Furstenberg and Miu Miu.[11] Yet, with inflation running over 8 per cent (which is almost twice the official target) and sluggish growth, Brazil's economy is moving at a much gentler pace than anticipated. So much so, that it recently slowed sharply after growing by as much as 7.6 per cent in 2010 and faced a technical recession for the second year in a row in 2016, its deepest recession since official records began.[12] Furthermore, Brazil's overreliance on commodities is gaining prominence given that over the past year, commodity prices have been severely depressed as its largest trading partner China continues to struggle with its economy. Case in point, in 2016 Brent crude oil fell more than 40 per cent, soya beans by more than a third and iron ore by almost half.[13] With Brazil's exports accounting for just 12 per cent of GDP compared to Mexico, where they account for a third of GDP, even the real's recent depreciation of nearly 40 per cent against the dollar has had little effect on making Brazil more attractive to outside investment.[14] This is because over the past decade, Brazil continues to be beset with 'custo Brazil' or the 'Brazil cost'. A host of challenging factors which require speedy attention, such as an over-regulated labour market, poor educational performance, inadequate infrastructure investment, a complicated tax system plus numerous trade restrictions and protectionist measures that still linger from its past military rule which only ended in 1985, has made the country one of the most expensive places to manufacture and purchase fashion products in the world. Taking wages as an example, hourly wages in dollar terms remain approximately 40 per cent above those of Mexico and China. Furthermore, the ease of doing business is also a major deterrent, as it takes 102.5 days to open a firm in São Paulo and 2,600 hours to pay corporate taxes, compared with an average of just over nine days and 175.4 hours in Organisation for Economic Co-operation and Development (OECD) countries.[15] This has led to the rapid rise of the 'despachante', an intermediary hired by firms and individuals who pay a fee to secure documents rather than queue themselves. Though this makes life easier for many users, it probably further entrenches an obstructive and already bureaucratic system. In the long term, following Mexico's lead, Brazil does provide cause for optimism as it has many favourable attributes, such as a good demographic base with increasing numbers of millionaires, a likely proliferation in energy production, a strengthened appetite in foreign direct investment and increasing exports of services. For this to work in Brazil's favour requires trust, technical expertise, a political and economic vision from all its key stakeholders and most importantly, from its highly interventionist government. Whilst austerity is painful, the price of not acting is even higher and if the past is a guide, change will take decades rather than years to put into effect.

India is the world's largest democracy, the fastest growing military power and the third-largest economy after China and the United States in terms of PPP. However, India is on a slow path towards free-market capitalism because of a lack of coherent policy making and an obstructionist opposition. With less reliance on trade than China, it is also in a similar position to Brazil as it also has previously experienced a near double-digit annual rise in annual GDP, although this is now slowing down and will require radical structural reforms if it is to sustain its past trajectory. In particular, as a multi-ethnic and multi-cultural society with over 22 official language groups, India faces significant social problems, including chronic widespread poverty, low food security, poor health and a labour market, which entails a large population of unemployed but skilled young people. This poses a real barrier to increasing its competitiveness and productivity as it struggles to create enough employment. Specifically, with a rapidly growing population of which more than half is under the age of 25, India needs to create around one million jobs each month just to employ those reaching working age, let alone serve the unemployed or those migrating from rural areas to its cities.[16] This is intensified further, as in a land of old-fashioned workshops, there is an lack of large-scale manufacturing jobs compared to China, with Indian manufacturing making up only 16 per cent of its GDP in 2015.[17] India's industrial weakness has meant that it has failed to emulate other developing nations such as South Korea and Thailand. Two broad opposing views centre on India: first, it is focusing too much on economic growth and GDP, neglecting education, health and equality; and second, there has been too much emphasis on social development and not enough on economic growth. Whichever is the correct view, India has an immense opportunity to catapult itself onto a global platform if it can overcome some of its structural challenges. This denotes that a cash-centric economy must enter the digital age, increase investment in transport and infrastructure, and fix state-owned enterprises. In addition, loosening onerous labour laws, streamlining governance controls and opening up capital markets will help to further drive foreign investment.

In sum, the BRIC countries being coined as emerging markets was probably correct in 2001, but today the term has outgrown its usefulness and is not an accurate reflection of the state of their development. For example, in terms of PPP, China is the world's largest economy and yet is still classified as emerging. Moreover, with a 96 per cent literacy rate, more high-speed rail tracks than all other countries combined, more college students than any other country and with the world's second-largest stock market, it seems contradictory and confusing that it is still classified as such.[18] This is because since its inception, the term was not designed with any real specific criteria. Instead, it sounded more aspirational than saying 'Third World' and provided connotations of potentially being on a journey to something better, which was designed to lure potential investors seeking high returns.

Beyond BRIC: the new world

The **Next Eleven (N-11)** has been identified by Goldman Sachs as the next cluster of countries that will shape globalisation. Due to their low-cost location and expanding consumer markets, they are destined to be the future drivers of the global economy. The N-11 consists of Bangladesh, Egypt, Indonesia, Iran, Mexico, Nigeria, Pakistan, the Philippines, Turkey, South Korea and Vietnam. Traditional economic markers coupled with new measures such as the examination of increases in rail cargo volume, electricity consumption, the availability of financial credit and real estate construction have moved the spotlight on to these countries and have provided a holistic reference for growth rates. Given their size and continued rapid growth, the N-11 countries present an attractive opportunity for international firms to spearhead new market development by attracting new consumers and capturing market share, even though this may not be profitable in the first instance. Expansion into N-11 countries will not only be in mega-cities such as Lagos, Manila and Istanbul, but also in second-tier metropolises with large populations that today are unfamiliar to many, like Busan, Faisalabad and Chittagong.[19] The global paradigm shift towards emerging markets and mega-cities does not automatically mean that economic growth equates to consumption development for both domestic and international firms. Specific factors that vary by country and city, such as birth rate, wealth distribution and proportion of working women, correspondingly affect growth in categories such as beauty products, home, luxury goods and mass-market fashion. Firms will need to identify and position themselves against the largest and fastest-growing markets and cities with regard to their own product offering and how they are structurally organised.

The combined population of the N-11 countries is still not on a par with the inhabitants of China or India and therefore growth will be broader and less reliant than it was in the BRIC countries. This will also impact the rest of the world indirectly, as the N-11 is now richer than the BRIC countries were in the past, meaning that the continued potential for growth will be less impactful, as larger absolute increases in output are required. The rise of these countries signifies that the future growth of the fashion market will be concentrated in these growing clusters as demand from some of these populous cities outstrips some entire countries. These rapidly modernising markets are still vulnerable, as if global economic growth slows down, many consumers risk falling out of the fragile middle class and back into poverty. This poses a real threat for the economic competitiveness of these countries. Consequently, many firms are strategically positioning themselves via gateways to gain access to lucrative markets by investing in Malaysia, Indonesia, South Korea or Vietnam to enter China or India, or investing in Poland as a path to Russia. On the other hand, many countries are much more cautious about globalisation than they were a decade ago and are taking a more controlled standpoint by maintaining their interest in export competitiveness rather than relying too much on imports.

A good emerging market strategy guides the firm to balance its efforts and to ensure that it does not devote too much time to penetrating emerging economies at the expense of ignoring domestic demand. De-emphasising its presence in its traditional centres of demand could mean missing out on potentially rewarding opportunities for growth. This is because many brands already have a relatively weak top-of-mind presence among consumers in their home country. However, many opportunities still exist in these new markets especially for first-mover firms, particularly global brand owners, niche high-value-added manufacturers and retailers with strong franchise and distributor models. Conversely, challenges exist for mass-market manufacturers as China and others move up the value chain. Finally, as developing markets can be unsettling in terms of conducting business in, it is crucial that executives appreciate the nuances of doing business. Understanding local regulations, customs, cultural norms and political differences plus finding the right entry strategy and devising products that meet local consumer tastes and behaviours are decisive factors in achieving success. This is facilitated by a well-governed country with policies and institutions that are supportive of stability and growth. Crucial factors that were exposed during the financial crisis as politically manipulated markets, bad governance, wide-spread corruption, weak public services and poor infrastructure came to the forefront and to the detriment of many firms.

Review questions

Questions for debate regarding emerging markets are as follows:

- What type of due diligence can foreign firms undertake when entering emerging markets?
- Will operating in selected mega-cities require the firm to have its own profit-and-loss responsibility and freedom in design, product development, pricing, communication and sales strategy for these locations?
- What can developed countries do to increase growth to a level of 5–7 per cent a year?
- How do firms weigh the balance of effort between domestic versus international investment?

- Will local brands eventually overtake foreign brands in emerging markets?
- What other countries do you think will become key players in the future?

Further reading

1 Audino, H. and Hawksworth, J. (2017) *The Long View: How Will the Global Economic Order Change By 2050?* London: PricewaterhouseCoopers.
2 Bremmer, I. (2015) 'The New World of Business', *Fortune*, 22 January.
3 *The Economist* (2013) 'China Approaching the Turning Point', www.economist.com/blogs/freeexchange/2013/01/growth-and-china (accessed 4 May 2017).
4 Bremmer, I. (2015) 'The New World of Business', *Fortune*, 22 January.
5 Chamie, J. and Mirkin, B. (2014) 'Russian Demographics: The Perfect Storm', Yale University, http://yaleglobal.yale.edu/content/russian-demographics-perfect-storm (accessed 4 May 2017).
   The World Factbook (2016) *Russia*, www.cia.gov/library/publications/the-world-factbook/geos/rs.html (accessed 4 May 2017).
6 Transparency International (2015) 'Corruption Perceptions Index 2015', www.transparency.org/cpi2015/results (accessed 4 May 2017).
7 *Bloomberg* (2017) 'USDRUB:CUR Exchange Rate', www.bloomberg.com/quote/USDRUB:CUR (accessed 4 May 2017).
8 Beyrle, J. (2009) 'Russia and America's Shared Economic Future', Moscow Higher School of Economics, https://moscow.usembassy.gov/beyrlerem042909.html (accessed 4 May 2017).
9 Bremmer, I. (2015) 'The New World of Business', *Fortune*, 22 January.
10 Jackson, T. (2016) 'Walpole Luxury Summit 2016: The Americas', London: Walpole.
11 Clark, E. (2012) 'Top 10 Emerging Markets', *WWD*, 19 November.
12 Leahy, J. (2016) 'Brazil's GDP Shrinks 3.8%', *Financial Times*, 3 March.
13 International Monetary Fund (2017) 'Commodity Market Monthly: 25th January 2017', www.imf.org/external/np/res/commod/pdf/monthly/012617.pdf (accessed 4 May 2017).
14 Lex (2015) 'Brazil: Turning the Clock Back', *Financial Times*, 12/13 September.
15 Wheatley, J. (2015) 'Brazil Competitive Profile: Scandal Mars Efforts to Tame Bureaucracy', *Financial Times*, 26 March.
16 Mansharamani, V. (2016) '"Make in India" Promises Manufacturing Jobs for Millions. Here's Why it Won't Work', *PBS*, www.pbs.org/newshour/making-sense/make-in-india-promises-manufacturing-jobs-for-millions-heres-why-it-wont-work (accessed 4 May 2017).
17 India Brand Equity Foundation (2016) 'Manufacturing Sector in India', www.ibef.org/industry/manufacturing-sector-india.aspx (accessed 4 May 2017).
18 Kynge, J. and Wheatley, J. (2015) 'Emerging Markets: Redrawing the World Map', *Financial Times*, 3 August.
19 Dobbs, R., Manyika, J., Remes, J., Restrepo, A., Roxburgh, C. and Smit, S. (2011) 'Urban World: Mapping the Economic Power of Cities', McKinsey & Company, www.mckinsey.com/global-themes/urbanization/urban-world-mapping-the-economic-power-of-cities (accessed 4 May 2017).

3 Strategy
Creating and capturing a competitive advantage

> **Chapter goals**
>
> This chapter defines the role of strategy and explores several constructs on how the firm can create a continued competitive advantage. The key areas covered are:
>
> - What is strategy?
> - Creating and capturing a competitive advantage
> - The strategy development process
> - Strategy implementation

What is strategy?

Etymologically, the word **strategy** has strong connotations to the Greek word 'strategia', meaning generalship. Its close relationship with the word 'stratos', denoting the army, has long inferred its association to military planning and this is evident through terms such as 'headquarters', chief executive 'officer', 'chief of staff', 'attacking markets' and 'defeating rivals'.[1] However, the widespread use of the concept in management literature did not emerge until after the Second World War. In 1944 the classic work of mathematician John von Neumann and economist Oskar Morgenstern, *Theory of Games and Economic Behavior*, was seen as being the first to link strategy to business activity and the management lexicon.[2] Since then, strategy has attracted a plethora of contributions. A multitude of expressions have led to various definitions of strategy being applied to a range of business issues and situations. This is reflected both in the literature and in practice as definitions of strategy are not common, have little consistency in their use and tend to be over-used by executives. Consequently, strategy is a process that requires careful management and should not be confused with tactics. To decipher this, strategy can be clarified and segmented into three distinct types, all of which are implemented simultaneously, but which affect the firm differently.

Business strategy focuses on how firms compete through the integration of functional strategies for a distinct set of products and services that are intended for a specific group of consumers. Here, successful executives understand the trajectory of their industry as well as the position of their own firm. **Functional strategy** is concerned with the specific operational aspects of the firm, for example, marketing, finance and human resources, and emphasises the integration of disparate parts of the business so that they are consistent and supportive of the business strategy. **Corporate strategy** formulates the overall direction of the firm through the identification of the businesses in which the firm will compete and the allocation of resources. The aim is to align business strategies and coordinate operations so that synergies are captured. Corporate strategy has always been the major unit of analysis for the firm, as it is corporate strategy that directs and creates focus for firms searching for the creation of new value-laden opportunities. Firms that can capture and exploit this value in the mercurial business environment are well rewarded. As a result, corporate strategy can be said to be the linking process between the management of the firm's resources and its key stakeholders, so that it has a sense of purpose with the required actions of searching, doing, learning and adapting.[3] It should also be competitive and add 'value' to the various stakeholders by yielding new ideas. In its strictest sense, this usually provides a common goal of at least survival for the firm or maximising one or more of the following: the efficiency of the resource-conversion process so that marginal revenues equals marginal cost and profit maximisation attained; or the maximisation of its net present worth or its market value.

Creating and capturing a competitive advantage

A strategy is of no use if it does not deliver an increased advantage to the firm and its shareholders. For this to happen, the firm's strategy should be competitive against the actual competitors or potential competitors it wishes to challenge, as normal competition occurs when several firms strive to make a profit by satisfying the same demand. A competitive strategy explains how the firm will configure and position itself to do better than the competition to earn superior profits. Another way to evaluate this is to see if the firm earns above the average profitability for its industry and therefore can be said to have a strong competitive position or disadvantage. In order to analyse **competitive advantage** (value creation and value capture), strategists start by dismantling a firm's primary and secondary activities, commonly referred to as the **value chain** (processes and components). The activities undertaken to design, produce, market, deliver and service goods are a reflection of the firm's strategic choices in terms of how these activities are configured and linked together. These choices then contribute to the firm's relative cost position and what customers are willing to pay.[4] By doing this, executives can understand disparities in the profit formula and why their firm does or does not have a competitive advantage, albeit at the level of the individual business unit. Executives who can make choices on how the firm will operate differently by re-engineering the value chain for the desired position and understand its dynamics are well placed to gain a competitive advantage. However, as financial data is historical, relying on this implies that it is probably too late if the firm bases its future advantages solely on past information. Therefore, good strategists are the architects of the firm's purpose and can project out the future industry structure as well as their own position in order to drive a positive transformation in industry structure. As disruptive thinkers, they can spot opportunities to increase a firm's competitive edge and can also foresee future shifts in competitive advantage by changing the basis of competition and the number of rivals they have. For this reason, a competitive advantage is an advantage one firm has over a competitor or group of competitors in a given market, strategic group or industry.[5] As a competitive advantage is a static concept, real advantages are those that focus on dynamic capabilities, are sustainable and add value.

Defining and measuring **value** is a complex issue as it focuses on the perceived, anticipated or actual utility, plus the satisfaction and total benefits to be accrued from a purchase. This highlights a central message in describing value in the fashion industry, in that purchases made by different consumers of the same item, for the same purpose and for the same price may result in widely differing levels of satisfaction and therefore value. Consequently, the concept of value continues to evolve from being entirely based on cost pricing to value pricing, and one that incorporates quality and features that go beyond standard expectations. Therefore, value can emanate in several forms. From a financial perspective, this can be the difference between the customer's willingness to pay and the supplier's opportunity cost, the floating average of return on investment or internal total shareholder return. From a consumer viewpoint, this can be gauged through market share, retention rates or brand recognition. In addition, internal value to the firm can concern brand value, quality per expended currency over time and new product development rates. The **value net** as shown in Figure 3.1 can provide clarity to a firm's value proposition and the resources and strategic actions needed to deliver it, since it incorporates three important constructs that are significant when operating in this industry.

Examples of **operational excellence** include Hong Kong-based Li & Fung, which is the world's largest sourcing firm and the multi-brand group VF Corporation. This vector aims to pursue cost leadership by focusing on efficiency, streamlining activities and managing volume dynamics. The aim is to achieve economies of scale and scope in order to ultimately meet the needs of the end consumer, whether this is a manufacturer, wholesaler or retailer. This usually involves a high degree of ICT being used throughout the firm's operations and supply chain. Techniques such as Just-in-Time (JIT) and Collaborative Planning, Forecasting and Replenishment (CPFR) are used to electronically share real-time information with key stakeholders so that

Product Leadership

❑ Constant innovation
❑ Market and offering-driven
❑ Superior brand image
❑ Short time to market

Operational Excellence

❑ Cost leadership
❑ Agile and lean structure
❑ Continuous benchmarking
❑ Digital supply chains/networks
❑ Cutting-edge use of ICT

Customer Intimacy

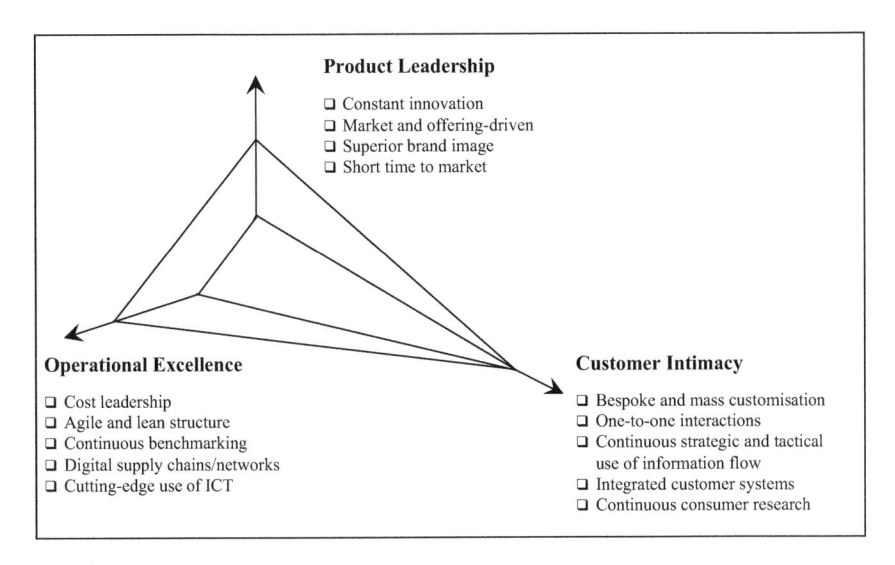

❑ Bespoke and mass customisation
❑ One-to-one interactions
❑ Continuous strategic and tactical use of information flow
❑ Integrated customer systems
❑ Continuous consumer research

Figure 3.1 The value net
Source: adapted from Treacy and Wiersema (1996).[6]

visibility is improved and the firm is nimble and responsive to customer needs and trends.

The second sharp point, **product leadership**, aims to be the first to offer superior products and services. These firms believe that product excellence is paramount to business success and use their deep knowledge and resources, such as a unique core technology, to position themselves as inventors and brand marketers, constantly experimenting with new offerings that deliver great experiences. Nike is an expert in this field and frequently pursues game-changing innovations that generate immense brand heat in a consistent way. Examples include its sock-like Flyknit technology, which eliminates the stitching of the shoe's upper to the sole, thereby reducing the number of production operators needed and, more recently, its HyperAdapt trainers, which incorporate an electro-adaptive self-lacing function based on an algorithmic pressure equation that adjusts the fit until it senses friction points.

Customer intimacy aims to be the most dependable and responsive to the needs of the customer and is well depicted in the luxury goods industry, where customers are given personal attention. The Japanese department store Isetan exhibits this well and offers a 'customer first' philosophy which aims to build loyalty and long-term relationships. This can make a significant contribution to the bottom line by creating extra sales not just in clothing, but also in other areas like hairdressing or lunch appointments. In addition, retailers such as La Rinascente, Matahari and Harrods use store cards as a tool for customer intimacy by rewarding their customers with exclusive services, including free delivery and personal shopping, sale previews or extra discounts. Moreover, in Turkey, Hopi, a mobile shopping assistant app with over a million users, has collaborated with multiple fashion brands and two leading department stores, YKM and Boyner. The app offers personalised product offers, promotions and discounts, and allows users to view new product ranges first whilst also integrating the retailers' loyalty programmes to strengthen customer relationships.

Though the value net model shows a triptych of various ways to create value, most firms over-estimate their capability to execute these value drivers, which can derail their competitive success. The majority of firms are only capable of configuring themselves to create a sole or at best dual competitive advantage. Therefore, a firm will have to make decisions on what strategic trade-offs it is willing to make based on the available resources and processes to deliver the value proposition and ultimately to maximise the profit formula. This is crucial as the firm cannot meet all the needs of the customer, especially when customers are happy to accept improved products and services, but are often unwilling to pay a premium price to get them. For this reason, the type of improvement for which customers will pay should be carefully calibrated to avoid value being lost.

Intense competition exists among designers, manufacturers, distributors and retailers. Conventionally, they have tried to shift costs or add value through zero-sum competition. As one firm's gain requires another firm's loss, through for example reducing prices to increase market share, this form of competition only dissipates industry structure and profitability. Moreover, modern discourse focuses on positive-sum competition. In this, in order to be really competitive, a successful firm should be concerned with inventing value through a distinct strategy and should not attempt to match its competitor's every move. This needs to be sustainable not in terms of a particular period of time, but rather the possibility and extent of mass competitive duplication by taking into account likely future changes. This is because as positive-sum competition expands the customers served and the overall value pool, more than one firm can be successful.

The strategy development process

Traditionally, the fashion industry had a distinctive structure that shaped the nature of the competition and the level of long-term average profitability. Yet, industry boundaries may fall into different categories in different countries. A firm can be an export business in one country, but be largely dependent on its domestic business in another country. Consequently, it is important to contextualise competitive strategy in a broader sense so that it incorporates other 'arenas' and competitor analysis goes beyond existing rivals. Take, for example, China's Taobao e-commerce platform or India's Myntra. Who would have thought they would become major competitors to established players? As industry boundaries continue to become increasingly blurred, this can be considered not a technological revolution, but a cultural revolution.

Therefore, smart executives focus on the most threatening competitors, especially those who might not be currently operating in their industry, but have the motivation, capability and opportunistic personality to do so. Amazon did this when it was in talks to acquire Net-A-Porter and this underscores the technology industry's growing interest in fashion. Therefore, understanding these arenas and the forces that determine firm behaviour now and in the future essentially provides more levers to work with and is a core discipline in strategy formulation for executives to understand.[7]

Strategic planning is not as informed and as accurate as cost planning, as it often takes a considerable amount of time for a comprehensive strategy to be formulated and implemented and for the effects to become known. This is because human beings have their own individual judgements on business issues concerning strategy. For this reason, to influence and achieve a common viewpoint as well as change the initial decision and subsequent actions often takes a long time. Moreover, the dynamic business environment can result in sweeping changes that can make the chosen strategy defunct. Therefore, **strategy development** must take into account the **context**, which is the environment in which the strategy will operate and is developed. An example of this would be whether it will operate in the fast-paced environment of teenage fashion, where products are 'chased' during production like Topshop, or the gentler-paced environment of corporate workwear, where products are 'shaped' in advance like those of Designs By Marc, a successful Jamaican family-run business. In addition, the main actions of the proposed strategy known as the **content** must be taken into account, and this relates to the distinct elements of the firm's strategic plan and how it proposes to win. For example, at one point in time, Nike as a new entrant centred its football apparel strategy on innovations such as seamless moisture-wicking body-mapped jerseys. Conversely, Adidas' strategy was based on its heritage and long-standing association with major football clubs and tournaments, which dates back to the 1950s. Finally, the **process** of how the actions link together and interact relates to how the strategy will be developed and achieved. Although the three elements are highly inter-related, a high degree of creativity is needed to ensure that the strategy is unique, engaging and followed. Because of this, the process element is often considered to be the most difficult to articulate. This is because as the environment is dynamic, the viewpoint on strategic issues is often convoluted and disparate between executives. Consequently, the complexities and differing views associated with strategy development have resulted in many researchers trying to pinpoint strategy, as it is still a relatively elusive concept that is expensive in terms of managerial time and money and is one that is rarely shared throughout the firm. Whether such an abstract concept can be useful to the firm's performance in today's results-orientated environment is often questioned. This has led to intense debates between academics, executives and practitioners in relation to the different approaches to good strategy development. For instance, some researchers argue that a firm's strategy should be implicit, as it is concerned with the unique position of the firm and so should only be known to the executive leadership team. Others have argued that as strategy concerns business coherence and direction, it should be made explicit, otherwise how is it then possible for a firm to achieve coherence and coordination without making the strategy explicit? Additional research has added to the debate, stating that a strategy is only needed when a firm faces competition and that no competitive threat, such as in a monopoly situation, denotes no need for a strategy.[8] This perplexing paradox has resulted in analysing the nature of a firm's growth as the answer to formulating a strategy. Accordingly, two main schools of thought have emerged.

The first school of thought, supported by rational strategists such as Igor Ansoff and Michael Porter, views strategy formulation as a pattern of conscious actions and is known as the **prescriptive** viewpoint.[9] This approach allows firms to examine the environment and engage in a measured approach to strategy development as objectives are defined in advance and the main elements are developed before the strategy commences. This is achieved through the **strategic planning process**. At best, this is typically an annual process that is undertaken in firms such as Levi Strauss & Co and can be viewed as a series of comprehensive business unit and corporate strategy reviews. Its purpose is to determine what the firm should become and how it can best achieve this goal. This is often driven by the history of the firm and is usually not very creative, whilst being heavily directed by the chief executive officer (CEO) and chief financial officer (CFO), with support from senior business unit executives. This includes the **mission statement** and through the firm's **vision**, its desired strategic intent and fundamental values are formulated. This defines the present and desired position of the firm and how the firm will use its resources and distinct competencies to differentiate itself from its competitors to produce incremental gains. This is not usually communicated well enough. Instead, it should be conveyed in a vibrant and inspirational way so that everybody within the firm understands and is inspired by the corporate direction. Here, it is key that this part of the process should not be confused as the firm's complete strategy. Next, internal strengths and weaknesses and external opportunities and threats are analysed. For example, data on market growth rates, market research feedback on customer needs, shifts in the retail landscape and competitor strategies. In doing so, the firm generates scenarios and contingency plans on how the world might turn out tomorrow. This is not an exact picture, but is one that drives better decisions about the future and their strategic implications. This encourages the development of forward-looking market intelligence, which acts as a key enabler for ensuring that strategic decisions allow the firm to stay ahead of the competition. From this analysis, three to five qualitative and quantitative possibilities are offered over a measurable timescale. This usually guides the annual budget along with a rolling three-year plan, with the latter covering its strategic grouping, what the firm's architecture should be and its intended scale and scope. For example, by function, channel, market, geography and product. Next, the initial annual plan is usually rolled up from a regional base into a corporate level plan and tracked on a quarterly basis during the fiscal year in order to monitor progress. This is measured by top-down **Key Performance Indicators (KPIs)** that reflect the critical success factors for each business unit within the firm, such as top-line sales growth, net profit, attracting new customers, expansion into new markets and rate of product innovation. It is important to note that the process should entail a mixture of data and ideas that drive quality decisions and not just opinions. Because of this, the process should be a stimulus to collective thought, as it is the quality and depth of the dialogue, not the document which is usually a lengthy PowerPoint presentation that matters.

In well-run firms, strategic planning is aligned with but separate from budgeting and compensation discussions, as this can stifle the dialogue and hence opportunities for growth. The strategic planning format should vary enough over time so that executive teams do not simply cut and paste the previous year's strategic playbook. In addition, external parties may be involved with input and there should be a heavy focus on external considerations such as customers, competitors and the environment in general. Overall, using the prescriptive approach can pose a real problem for the firm if the strategy does not go according to plan or the environment changes too quickly, as a competitive advantage can evaporate in less than a year. Therefore, spending months crafting a long-term strategy can be a costly exercise in terms of resource allocation in today's increasingly competitive world. However, this approach does provide the advantages of giving a complete overview of the firm, the resources needed and the ability to compare the strategy to the defined objectives. The context of the prescriptive approach is best suited to environments and product groups that are relatively stable and mechanistic in nature. They are typically populated by mature firms selling standardised products and tend to be mostly hierarchical, ossified and bureaucratic in nature.

The second school of thinking, advocated by generative strategists such as Henry Mintzberg and Peter Senge, supports strategy as a pattern of decisions. As the final objective is unclear, the main elements of the strategy are formed as it develops. This type of approach, advanced from the work on *Organizations* and *The Behavioral Theory of the Firm*, and is termed the **emergent** approach.[10] It was during the oil crisis in the 1970s that this style became prominent as the traditional technique of producing a single-base case forecast and assuming that the current state of affairs would remain the same became unreliable. Management deemed the environment too volatile to predict and moved to an emergent approach where strategy formulation was 'naked', in that it was evolving, tactical and experimental in nature. Importantly, as the emergent approach was better aligned with the rapidly changing business environment, it became the preferred option, because it not only reduced strategy alienation and myopia, but through continuous recalibration it leveraged exploitable opportunities quicker than the prescriptive approach.

In advancing strategy development, many executives favour repeating a 100-day exercise and when the effectiveness of their primary strategies are recognised, they are then formalised and implemented into deliberate directives. These primary strategies are supplemented with contingency plans that can be triggered quickly should circumstances change, as trying to forecast the future has become an impossible task for many. Given that a fully emergent strategy is less documented than a prescriptive strategy, it can be difficult to articulate the strategy to the wider firm. This is partly overcome by communicating the strategy through monthly board meetings, the formation of steering groups, frequent intranet updates and departmental gatherings. However, it is unrealistic to expect senior management not to have a stronghold on the direction of the firm, especially if it is global in nature and publicly traded. This is because valuable resources need to be effectively managed to avoid incoherence and this requires some form of responsibility, central strategic overview and rationale for usage. In a highly ambiguous environment, it is best to have a strategy that leverages dynamic capabilities and resources with a strong culture. Therefore, the emergent strategy is best suited to early-stage and high-growth firms that are decentralised, as well as those that operate in relatively new areas of the fashion industry where the future is hard to read, as a great deal depends on trial and error.

Sometimes senior executives refrain from making clear **core strategic choices** and claim that the future business environment is too unpredictable and volatile. They prefer to wait for the environment to settle down and become sufficiently clear as the anxiety and pressure to make tough decisions diminish. But if the future is unstable and fickle, then how will executives know when it will improve? As we cannot predict the future, the emergent strategy has become a common way for executives to avoid making difficult and courageous choices that affect a firm's competitive position. Rather, many executives hide behind the **fast follower** approach and replicate choices that appear to be successful for competing firms or employ copycat products and services, which avoids creating any real value. Though being in the 'lead pack' is a valid and well-utilised strategy, it is not entirely what the emergent framework is intended to do. In addition, many leaders still focus too much time on tactics and not enough on strategy. For them, the current year is chiefly about the anniversary of last year's sales at a lower cost and with a better net margin. Whether strategy development is prescriptive, emergent or a hybrid, it can be summarised to be in its rawest form a bet and is probably better replaced by the **strategic learning process** as there is no right way to form a strategy. Consequently, executives can shorten the odds by linking strategic choices closely together and by channelling their efforts on the choices and actions that most influence the customer in order to obtain a superior sustainable competitive advantage.

Strategy implementation

> Some companies have great strategies and do a lot of talking, but they don't get it done. (Domenico De Sole, former Gucci Group CEO).[11]

Much time is wasted in the boardroom and little is spent on strategy. It is not enough to lay out grand vision statements and multiple goals without addressing the critical question on how to reach these objectives. Firms that are leaders now may become laggards in the future if strategy is not effectively implemented, as any rival can duplicate a strategy. In great firms', their products and services may alter due to a change in firm strategy, but the overall vision of the firm will remain relatively stable. Many firms have similar goals, such as 'to provide the best customer experience' or 'to create the most desirable product', but what separates high-performing firms is their ability to devise a strategy that engages its executives to execute it better than the competition, particularly as in the financial community, analyst opinion is rarely influenced by strategy, but nearly always by successful execution. With this in mind, it is the executive's role to get results and champion constant renewal for the firm, which requires persistence and drive. As time pressure intensifies, senior executives must make sure there is enough time and the right mechanisms for the wider firm to catch up with their thinking so that implementation does not become problematic. This is facilitated by clarifying decision rights and making sure information flows where it needs to go by having a correct organisational structure and reward system. One way to look at **strategy implementation** is to identify where strategy is missing. The absence of strategy is often characterised by executives stating that 'this firm lacks strategy and direction', one where the core strategic choices of the firm make sense by themselves, but when combined, they are not coherent and lack consistency. By identifying this, the firm can introduce measures to align the implementation of its strategy. These measures ensure that the strategy is not overly broad in its objectives, such as 'maximising shareholder return', and should also be flexible enough so that it is adaptive to the changing environment. Because of this, the firm's core strategic choices become an effective decision and coordination tool. In determining central choices, it is important to identify what other decisions they interact with and how this can influence future decisions. Highly central preferences like a firm's scope simultaneously guide many other choices and are effective and strategic in nature as long as they minimise overlap with each other and guide the same decision. Strategic choices should aim to be reliable so that the final choice coincides with the original intent. If not, then it is incongruent and there will be little reason to follow the strategy, something disgruntled employees are quick to pick up on, as a firm whose choices are internally inconsistent is very unlikely to succeed.

Strategy implementation in the fashion industry is a commonly ignored area of research.[12] The best firms understand that strategy formulation and implementation offers major opportunities for learning curve improvements and consciously builds expertise in the process by learning to think and act at the same time. They leverage this to drive down the learning curve in order to be more efficient and faster than the competition. Strategy consultants have made a lucrative business out of helping firms with strategy development and implementation. Nevertheless, though these consultants are good at formulation,

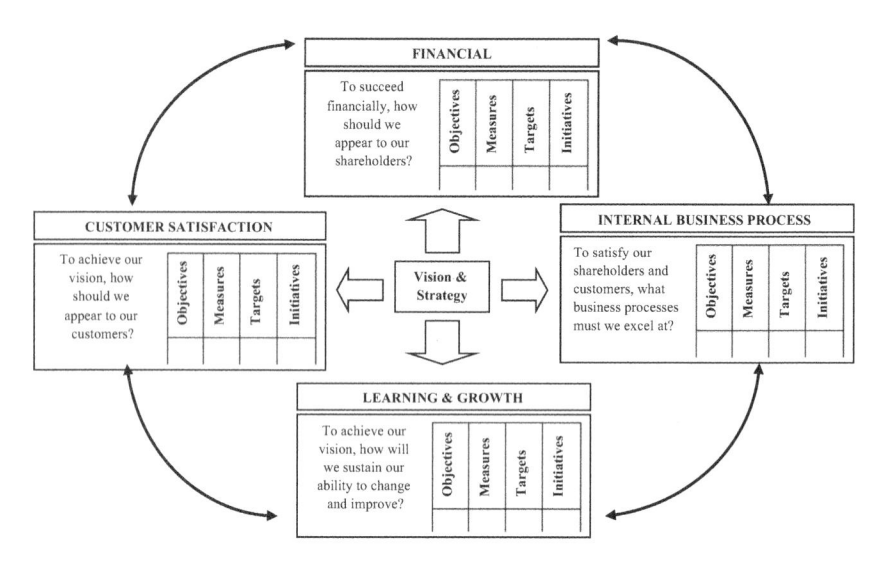

Figure 3.2 The Balanced Scorecard framework
Source: adapted from Kaplan and Norton (1992).[13]

they are not as successful at implementation as they do not usually know the firm and its nuances well enough in terms of its process, assets and architecture.

There are various frameworks such as Six Sigma, Total Quality Management and the Balanced Scorecard that have been created to help with implementation. Taking the **Balanced Scorecard** as shown in Figure 3.2, this framework is essentially a performance measurement system concerning four areas. In today's competitive environment, fashion firms rarely compete solely on their physical tangible assets, but rather through their intellectual and knowledge assets. However, many intangible assets have no value in themselves and need to be complemented with physical assets to create a value system. In doing so, the scorecard covers areas traditionally left off the balance sheet and helps drive the firm's strategy down to the front line. It also provides critical information in a single report to senior management in assessing the firm's progress to achieve its strategic vision and objectives, both now and in the future.

Aggregate **financial** measures of business unit performance such as operating income or return on investment allow a firm to examine its outlook to key stakeholders and analyse if its choice of strategy, its implementation and its execution is successful. Though not perfect by themselves, financial measures are well understood and provide clear objective goals on which executives can focus. For many fashion firms, such as Maison Margiela, important assets include technical know-how, creative ethos and a strong heritage, but all of these are drivers of firm performance that do not appear on the balance sheet.

Operational measures of **customer satisfaction** allow a firm to understand how customers view the firm and whether its efforts regarding service and customer satisfaction are affecting sales and net profit. One way in which firms are monitoring this is through calibrating the effect of retaining or losing customers by projecting their lifetime value or by simply analysing conversion and product return rates. In the digital world, this can be interpreted through click-through rates, scroll-down usage and abandoned orders.

Internal business processes allow a firm to understand what it excels at and how successful it is in setting up and managing existing and entirely new business processes to meet and deliver future customer demand and its financial objectives.

Learning and growth identifies the infrastructure that a firm must build through its people, systems and procedures in order to create long-term value and achieve breakthrough performance. This measurement area is the most difficult to capture quantitatively, but can be achieved through performance-to-goal percentages, for instance, where a firm can set a target of launching five new innovative products per year and then measure their success rate.

The scorecard can also be used as a structured change management tool. For effective strategy implementation, this requires a high level of soft skills and the know-how to navigate formal and informal networks within the firm. The smart business executive knows that a disproportionate amount of time should not be spent on cascading the scorecards throughout the firm as a bolt-on activity to the change management process. Instead, involvement by all the key stakeholders is required in order for it to be a success. These stakeholders are seen as process champions and are tasked with the change management initiative. They are accountable for the implementation of the scorecards and use reporting dashboards to track and show KPIs to senior management. If implemented well, the advantages of the scorecard can generate many positives. For example, by focusing on the four essential measures, the system restricts information overload and brings together often disparately reported elements of the firm's strategic position, enabling management to optimise and align the resource allocation process. In addition, the scorecard requires management to convert their mission statements for each dimension into a series of specific measures that reflect critical factors of strategic concern. Moreover, the risk of the consonance concept the 'fit' between the firm and its environment is reduced due to the utilisation of relevant information. Finally, real-time information can be used to capture and react to the changing fashion trends in the marketplace, as is used by the British value retailer Primark. Overall, the scorecard is a useful tool in highlighting to the management team that if the firm cannot measure factors, then it cannot improve on them.

Although there is nothing new about the call for measurement of non-financial markers, senior management are still more likely to be biased towards putting financial instruments and methods that executives can control, they are good at and compensated for on the scorecard. Likewise, institutional investors, so vitally important to firms, are still largely concerned with conventional financial metrics based around profit and growth. The framework can also be considered fairly rigid as key success factors that do not lie in a single category can be easily missed. The scorecard also omits the external perspective of the customer and the firm's employees, who are perhaps its most important asset. As the scorecard is based on data, there has to be sufficient information from all measures to base decisions on and an ICT system capable of providing accurate reporting and analysis in a timely manner. Subsequently, there is a danger that inaccurate or lagging information that is slow to navigate the system loses its value in the decision-making process and provides little guidance in how to navigate the future. Also, like most frameworks it does not take into account how to deal with uncertainty, which is a major factor in the strategic process. Finally, though the scorecard may result in sizeable operational gains, it may not be possible to translate many of these improvements into sustainable profitability due to the rapid diffusion of best practices, and therefore the benefits are mostly incremental and not revolutionary. Because of this, it is important to note that management tools do not take the place of strategy and the strategically competent executive. This is because it is hard to tell if weak firm performance is due to the good implementation of a bad strategy or the poor implementation of a good strategy.

Case study: W.L. Gore & Associates

W.L. Gore & Associates was founded in 1958 in Newark, Delaware by Wilbert and Genevieve Gore. With over $3 billion in annual sales and 2,000 patents worldwide, it pairs deep technical knowledge with a thorough understanding of its customers' needs to deliver innovative and high-performing products, such as fabric laminates, membranes, venting and fibre technologies, to a number of diverse industries. Using polytetrafluoroethylene polymers, it is best known as the creator of the famous windproof, waterproof and breathable fabric GORE-TEX®, which has forever changed the standard of performance outerwear and footwear. Gore depicts the concept of strategic flexibility, making core strategic choices that are sustainable, in that its development team uses a three-stage cross-functional review process termed 'Real-Win-Worth'. First, a 'real' and tangible market opportunity must exist for a unique product or business idea. The proposition is then evaluated in terms of whether it can be successful and 'win' in the marketplace, given the potential substitutes, and whether there is any potential demand from customers. In order to win, the product should have a competitive advantage, and be sustainable and protectable by intellectual property rights. Lastly, depending on the size of the opportunity and the return on investment, the economics need to make sense so that the idea is 'worth' pursuing.[14]

Review questions

Questions for debate regarding strategy and competitive advantage are as follows:

- How do firms plan for the long-term in a short-term world?
- On what axis does the modern firm compete on, for example, price, quality or service?
- Should firms expand during an economic downturn?
- How can strategic frameworks deal with uncertainty in a better way?
- Does the economics of being a global provider offset the added complexity of running the firm?
- Should the firm focus its efforts on value creation or value appropriation?

Further reading

1. Von Clausewitz, C. (1976) *On War*. Princeton: Princeton University Press.
2. Morgenstern, O. and Neumann, J.V. (1944) *Theory of Games and Economic Behaviour*. Princeton: Princeton University Press.
3. Kotter, J.P. (2014) *Accelerate: Building Strategic Agility for a Faster-Moving World*. Boston: Harvard Business Review Press.
4. Porter, M.E. (1985) *Competitive Advantage; Creating and Sustaining Superior Performance*. New York: Collier Macmillan.
5. Kay, J. (1993) 'The Structure of Strategy', *Business Strategy Review*, Vol. 4, No. 2, pp. 17–38.
6. Treacy, M. and Wiersema, F. (1996) *The Discipline of Market Leaders: Choose Your Customers, Narrow Your Focus, Dominate Your Market*. London: HarperCollins.
7. Porter, M.E. (1980) *Competitive Strategy: Techniques for Analysing Industries and Competitors*. New York: Collier Macmillan.
8. Ohmae, K. (1982) *The Mind of the Strategist*. New York: Penguin Books.
9. Ansoff, I. (1988) *Corporate Strategy*, revised edn. Harmondsworth: Penguin Books.
   Mintzberg, H. and Waters, J.A. (1985) 'Of Strategies, Deliberate and Emergent', *Strategic Management Journal*, Vol. 6, No. 3, pp. 257–272.
   Mintzberg, H. (1990) The Design School: Reconsidering the Basic Premises of Strategic Management, *Strategic Management Journal*, Vol. 11, No. 3, pp. 171–197.
   Senge, P.M. (1990) *The Fifth Discipline: The Art and Practice of the Learning Organization*. New York: Doubleday.
10. Cyert, R.M. and March, J.G. (1963) *A Behavioral Theory of the Firm*. Upper Saddle River, NJ: Prentice Hall.
    March, J.G. and Simon, H.A. (1958) *Organizations*. New York: Wiley.
    Simon, H.A. (1947) *Administrative Behavior: A Study of Decision-Making Processes in Administrative Organization*. New York: Macmillan.
11. Rice, F. and Sole, D.D. (1997) 'The Turnaround Champ of Haute Couture Gucci Group CEO Domenico De Sole Tells How He Rescued a Dying Brand – With New Marketing, Lower Prices, and "Terminator Tours"'. *Fortune*, 24 November.

12 Buckley, C. and Vecchi, A. (eds) (2016) *Handbook of Research on Global Fashion Management and Merchandising*. Hershey, PA: IGI Global.
13 Kaplan, R.S. and Norton, D.P. (1992) 'The Balanced Scorecard: Measures that Drive Performance', *Harvard Business Review*, Vol. 70, No. 1, pp. 71–79.
14 Day, G.S. (2007) 'Is it Real? Can We Win? Is it Worth Doing? Managing Risk and Reward in an Innovation Portfolio', *Harvard Business Review*, Vol. 85, No. 12, pp. 110–120.

4 Creating winning business models
Past, present and future

Chapter goals

This chapter examines the importance of the firm's business model, the underling architecture needed to create and maintain value through the value linkage model, and explains what types of business models may exist in the future. The key areas covered are:

- What is a business model?
- The new business model paradigm
- The efficiency-centred business model
- The novelty-centred business model
- Creating shared value through business model innovation
- Future business models
- Strategic congruence through the value linkage model

What is a business model?

The concept of a firm's **business model** can be considered to conflate corporate strategy, economics, entrepreneurship and organisational design literature. Until recently the presence of the term has generally been slow to permeate the strategic management literature and therefore is not short of confusion and ambiguity. A business model in its simplest form can be defined as the core architecture of a firm. Specifically, how its products, services and information flows deliver differentiated value as defined by the customer.[1] This is similar to the concept of 'strategy', as this is also concerned with utilising resources to create value for various stakeholders. However, a business model is different from strategy as the business model describes a system of how the pieces of the firm fit together, but it does not factor in one critical dimension of performance: competition. Dealing with this reality is strategy's job.[2] This holds true, as traditionally the industry had a standard model in terms of market structure, organisational design or asset management. For example, for asset management, it was 'buy-move-sell' and in terms of organisational design, the retail format was the shop and the centuries-old flea market was the auction, whilst it was the use of strategy that ensured the firm remained competitive. Another difference between strategy and a firm's business model is the ability of the business model to react quicker to competitor actions than strategy can. A business model can also be used as a tool for assessing revenue viability as the old model has to provide the economic logic necessary for the new model.

The new business model paradigm

Today's strategy will not work tomorrow as competition intensifies and industry conventions emerge, ICT diffuses and consumer tastes converge. As industry profitability declines and weaker competitors exit, products become obsolete, customer profiles change and ICT renders the firm's business model uncompetitive. The question is not if, but when, as only the strongest can survive. Competition has become increasingly global and intensified as product development cycle times have shortened dramatically. Quality, innovation, delivery cadence and service have become key competitive requirements. The impact and importance of ICT as a principal driver of competition on business has been recognised from an early point. ICT plays a major role in changing industry structure and in creating new industries.[3] New technology equates to new products, which correspond to new markets. ICT is also a great equaliser, eroding the competitive advantage of even well-entrenched firms and propelling others to the forefront. In particular, the advancements in disruptive technology such as rapid 3D prototyping for small-scale manufacturing have exposed the advantages of the new economy, like low barriers to entry, global reach and lower contact costs. This is providing a platform for change in entrepreneurial management thinking and is leading to an increased willingness to experiment with both new organisational designs and the deployment of competitive strategies. Consequently, many of today's firms look vastly different from those of the past, as their scope, structure and relationships are redefined across increasingly blurred industry boundaries.

Though **new business models (NBMs)** can be applied to different industries, the profit formula is the same and usually follows long periods of incremental change punctuated by revolutionary change. If a firm faces no threat of competition, then NBM innovation will be slow and vice versa. The most successful executives know that when the business model shifts or expands, it creates gaps that need to be addressed. Subsequently, they make business model innovation a top priority and proactively manage the process to be forward-looking to capture the next big trend or innovation. Many firms have invested significant resources only to find their return on investment to be below expectations because they have followed trends until they are dead or are ready so late that they have missed the opportunity to capture heathy profits and are instead playing catch-up. For instance, there were many firms that were slow to recognise the rise of the slim-fit silhouette and athletic-leisure trend. Therefore, the best executives are always trying to balance the advantages of consistency and continuity with the need to react, evolve and change.

Historically, the rise of NBMs in the fashion industry has been relatively slow to materialise. This is because most firms were very labour and skill-intensive. In addition, the industry has generally been a follower of NBMs compared to other industries, such as the automobile and electronics industry. Since many fashion firms operate in a highly vertically integrated and siloed environment, the room for innovation and proactive responses to change has been limited. A lack of a good ICT infrastructure along with the skills and knowledge to embrace ICT has caused the firm's structure to move at a slower pace than that of technology. Change has also been impeded by the weaknesses of electronic business platforms. In particular, rampant experimentation has resulted in distorted market behaviour and economically unsustainable operations as spiralling marketing, technology and employee costs weigh heavily on earnings. This has resulted in some well-known casualties like the early web start-up Boo.com and more recently, Cocosa and Nasty Gal. In addition, the quandaries surrounding data security, the availability of a global distribution system and non-uniform industry standards, along with the appropriateness of the current legal framework and the ability to develop brand awareness have acted as barriers to entry. However, even though many e-commerce platforms are yet to turn a profit, the industry does host some of the world's most rapidly growing firms, such as Germany's Zalando, Britain's Farfetch, America's Gilt Groupe and Nigeria's Jumia.

A NBM may represent a better way than the existing alternatives. It may offer more value or it may simply replace the old way of doing business and become the benchmark for the next generation of entrepreneurs to beat. As a result, a NBM may be sheer entrepreneurial insight, an unintentional creation or a process innovation through a better way of producing, selling or distributing an existing product or service. In today's fast-paced, I-want-it-quicker, better, cheaper society, firms are devising a multitude of formats as shown in Table 4.1 to satisfy current demand, as well as designing new platforms to service unmet needs. This has meant that dynamic capabilities, such as flexibility, high speed to market, continued innovation and responsiveness, are crucial as products and services evolve. Characteristics such as consistency, reliability and efficiency are also high on the agenda, but too much emphasis on these can lead to the firm missing out on capturing the value of its early innovations due to it exhibiting resistance and inertia.

Despite the growth that NBMs can create, established firms rarely create innovative business platforms. Most are created by start-ups that are disruptive attackers in the industry. The array of NBMs shows a trend towards the development of highly innovative specialised services and models that use a high integration of ICT and are asset-light. As the industry has been a slow adopter of NBMs, much depends on the ability of senior executives to lead innovation, as some of these models are still developing whilst others are

Table 4.1 Taxonomy of business models

Business model	Characteristics	Benefits	Example
Physical store	Products and services offered in a unique environment serviced by sales associates	Expert advice and enhanced service/experience. Ability to try on products in real-time	Belstaff
Subscription	For a regular fee, customers are able to receive a curated supply of goods	Online or in-store style advice with potential international presence	Trunk Club
Mail order	Catalogue to promote a wide range of mono-brand or multi-brand products	Wide choice of brands, easy to use, with the convenience of quick delivery and returns	Next Directory
E-shop	Web marketing of a shop, used to promote products or services through a website	Low-cost route to global presence and cost reduction in promotion and sales	Vente-Privée
Pop-up shop	Temporary setting-up of store in various locations Offering limited edition products creates consumer interest	Brand heat and reduced fixed costs, constant demand creation obtained from high-value limited edition goods	10 Corso Como
E-mall	Electronic platform which consists of a collection of e-shops, enhanced by a common umbrella, e.g. well-known brand name, product positioning or target market	Ability to specialise in certain market segments and collective benefits of lower cost, a trusted umbrella brand name and increased traffic from 'neighbouring' e-shops	Tmall
E-procurement	Electronic tendering and procurement of goods and services on the Internet	Access to a wider choice of suppliers and lower transaction tendering costs	Ministry of Defence
E-auction	Electronic bidding auctions on the Internet, where the product or service is awarded to the highest bidder	Increased efficiency and time savings, global access to a variety of suppliers and buyers	eBay
Reverse e-auction	Electronic bidding auction where prices go down as more people bid. Usually for low-value items	Increased efficiency and time savings, global sourcing, reduced surplus stock/made to order and better production capacity	N/A
Infomediary	Virtual brokers who gather product and service information from suppliers, normalise the data and then create one centralised point of access for buyers	Enhanced service-based offering that reduces search time and provides contemporary information/reviews	WGSN
Value chain integrator	Integrating multiple steps in the value chain, with potential to exploit information flow between steps to add value	Added value to the firm from transaction data and information flows	JDA Software
Value chain service provider	Specialisation in a specific function in the value chain, such as electronic payments or logistics	Distinct competitive advantage to be gained from specialising in the activity	DHL Logistics

copious and fully commercial in operation. These models may also offer separate platforms for different markets and products. They extend a high degree of networked relationships with a focus on value for the end user and may not necessarily operate mutually exclusively of one another. As a result, most executives agree on a unified commerce thought process as shopping is no longer a linear process. Armed with online pre-purchase information, most consumers switch across channels, **showrooming** the benefits such as feedback on in-depth product features gained from a sales associate, whilst searching for key purchase drivers like the lowest price, instant availability and free delivery. This is particularly true for frequent shoppers and especially those planning high-value purchases. Because of this, **omni-channel** retailing, whether the firm operates in a business-to-business or a business-to-consumer market serves not only as a new source of competition, potentially leading to a redistribution of sales, but also represents a significantly more complex challenge than pure play. This is because firms, especially start-ups, need to be cautious not to get overwhelmed by trying to do more to sell in the same way, which can negatively impact margins and profitability. Omni-channel retailing also requires a frictionless experience and therefore a profound synchronisation due to the consumer journey using the same buying criteria across all channels, whether this be mobile, desktop, tablet, social site or physical store, which creates new touch-points and benchmarks. For this reason, a strategic approach to both selling and servicing the customer is required and though this is expensive to implement, it should not be seen as a logistics, ICT or back-office operational problem, but rather as a holistic organisational design issue.

Case study: Rent The Runway

Founded in 2009 by two Harvard Business School graduates, Rent The Runway is a New York based e-commerce start-up which has often been called the 'Netflix for fashion'. Having raised more than $125 million in venture capital, it has more than six million users and hires out designer dresses and accessories from over 350 brands for formal occasions such as weddings and parties. As an online business with over 65,000 items, it recently decided to add an offline platform by adding multiple bricks-and-mortar stores in key cities such as New York and Las Vegas, so that its customers can try on its garments to ensure they fit correctly. By letting customers try on clothes and order them for delivery, it aims to reduce the high cost of processing returns from customers who order a range of sizes, use their homes as fitting rooms and then return some or all of the items, which can be as much as 50 per cent. This also provides a valuable source of additional data to analyse and helps the firm optimise its offering, as well as a platform for ongoing customer engagement as the trend for online stores to build offline stores and vice versa continues.

The efficiency-centred business model

There is little codified understanding of the elements that form a business model or the processes of building them. An examination of configuration theory shows that these models operate primarily via two main platforms: efficiency (cost leadership) or novelty-centred (differentiation). The **efficiency-centred business model (ECBM)** is anchored in transaction cost economics (TCE).[4] TCE focuses on the cost of economic organisation and recognises that there are costs to using the market mechanism. When transactions costs are high, the advantages of vertical integration are promoted, thereby reducing search, negotiation and monitoring costs for all participants through the attenuation of uncertainty, complexity or information asymmetry. In achieving a cost leadership position, firms should have the resources and capability to reduce transaction costs when establishing the possession of scale-efficient plants, accessing superior process technology or identifying low-cost sources of raw materials, as well as accessing low-wage labour. This enables a competitive advantage to be achieved through economies of scale and scope. ICT has been proven to play an integral role in reducing transaction costs. For instance, the use of Radio Frequency Identification (RFID) tags to track goods from suppliers as used by C&A is helping to shorten and stabilise supply chains, thereby reducing search and monitoring costs. Firms like John Lewis are also using ICT to build strategic partnerships with their suppliers through Vendor Managed Inventory and CPFR, helping to reduce switching, search and coordination costs. This is achieved by making the flow of goods globally transparent, providing flexibility regarding transaction fluctuations and the ability to instantly replenish raw materials, components and inventory. It is imperative that a business model based on cost leadership is aligned with the firm's overall strategy. In doing so, the firm can optimise its performance by strategically positioning itself favourably against industry forces. This is because these forces are instrumental in setting the average profitability of the industry. Figure 4.1 depicts the ECBM through the interpretation of the **Five Forces** framework:

1. **Influencing the barriers to entry** – new entrants to an industry bring new capacity and aspirations to gain market share. This is being stimulated in the industry through, for example, the rapid rise of mobile commerce. When the threat is high, profits cannot rise too quickly without attracting new competitors, some of which will be players that are diversifying from other industries where they have a strong brand equity and can leverage existing capabilities to agitate the competition. Tesco the supermarket company did this with its F&F brand, as did Asda with its George range when it entered the United Kingdom fashion industry. Recently, Amazon has done the same and has launched its own branded apparel range called Buttoned Down, which with its global presence and efficient scale could have severe consequences for

Creating winning business models 49

- ☐ Switching costs can keep competitors out
- ☐ It is harder to compete with existing, efficient players

Threat of Potential New Entrants

Industry Competitors

Rivalry Among Existing Firms

Bargaining Power of Suppliers

- ☐ More margin to cope with price increases
- ☐ Being the lowest-cost producer can help strengthen alliances with buyers
- ☐ Cost leadership can provide access to more customers

Bargaining Power of Buyers

- ☐ Prices can only be lower at even more efficient competitors
- ☐ Switching costs can manipulate buyers
- ☐ Downward pressure from demanding buyers

Threat of Substitute Product or Services

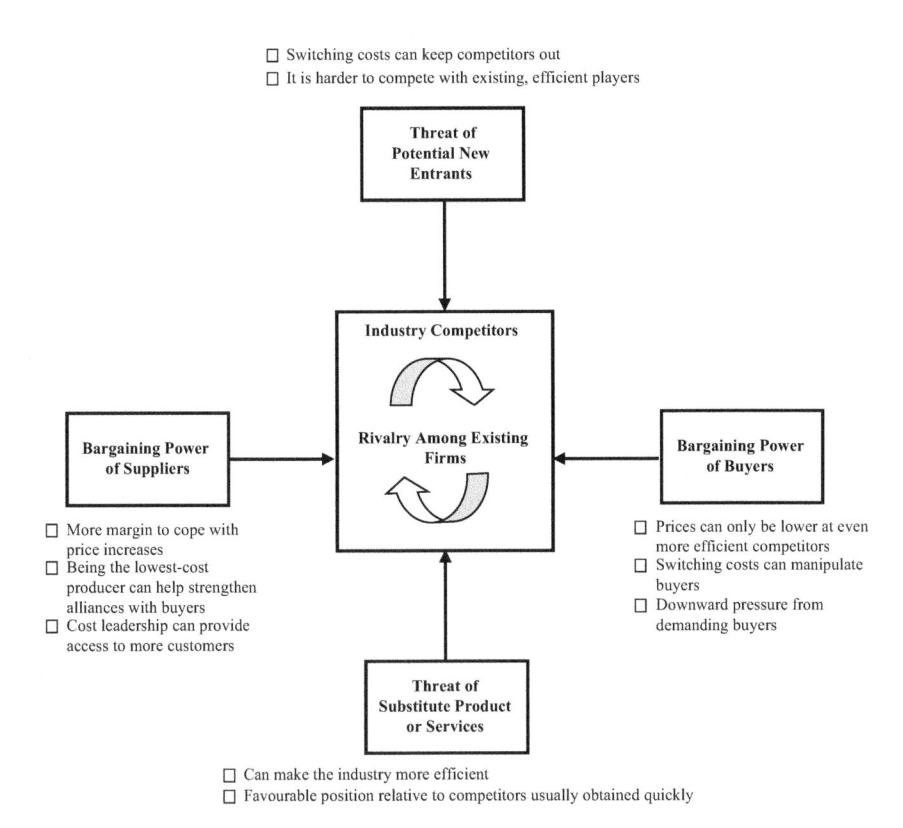

- ☐ Can make the industry more efficient
- ☐ Favourable position relative to competitors usually obtained quickly

Figure 4.1 Cost leadership and the Five Forces
Source: adapted from Porter (1995).[5]

existing players. Cost leadership can make it difficult for consumers to switch to alternative suppliers as these firms enjoy lower costs per unit, utilise ICT more efficiently or command better supplier terms. A buyer who switches vendors must, for example, alter product specifications, retrain employees and build up new processes or systems. Demand-side benefits, also known as network effects, can also be a barrier, as buyers value being in a network with a larger group of customers. For example, many customers are attracted to eBay when selling their clothes online rather than other auction sites because as the world's largest online marketplace, eBay offers more potential trading partners. New entrants are likely to be smaller than established firms as they usually find it difficult to compete with the most efficient player, since plenty of capital is needed for facilities, distribution, inventory and upfront advertising. In the beginning, this can cause a sustained price war, which can erode competitor margins and eventually force rivals to exit the industry as they burn through their capital.

2. Influencing the bargaining power of suppliers – suppliers can raise prices, shift costs downstream or limit the quality of goods and services they provide to exert bargaining power. Labour is usually the most important supplier factor and therefore profitability can be squeezed out of an industry that is unable to pass on these costs. A supplier group is powerful if it is more concentrated than the industry itself or if industry players face switching costs in changing suppliers. When switching costs are high, such as in the luxury goods industry, buyers find it difficult to switch and suppliers are then positioned to extract profits from the industry. A firm typically has more influence over the buyer experience than over the supplier experience, as suppliers are usually much more diverse than buyers. This has led to firms such as Prada purchasing Tannerie Mégisserie Hervy in order to acquire a vital strategic downstream supplier. Renamed Tannerie Limoges, this helps Prada to maintain a strict supply of quality lambskin and plongé leather, whilst enhancing its margin and reducing the threat of supplier competition. Moreover, the trend towards wearable and immersive technology has meant the introduction of powerful new suppliers, such as providers of smart sensors, software, connectivity, operating systems, data storage and smart analytics. Traditional manufacturers have historically never needed these suppliers, but now they are becoming essential to product differentiation and cost. The bargaining power and reputation of these new suppliers can be high. Therefore, seeing suppliers also as customers can really enhance the process of creating and capturing value.

3. Influencing the bargaining power of buyers – analogous to supplier power, commanding buyers can exert pressure on suppliers to cut costs, demand higher quality and play competitors against each other all at the expense of industry profits. As a cost-efficient leader, the firm can also eliminate conventional channels and reduce switching costs. For instance, traditionally the bargaining power of buyers was limited as goods were pushed along the supply chain, whereas now ICT has allowed goods to be demand-led and facilitated through techniques such as JIT and mass customisation, placing the bargaining power directly with buyers. Moreover, some buyers are moving into producing products themselves to retain greater power and control. Product differentiation or being a niche player moves competition away from price alone, and firms that are able to understand their customers and how they use their products can then better segment and customise their offering to capture more value. However, following a differentiation strategy usually requires more capital expenditure, so the cost in the long run can be higher to the firm, although if executed well, the net profits will be larger.

4. Influencing the threat of substitute products or services – substitute products or services do not react to the firm's actions, whereas immediate competitors do. Substitutes can cap an industry's profit potential by making the industry more efficient and therefore limit the prices that firms can

Creating winning business models 51

charge. Players must distance themselves from substitutes by focusing on the needs they serve rather than purely product characteristics or they will incur heavy sunk costs and suffer in profit. Harnessing cost leadership enables new approaches to meeting needs and performing functions. For instance, direct access through the Internet to suppliers discards any intermediaries in the process, creating new substitute business processes. Substitute products and services that require strategic attention are those that are subject to trends and improve the price-performance trade-off or that are produced by substitutes, reaping high profits that may erode with competition. A favourable position can be achieved relative to the competition through first-scale advantages and learning experiences from agile incumbents. By collecting key data, the firm is responsive to improve products and service quality. This can stimulate loyalty and increase switching costs, further raising the barriers to entry.

5. Influencing the rivalry among existing competitors – the composition and interplay of the competitive forces collectively determine the nature of competition and the profitability of the industry. The ECBM can change the basis for competition by creating high barriers to entry, forcing out existing inefficient players through, for example, introducing high fixed-cost activities, focusing on niche markets or selecting scale-sensitive ICT. Rivalry often intensifies naturally over time and industry competition is greatest when a product is subject to trends and when competitors are numerous or roughly equal in terms of size and power. This is amplified when industry growth is slow as the battle for customers and market share intensifies. Price is typically the most destructive form of competition for industry profitability as it transfers profits directly from an industry to its customers. In order to retain customers, increased choice and price transparency have led to firms both lowering their prices and adding on extra services, such as complimentary extended warranties and free delivery and returns. This causes a price war where only the consumer wins and the most efficient player survives, making the industry unattractive for new entrants. Consequently, industry consolidation is increasing as firms choose to compete on either low-cost or high-value strategies. Furthermore, when exit barriers are high, such as heavy upfront investment in specialised assets or management's commitment to a business, these barriers keep firms competing even though they may be achieving low or even negative revenue. This is evident when a firm has a key strategic footprint, is restructuring or has recently been bought by another firm. Because competition plays out over time, it can be difficult to pinpoint and make granular statements on when competitive advantage arises and when it does not, particularly as competitive responses are often both a mixture of rational and irrational actions.

The ECBM can be said to be best suited to mature environments where a prescriptive strategy along with incremental innovation is used and where the firm is focused on positioning choices in terms of where and how to compete.

This type of model can be associated with higher firm performance when resources are scarce than when they are abundant, as cost savings are higher on the management agenda. One of the main issues with this model is the lack of transparency in calculating the actual costs of a competitors' products and services, which makes it difficult to devise cost strategies.

The novelty-centred business model

The **novelty-centred business model (NCBM)** emanates from Joseph Schumpeter's theory of different forms of innovation.[6] This design focuses on either creating a new market or innovating new ways of conducting economic exchanges through the recombination of resources, such as connecting previously unconnected entities by linking transaction participants in new ways or by designing new transaction mechanisms. Levi Strauss & Co achieved this when it revolutionised the jeans market by offering customised products. This type of model requires the product or service to appeal to customers in ways that are different from current competitor offerings and usually involves increased investment in terms of research, design, materials and service. By focusing on activities in the value chain where the immediate customer is not yet satisfied with the product or service proposition, this type of model can often capture super-normal profits by charging premium prices. A case in point has long been offered by Savile Row tailors such as Richard James, where the choice of designs, colours, fabrics and fits are offered on a bespoke basis and hence at a premium price. Similarly, many firms like MTailor, a San Francisco start-up, are leveraging ICT in their business model. MTailor raised $2.1 million in seed funding and produces bespoke men's shirts starting at $69. In under 30 seconds, customers use its app to take a video of themselves turning in a circle for a 360-degree view. Algorithms calculates measurements from the video to create a 3D model and within three weeks, the item is manufactured and delivered.[7] Other NCBM include 'pop-up' or 'flash retailing' and are increasingly becoming a part of the changing retail landscape. By selling a selection of products, in a concept store such as Supreme, brands like Comme Des Garcons and Lacoste can showcase their products, which are often exclusive and sought-after limited edition goods in new distribution channels to new consumers. The innovation in physical bricks-and-mortar stores has now firmly moved to the digital world, where online pop-ups such as Marc Jacobs are using their 'Tweet Shop' to entice consumers to exchange tweets for merchandise to drive brand awareness, footfall and revenue. In doing so, these brands and stores have evoked a huge following with the trendiest consumers in search of the latest fashions. Moreover, there is a movement towards membership and subscription-based business models such as Avenue A by Adidas, which is a women's subscription service that delivers four boxes of premium athletic apparel and footwear for $150 a year. A NCBM is best suited to environments where an emergent strategy is used and where the firm aims to provide a vision of industry structure and standards to other players. It will also have greater importance when resources are plentiful and readily available. Key drivers are strategic flexibility, capital and being able to leverage ICT to facilitate innovation.

Creating shared value through business model innovation

Philanthropy and CSR can only play a limited role in impacting society, as both are unable to achieve sustainable scale and do not fully solve society's main problems. As shown in Table 4.2, **creating shared value (CSV)** is a new business model that moves from a narrow focus to a game-changing approach because it does not see a trade-off between economic gain and social progress. CSV is not a redistribution approach to value sharing or at the periphery of the firm's activities. Instead, by reconceiving society's needs and challenges to become the core of the firm's business model and corporate strategy, the firm moves away from traditional neoclassical economic thinking to expanding the total pool of positive economic and social value. The majority of firms in the fashion industry are hesitant to talk about making a profit, as this is often viewed as taking away from someone else who is less fortunate. This is ill-advised thinking, as the capitalist method re-aligned to solving a social need is what makes CSV sustainable and is what will drive the next wave of innovation, productivity and economic growth. This requires fundamental symmetry in creating material economic impact and competitive advantage to society, and should be viewed as complementary rather than contradictory.

Firms that engage in CSV can pursue its opportunities at three levels:

1. **Reconceiving products and markets** – the aim is to better serve an existing market or target an unmet need in new markets. The focus is on incremental revenue, market share and profitability for the firm. Environmental, social or economic development benefits such as a reduced carbon footprint are delivered by the firm's products and services.
2. **Redefining value chain productivity** – this centres on utilising resources, energy, suppliers, logistics and employees in a different and better way, for example, improvements in internal activities such as securing a key supply of raw materials that helps improve costs, quality, reliability and productivity. Social results are achieved through environmental improvements in resource utilisation, including reduced water usage, improved supplier capability and increased investment in workforce skills.
3. **Enabling cluster development** – this derives from developing a strong competitive context by improving the external environment through community investments and strengthening local suppliers and infrastructure.

Table 4.2 Social impact through shared value

	Philanthropy	Corporate social responsibility	Shared value
MOTIVATION	Be generous	Be responsible	Be competitive
FOCUS	Community needs	Mitigating harm in the value chain	Strategic opportunity
RESOURCES	Contributions and volunteering	CSR budget	Corporate and R&D budget
DEPARTMENT	Foundation and corporate giving	CSR or sustainability	Strategy, cross-functional team or social innovation
FORMAT	External programmes	Corporate initiatives	Product innovation and new business models
SOCIAL VALUE	More resources for charities	Less social and environmental impact	Enduring, scalable solutions
BUSINESS VALUE	Goodwill	Reduced risk and improved reputation	Long-term profitability
VALUE CREATION	Low	Medium	High

Source: adapted from FSG (2015).[8]

This reinforces the link between the firm's success and the community's success, which helps create a mechanism for constructive business–government dialogue. Efforts to build a robust local cluster while raising regional competitiveness often require the firm to establish new partnerships with entities, which can often vary in terms of size and might involve working with competing firms because they have the networks and knowledge to navigate the larger environment better than the firm itself. Some firms are reluctant to bear the costs of improving the market ecosystem when it improves conditions for its competitors, but first-mover advantages are often sustained by the firm. By working with other partners, a firm such as Brunello Cucinelli through its 'Scuola dei Mestieri' or school of crafts has created specialised craftsmanship programmes to address its need to train future artisans. This has helped to reduce its costs, secure supply and increase its profitability, whilst improving jobs and income for the local Solomeo community in Italy, where the firm is based.

Other firms that express CSV well include Patagonia, the privately owned outdoor clothing firm with its initiatives like 'Worn Wear', which proactively supports consumers to adamantly reuse and recycle their Patagonia products in order to help save the planet instead of being a part of the disposable mindset group. In addition, Patagonia's 'Footprint Chronicles' has the goal of bringing transparency to its supply chain to help reduce the adverse social and environmental impacts of its products.

With CSV, there is no short-term fix to society's problems, as the relationship between business and society requires transformational thinking, which governments and NGOs alone cannot solve due to a lack of resources, skills and capabilities. Therefore, society's challenges are most likely to succeed if they are tackled by private sector firms that have the legitimacy to initiate social progress by incorporating it into the core of their business strategy and can engage a variety of stakeholders to spur on shared value creation. This requires firms to be innovative in their business models and to rigorously track the interdependency of their activities and their impact on society so that results can be measured, validated and profitable opportunities scaled, as the definitive goal is to optimise the effectiveness of the firm's strategy. CSV is a major new business model to tackle the world's most pressing problems, many of which exist in developing economies like those of India and Africa. Here, executives should consider factors such as market potential, political stability and the regulatory context when making decisions about where to get started. Together with the challenge of bringing the message to the investment community, makes CSV less about managing the current path and more about creating the future of the fashion industry.

Case study: TOMS

TOMS was founded in 2006 by Blake Mycoskie as a for-profit firm. The firm designs and sells shoes based on the Argentine 'alpargate' design, a lightweight canvas shoe also known as espadrilles. They started out with the 'one-for-one' giving concept, where whenever a pair of TOMS shoes was sold, another pair of shoes was given to children from low-income families. To date, this CSV business model has resulted in over 60 million pairs of shoes being donated worldwide. TOMS also design eyewear and when it sells a pair, part of the profit is used to save or restore the eyesight of people in developing countries. Similarly, it launched the TOMS Roasting Company in 2014 and with each purchase of its coffee, the company works with other organisations to provide 140 litres of safe water to people in need. In 2015, the TOMS bag collection was conceived to help address the need for advancements in maternal health. Purchases of TOMS bags help provide training for skilled birth attendants and distribute birth kits containing items that help a woman safely deliver her baby. In addition to these product initiatives, TOMS is now also actively investing in local communities by opening production plants and creating jobs in poor neighbourhoods, strengthening its shared value ecosystem.[9]

Future business models

The ECBM and the NCBM are neither orthogonal nor mutually exclusive, as in the case of the retailer Zara, which operates an efficiency-driven and innovative business platform. Rethinking what the future could be points us towards the **networked firm**. The key characteristics of this platform are that the assets of the firm are clearly identified, but how they are assembled across the value chain varies according to the task and follows an 'ownership' versus 'shared access' model. Horizontal and vertical communication is encouraged and the use of ICT makes it possible for firms to dramatically decentralise their decision-making without giving up control. Consequently, internal links are capable of being rearranged quickly, easily and effectively, along with the roles of employees who utilise cross-functional team-centric networks based on knowledge and expertise.

This type of platform can be developed further so that operating in a non-linear ecosystem the firm is intentionally spatial and transient. The **ephemeral platform** as presented in Table 4.3 is centred on a firm that is 'borderless' and formed to create new products or services as required, only to be absorbed by sponsor firms or business units when its mission is complete. Using a data-driven risk-based approach, the firm is able to leverage its resources through an agile strategy which is organic and in a constant state of aligning itself to the environment to reap the benefits of this platform. This type of firm may take advantage of the burgeoning economy of freelancers on websites such as upwork.com to conduct a strategic assessment or leverage usage-based pricing and crowdfunding to introduce new products with a high degree of personalisation. Shared access means that the firm is asset-light and can act as an intermediary. This can reduce barriers to entry and therefore the firm can also enter a new country, change a brand or drop a manufacturing competence swiftly. In doing so, it is able to rapidly respond to competitive threats and opportunities as well as to shape them. Because of the increased awareness of the changing business environment and more importantly, customer needs, there will always be value-laden opportunities to capture, especially as consumer tastes and needs continually chase the revolving world of fashion trends.

Table 4.3 The ephemeral firm

Characteristic	Value driver
ORGANISATION	Web network of operating units
STYLE	Flexible and team-centric
STRATEGY	Emergent, agile and risk-based
STRUCTURE	Interdependent and flat
FOCUS	Efficiency or novelty-centred
LEADERSHIP STYLE	Inspirational
DEMAND CREATION	Consumer and innovation-driven
COMPETITIVE ADVANTAGE	Change and responsiveness
KEY RESOURCE	Data, analytics, knowledge and creativity
RESOURCE FACILITATOR	Cutting-edge ICT
OPERATION	Virtual integration
REACH	Global, 24/7 and instantaneous

The ephemeral business model could easily become reality as the commodity capital is no longer scarce, as venture capitalists or online crowdfunding services like Funding Circle or Indiegogo easily provide this. For proof of the concept, the Boston Boot Company, a small men's American 'micro-shoery', launched its Kickstarter campaign in November 2013 with a target of raising only $25,000. Instead, it achieved $248,108 through 1,646 patrons, of which 432 where first-time backers. The brand's first batch shipped in the spring of 2014 and in 2015 ShoeBuy, a leading global online retailer, acquired a minority stake in the company.[10] This is because what is scarce are the good ideas that can create real value. The ephemeral model may be too challenging to implement for large established firms as it is immensely difficult for them to quickly change their business model or imitate a competitor due to structural drift and a high reliance on existing branding, especially as these firms are not so flexible and major revisions in training, marketing, ICT, manufacturing and culture are required. Likewise, if the firm is constantly changing, then a new model of corporate governance and legislation is required, which takes a lot of time to create and dismantle, and all of these factors can be a non-starter if trade unions are involved. Therefore, the potential rewards of experimental concepts can be great for certain firms such as a start-up under certain circumstances, but for others, implementing them can be profoundly challenging or even destructive.

Strategic congruence through the value linkage model

For firms to succeed today and prepare themselves for tomorrow requires them to ensure that they create and sustain **strategic congruence**. This is because the relationship between a firm's corporate strategy and its business model is not one of diametric opposition. Instead, they are both inter-related as the firm's business model serves as a blueprint to understand how its core architecture will deploy its resources to create value by analysing the parties that can be bought together to exploit a business opportunity. Subsequently, it is the job of corporate strategy to apportion this value through the decisions and actions taken by the firm's executives to ensure that the firm is positioned competitively against rivals. Misalignment, also referred to as 'incongruence' or 'disequilibrium', is most common externally when the firm pursues strategies that are no longer competitive in the business environment or when over time it drifts off-mission as peripheral activities gain undue attention and the firm becomes inward-looking. Internal incongruence is mainly due to a failure to coordinate across business functions and insufficient support from other units and senior executives. Therefore, strategic congruence is a situation in which the firm's organisational structure, systems, processes, incentives and human capital support its strategic goals through common objectives. When these elements of alignment are synchronised, they not only support but also strengthen each other as more inputs pass through the system.

Typically, a firm is continually in and out of alignment in some form and key business units are almost always transitioning from one state to the other. Being internally consistent helps to act as a mechanism to create and sustain value, as the strategic consequences of misalignment include a lack of direction, inefficient resource allocation, poor financial performance and high employee turnover. The cogent orientation towards consumer-centric business strategies such as relationship marketing, service quality and mass customisation points to the exchange of value between the firm and the consumer as a fundamental construct in creating economic value added. When creating and sustaining strategic congruence, the firm should not only be aligned internally where strategic and tactical decisions are communicated and acted upon throughout the firm but also exogenously, in the sense that opportunities are maximised and threats are minimised. Moreover, there should be a suitable platform whereby a firm's inputs can be transformed into added value outputs to which the consumer is attracted and willing to pay for. This should be economically viable and delivered ethically and legally. Many well-known business activities are built on the principle of alignment. Examples cover KPIs, management by objectives, the 7S Model and strategic planning.

Creating winning business models 59

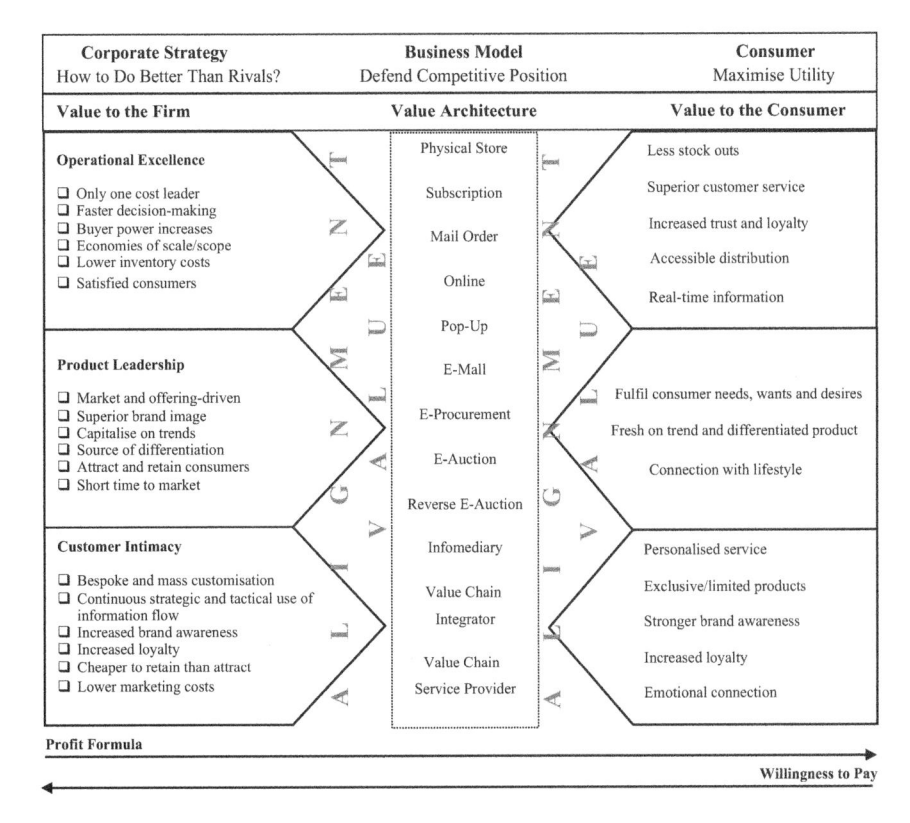

Corporate Strategy How to Do Better Than Rivals?	Business Model Defend Competitive Position	Consumer Maximise Utility
Value to the Firm	**Value Architecture**	**Value to the Consumer**
Operational Excellence ☐ Only one cost leader ☐ Faster decision-making ☐ Buyer power increases ☐ Economies of scale/scope ☐ Lower inventory costs ☐ Satisfied consumers	Physical Store Subscription Mail Order Online Pop-Up	Less stock outs Superior customer service Increased trust and loyalty Accessible distribution Real-time information
Product Leadership ☐ Market and offering-driven ☐ Superior brand image ☐ Capitalise on trends ☐ Source of differentiation ☐ Attract and retain consumers ☐ Short time to market	E-Mall E-Procurement E-Auction Reverse E-Auction	Fulfil consumer needs, wants and desires Fresh on trend and differentiated product Connection with lifestyle
Customer Intimacy ☐ Bespoke and mass customisation ☐ Continuous strategic and tactical use of information flow ☐ Increased brand awareness ☐ Increased loyalty ☐ Cheaper to retain than attract ☐ Lower marketing costs	Infomediary Value Chain Integrator Value Chain Service Provider	Personalised service Exclusive/limited products Stronger brand awareness Increased loyalty Emotional connection

Profit Formula →

← Willingness to Pay

Figure 4.2 The value linkage model

Figure 4.2 shows the **value linkage model**, a conceptual framework for creating and sustaining an alignment-driven approach. This model identifies that a central concept in successfully creating and apportioning value is when a firm's strategy is aligned with its business model and the consumer in a holistic manner. In particular, a firm should focus diffusing its resources initially on one of the value drivers of product leadership, operational excellence or customer intimacy. Once this becomes a significant distinctive core competency, the remaining drivers should be leveraged or clear trade-offs identified. These value drivers should reinforce and align to the key areas in which the firm wishes to be competitive via an appropriate and profitable business model, either as a single or omni-channel platform. The correct business model helps to create an emotional connection that the consumer values and is willing to pay for, such as brand image, excellent quality, speed of delivery or an enhanced store experience. This aids in creating, capturing and sustaining reciprocal value for the firm and the consumer, which can prolong brand advocacy.

Firms such as French Connection, Tommy Hilfiger, Benetton and Li Ning have all experienced misalignment as their strategy was unclear, their business model uncompetitive and their outputs undesirable, but many firms have successfully re-aligned themselves. Taking Burberry as an example, analysts once described it as 'an outdated business with a fashion cachet of almost zero'. With the help of a new management team, it redesigned its product range and positioned itself as a luxury brand, opened stores in strategic locations, controlled its licensing strategy and managed to reposition itself as a sought-after global brand.[11] In pursuing alignment, firms should make sure they do not succumb to the pressure to deliver short-term quarterly earnings in order to satisfy shareholders by undertaking activities that are inconsistent with their long-term objectives, such as heavy discounting or promotions. This is why some of the most progressive firms in the fashion industry are privately held and remain so.

In order for strategic congruence to be successful, the firm must recognise the importance of its human capital, as it is their unique cognitive skills and experience that are responsible for implementing and executing the firm's strategy in a way that rivals cannot. The firm should aim to become an employer of choice by attracting and retaining the most talented personnel who exhibit the required know-how and fit its culture. This is supported by the implementation of a robust performance management programme that is explicit throughout the firm and that rewards employees for their effort in facilitating and executing alignment. Through effective management, the firm can deliver consistent short-term financial goals, such as solid revenue and earnings per share growth, increased return on invested capital and accelerated capital flows. In the long term, the successful strategic positioning and strength of the brand is often an important construct for senior executives in tracking the success of strategic congruence, along with other key financial measures such as its compound annual growth rate and increase in share price. However, the firm needs to reward creativity and initiative, as both behaviours can sometimes be stifled due to a relentless focus on alignment and execution. This can mean that fleeting opportunities are unexploited and the next competitive frontier is missed.

Review questions

Questions for debate regarding creating winning business models are as follows:

- Are new business models more focused on demand-side or supply-side economics?
- Do new business models create more value than new products and services?
- Which is more important – an ecosystem or the business platform?

- Will a lack of data security and ethical control exclude firms from participating in digital platforms and ecosystems?
- If every firm practised shared value, what would the world look like?
- What new business model would you create and why?
- What are the advantages and disadvantages of the value linkage model?

Further reading

1 Timmers, P. (2000) *Electronic Commerce: Strategies and Models for Business-to-Business Trading.* Chichester: John Wiley & Sons.
2 Magretta, J. (2002) 'Why Business Models Matter', *Harvard Business Review*, Vol. 80, No. 5, pp. 86–92.
3 Porter, M.E. (1980) *Competitive Strategy: Techniques for Analysing Industries and Competitors.* New York: Collier Macmillan.
4 Williamson, O.E. (1979) 'Transaction Cost Economics: The Governance of Contractual Relations', *Journal of Law and Economics*, Vol. 22, No. 2, pp. 239–61.
5 Porter, M.E. (1985) *Competitive Advantage; Creating and Sustaining Superior Performance.* New York: Collier Macmillan.
6 Schumpeter, J.A. (1934) *The Theory of Economic Development: An Inquiry into Profits, Capital, Credit, Interest and the Business Cycle.* Cambridge, MA: Harvard University Press.
7 MTailor (2016) 'Stop Wearing Another Man's Clothing', www.mtailor.com (accessed 4 May 2017).
    Crunchbase (2016) 'MTailor Overview', www.crunchbase.com/organization/mtailor#/entity (accessed 4 May 2017).
8 FSG (2015) 'Creating Shared Value', www.fsg.org (accessed 4 May 2017).
9 TOMS (2016) 'TOMS Company Overview', www.toms.com/about-toms#companyInfo (accessed 4 May 2017).
10 Kickstarter (2014) 'Boston Boot Co. A Craft Approach to Men's Boots', www.kickstarter.com/projects/bostonbootco/boston-boot-co-a-craft-approach-to-mens-boots (accessed 4 May 2017).
    Hurst, S. (2015) 'ShoeBuy Acquires Minority Stake in Kickstarter's Boston Boot Company', *Crowdfund Insider*, www.crowdfundinsider.com/2015/01/61719-shoebuy-acquires-minority-stake-in-kickstarters-boston-boot-company (accessed 4 May 2017).
11 Birtwistle, G. and Moore, C.M. (2004) 'The Burberry Business Model: Creating an International Brand', *International Journal of Retail and Distribution Management*, Vol. 32, No. 8, pp. 412–442.
    Ahrendts, A. (2013) 'Burberry's CEO On Turning an Aging British Icon into a Global Luxury Brand', *Harvard Business Review*, Vol. 91, No. 1, pp. 39–42.

5 Brand management
Leveraging the fundamentals

Chapter goals

This chapter analyses the key characteristics that define successful brands and how, under the lens of consumer-orientated marketing, firms can create a marketing strategy that delivers prolonged value. The key areas covered are:

- Brand purpose
- Consumer-orientated marketing
- Marketing strategy formulation

Brand purpose

> Success needs coherence of the brand. (John Galliano, fashion designer).[1]

The fashion industry is potent because most people think of it as pretentious clothes, glamorous parties, self-centred designers, superficial media and glossy marketing. This is partly true, but there is another side to the industry that drives a more balanced and grounded approach. This is the strategic side of managing a brand. Traditionally, fashion brand management focused on product design and the aesthetic content because of the ever-shortening life cycle of products. However, as strong brands endure, the locus of attention has moved to managing the brand strategically. Successful brand strategists are those who create products and services that render positive associations, evaluations, recommendations and repeat purchases with the consumer. This is an ecosystem that only the best brand management executives can formulate and execute. This lends itself to brands being the reason why firms exist and not the other way around. Nike is a good example of this and has shifted away from being traditionally known for cool footwear and apparel to now becoming a world-class health and fitness brand, and can even be categorised as a firm striving to create shared value. Consequently, Nike has not only won the hearts, minds and wallets of many new consumers across the globe, but has also made consumers, families, cities and even countries healthier through the power of sport.

A **brand** in its simplest form can be described as a name, term, sign or symbol, or a combination of these used to identify the products or services of a seller to differentiate itself from the competition.[2] The best brands form an emotional bond and own a place in the consumer's mind. Therefore, it can be said that a strong brand provides an autonomous status between consumer and product. The rapidly changing nature of fashion trends and the dynamic business environment mean a lack of long-term security for both the firm and the consumer. It is the job of managing the brand in a 'brand-right and business-right' manner to ensure the longevity and equity of the firm, as there is always tension between growth and quality. This can be answered by asking the following simple question: 'we can do it, but should we do it?' This is important as the brand generally accounts for between 30 and 70 per cent of a firm's market value in the fashion industry. For some luxury brands, it can be even higher and plays a central theme for customers in their decision-making process. For example, Tom Ford launched his firm in 2006 based largely on the recognition of his name, which he earned whilst working for Gucci as its creative director, and is now reportedly a $1 billion business at retail value.[3] Yet, consumers choose brands just like they choose their friends. This is on the basis of whether they connect, believe, trust and love them. As a result, the role of managing a brand becomes fickle and arduous if the relationship is not carefully cultivated and respected. Accordingly, great brands are consumer-centric. They do not simply just talk to consumers, they inspire participation and invite them into a rich emotional experience. These brands are three-dimensional as they start new interactive conversations to generate demand, create innovate business models and are masters at surprising and delighting the consumer to participate in the cultural experience we love and call shopping. Constantly evolving, these brands are willing and understand the need to change. They know that consumers do not buy what a firm sells; instead, they buy what the firm stands for, meaning its brand, its culture and how it conducts its business.[4]

As consumers become more knowledgeable about their choices, they are demanding better reasons to buy. A **brand purpose** is the functional and emotional benefits and how this is nurtured to stand apart from the crowd so that there is a reason to purchase. A clear brand purpose is self-certification of its values and an enduring narrative. Internally, brand purpose provides a single voice with the aim of improving alignment throughout the firm. Externally, it aims to provide a consistent message for the consumer across various touchpoints. If the brand purpose is supported by a good strategy, it can really propel the firm to capture super-normal profits. Subsequently, strong brands are proven to be commercially successful and vice versa. Figure 5.1 encapsulates the main characteristics of a strong and coherent brand purpose.

64 *Brand management*

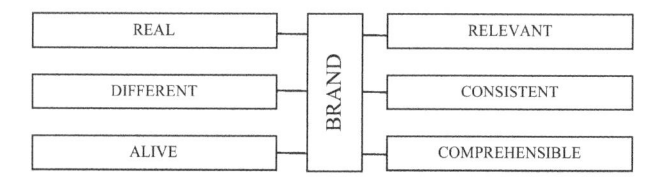

```
┌──────────────┐      ┌──────────────────┐
│     REAL     │──┐┌──│     RELEVANT     │
└──────────────┘  ││  └──────────────────┘
┌──────────────┐ ┌┴┴┐ ┌──────────────────┐
│  DIFFERENT   │─│BR│─│    CONSISTENT    │
└──────────────┘ │AN│ └──────────────────┘
┌──────────────┐ │D │ ┌──────────────────┐
│    ALIVE     │─└┬┬┘─│  COMPREHENSIBLE  │
└──────────────┘  ┘└  └──────────────────┘
```

Figure 5.1 Brand purpose
Source: adapted from Frampton (2009).[5]

In order to offer a meaningful experience, a brand needs to be **real** in what it does. It should have a defined heritage and be well grounded in its core values that deliver against the high expectations of the consumer. This is very important for items that carry a price premium such as luxury goods and bespoke products. However, the varying needs of heterogeneous consumer groups have resulted in different perceptions on what this entails. The flexibility and agility to stay authentic and genuine to the brand DNA is paramount as consumer tastes evolve. This is particularly true with Millennials, who search for brand and product legitimacy when shopping, but are less concerned with having a deeper level of engagement as their lives revolve around short-term 'Instagrammable' moments and maximising immediate utility.[6] As good brands take time to create, there has been a trend towards resurrecting dormant or underperforming brands. These firms have a strong heritage with an intact brand DNA and have the potential to be scaled up globally if they can be aligned with a sound strategic direction and supported with enough financial power.

Different, this is the degree to which the consumer perceives the brand to have a distinguished positioning divergent from the competition. One that they can rely on to guide their choice in order to minimise the risk when competing products or services cannot be easily differentiated, as in the case of multi-brand environments, where rival brands sit adjacent to one another. One way to really test this is to remove the brand name or logo and 'blind-test' the firm's products against its competitors in order to identify the difference between the brands. The infatuation with constant newness in the fashion industry, along with increased counterfeiting and trademark infringement, has resulted in blurred boundaries of differentiation in the form of mass imitation and fakes. This has hampered growth for many firms, especially in lucrative markets like China. For example, Kering alleges that Alibaba, the Chinese e-commerce group, encourages and profits from the sale of counterfeit goods on its site. Search suggestions including 'replica', 'cucci' and 'guchi' lead potential customers to fake products and damages its brands such as Gucci, Balenciaga and Saint Laurent.[7] One way in which firms are differentiating themselves is through sponsorship and product placement. N.Peal luxurious cashmere sweaters were worn by Daniel Craig, who played the secret agent James Bond in the box office smash hit *Skyfall* and more recently in *Spectre*. This helps consolidate its position as an English style icon by leveraging both its heritage and the lucrative halo effect of the Bond aesthetic, which creates a story that can be seeded across multiple media formats from Twitter to glossy magazines such as *Vogue* and *GQ*.

Brands are built, lost and rebuilt. Many brands had to sharpen their focus during the recession to remain **relevant** to their customers. Most firms at some point in their history have lost their footing in the contemporary world and have gone through a stage of reinventing themselves. From J Crew to Gianfranco Ferre to Christian Lacroix, each firm has experienced a point in time when its brand went through a rebirth, some of which were successful and others not so much. Brands, especially iconic ones, need to complement or enhance their historical identity and not erode their original meaning. To remain relevant, today's brands must aim to fit with the customers' needs, wants, desires and lifestyles across all relevant demographics and geographies. The globalisation of Western brands has increased this phenomenon, especially in developing markets like China, where consumers are largely younger than those in the West and habitually think 'why do I need that?', 'why is this brand important to me?' and 'what will other people think?' As a result, firms should track the sources of information their customers turn to and find the right combination of marketing channels and messaging to attract and connect these customers to the firm's products. Though a compelling value-for-money narrative remains crucial, the long-standing metric of 'share of wallet' has moved on to 'share of experience'. The old way involved taking an image, writing an editorial, placing it in a store and hoping it would sell. The new way involves shooting a video and posting it on YouTube or live streaming content, getting bloggers to do the editorial, customers to generate user content and being able to buy the product through multiple platforms. Brands like Michael Kors have over 17 million followers on Facebook, which is more than the circulation of some magazines and viewers of television shows. It is important to note that the monetisation of products through social media platforms like Facebook is yet to take off, as many consumers are keen to keep their social media and online shopping activity separate. Traditional bricks-and-mortar retailers cannot stay idle as online retailers dominate on big shopping days across the globe such as 'Black Friday' and 'Cyber Monday' in America, 'Singles Day' in China, 'El Buen Fin' in Mexico and 'Click Frenzy' in Australia. As consumer empowerment and the need for instant gratification intensifies, consumers have come to expect a convenience factor which differs according to generation and geography, but is crucial if brands are to stay relevant. Consequently, strategic contradictions such as not offering worldwide shipping or investing heavily in a website but failing to correct the site's compatibility across multiple media platforms can lead to an exodus of customers.

In today's networked world, to be a brand that is **alive** has meant reimagining the old-fashioned and static concepts of brand, trust and customer loyalty, as they no longer have the same traction that they did in the past. The reason for this is that the younger the consumer, the less loyal they are to brands as they prefer to mix and match products and continue to seek out non-mainstream brands. Millennials and Generation Z are the least-trusting groups and increasingly refer to reviews of products and services from their peers or an online shopping app rather than recommendations made by sales associates. Sports stars, influencers and celebrities continue to have an enormous impact, even though many consumers may deny that it is a key driver in the decision-making process for their purchase. Take, for example, the Italian fashion blogger Chiara Ferragni, creator of The Blonde Salad, who has eight million Instagram followers, 500,000 daily Snapchat story viewers and whose website generates over 500,000 unique visitors a month. Even bigger are Taylor Swift, Beyoncé Knowles and Kim Kardashian, who have more than 280 million Instagram followers between them and wield extraordinary influence over consumers. This is a delicate issue as user-generated content such as a Twitter or Instagram post is capable of exploding virally and tearing apart a brand name in a matter of hours. In 2014 ASOS encountered a 'Twitterstorm' after it compared the former model Jodie Marsh's physique to that of a man. Numerous ASOS customers threatened to boycott the website, resulting in its CEO offering a grovelling apology. Consequently, firms must engage with consumers in two-way conversations, regardless of whether they are positive or not. Table 5.1 shows a timeline on how the rapid development in social media is being leveraged to interact with consumers.

Consumers are trading experiences across various channels to create new rules of engagement and benchmarks. The long-term **consistency** of the brand proposition is crucial for a sustained competitive advantage before, during and

Table 5.1 Social media developments in 2016

Jan	Periscope begins broadcasting directly within Twitter
	London Fashion Week utilises live streaming of catwalk shows
Feb	Facebook launches Canvas, a full-screen and immersive mobile advertising experience
Apr	Facebook allows chatbots to be used within its Messenger function and launches Live to all users
Jun	Instagram introduces new features which allow customers to call or email businesses they follow
Jul	Instagram rolls out keyword blocking to everyday users, giving greater control to brands
Aug	Instagram launches Stories, which allows photos and videos to disappear after 24 hours
	Pinterest launches promoted videos for brands
	Snapchat launches Geo Stickers, offering brands the option to sponsor stickers at targeted locations
Sep	Snapchat launches Spectacles, which allows users to record video snippets to their Snapchat Memories
Oct	Facebook launches Marketplaces, an online exchange

Source: adapted from Gaunt (2016).[8]

after the actual purchase. Consistency is closely linked to being 'real' and is one of the major reasons why successful firms derail. Distinguished brands are cohesive and provide reassurance and confidence to the consumer. They are at ease when articulating their philosophies in the marketplace and avoid superfluous activities that detract from their core message and beliefs. Established brands provide stronger multiples and their brand durability provides equity for its stakeholders. For further justification of this, imagine if the same Canada Goose jacket had a different quality standard from the last one. The brand would have no meaning or integrity and customers would lose their trust in the brand very quickly. By protecting the brand, brand consistency also provides barriers to entry and acts as a sign of economic resilience.

Comprehension relates to the understanding of the distinct qualities and characteristics of the brand, its owners and its voice to the world. Internal comprehension relates to what the brand stands for and its exclusive values, positioning and proposition. External comprehension focuses on who its target customers are and what drives them from a quantitative and qualitative perspective. This ought to be communicated clearly throughout the firm so that everyone is aligned and resources are utilised effectively. Comprehension is often characterised by the creative director or the CEO's personality, as brands can be seen as warm as in the case of Disney, controversial in the case of Rick Owens or innovative in the case of Stone Island. However, if the brand's voice is not consistent with how consumers perceive or experience the brand, the strategy has no meaning and can be damaging. Therefore, it is important that the creative director is matched with a strong and complementary CEO to ensure that comprehension is clear, as getting this duo right keeps the strategic and creative vision aligned. This is because as a brand grows, execution becomes really important and the creative director should focus their talents on the creative tasks and not be distracted with operational responsibilities for which they usually lack the business acumen and time to deal with. A case in point is Burberry, which appointed designer Christopher Bailey to the position of joint CEO and chief creative director, only to see a one-fifth decline in its value, which resulted in investors losing faith in Bailey's ability to market the brand around the world and forced the board of directors to split his role and hire a new CEO.[9]

Case study: Moynat

The French luxury trunk and accessories maker Moynat was founded in 1849 during the great era of rail travel by Pauline Moynat, the only female trunk maker of her time. With a rich and varied past, it registered plenty of patents, including the first waterproof canvas in 1854, and was well known for its curved shaped limousine trunks that were designed to be placed on top of the roof of a car. Despite its past successes, Moynat closed in 1976. Resurrected by Bernard Arnault, the Chairman and CEO of Moët Hennessey Louis Vuitton (LVMH), through his private vehicle L Capital in 2010, the hope was that the brand's illustrious history of designing desirable travel, leather goods and accessories would now once again be able to rival other great houses such as Goyard and Hermès. Nonetheless, even with the financial backing and resources of LVMH, challenges remain because so few pieces of Moynat exist and, as a result, the firm has had to reinvent itself. By putting up flyers at vintage car fairs asking for Moynat items and buying everything it could find, including antique pieces and catalogues, the firm started to build up an archive to identify the brand's purpose and house codes. This helped respect the brand's past and create new designs that shape the future of the brand in a modern way. Today, it produces goods that incorporate clean lines and refined silhouettes sold in boutiques across the world from Paris, London and New York to Tokyo, Seoul, Beijing and Taipei. Without undertaking any advertising, it has instead chosen to partner with key influencers such as Dover Street Market, Pharrell Williams and the visual artist Mambo to spread its brand message to a select clientele.

Consumer-orientated marketing

The most successful firms in the industry are evolving away from a product-driven business model towards a consumer-focused model. Broadly speaking, the heart of modern marketing is the process by which the firm creates value by focusing on products and services that benefit the customer. The exchange in value is captured through pricing and the customer's willingness to pay. This is depicted through three inter-related facets.

Market segmentation focuses on 'what customer segments exist?' and 'who could the firm serve in the marketplace?' The firm should also ask itself 'who are our current customers?' and 'why have we focused our efforts on these customers?' They should ask themselves 'who do we wish our customers were?' and 'why we do not have these customers?' These questions can be answered using the most widely used bases like demographic, geographical, behavioural and psychographic variables. As these are general descriptors, a more granular unit of analyses to describe a customer's behaviour or relationship to a product should be used. For example, buying patterns, user and loyalty status, perceived benefits sought and attitude towards the product help in creating products and messaging that really resonates with customers. This can be achieved using techniques such as the **Voice of The Consumer** developed by the Massachusetts Institute of Technology, which utilises the Japanese product development methodology of **Quality Function Deployment**. Additionally, another widely used metric is a firm's **Net Promoter Score**, which utilises a 1 to 10-point scale to assess customer loyalty and brand advocacy. This is vital, as the firm should aim to frame its products in the consumer's mind or risk being framed by them. Brands, especially luxury goods, are often seen as status symbols that reflect accumulated wealth. Subsequently, luxury brands play to this through segmentation strategies like licensing to reach a wider audience who aspire to the brand. Firms such as Tory Burch, Ferrari and Porsche Design deploy diffusion lines to capture this wealth, ranging from apparel to accessories to fragrance. But few get this absolutely right and often many firms like Moschino and Dolce & Gabbana have previously lost sight of who their real customers were and spread themselves too wide. The result is brand fatigue and the firm devalues itself as consumers move away from these products to new and exciting offerings.

The **target market** concentrates on who the firm will select and attempt to serve. This has important implications for which features to include in the firm's products and its communication efforts. Analysis and questions focus on the attractiveness of 'who do you choose and not choose to serve?' and 'what customer needs does the firm aim to satisfy?' In general, the chosen customers should have common characteristics and should respond in a similar manner to activities presented to them by the firm. Marketers are generally moving towards localisation and serving smaller segments using the power of data analytics and smart technology. Yet, there is many ways to choose a target market. This ranges from mass marketing and an economies of scale approach to a 'snowflake theory', in that every customer is different and so products are customised for them. Consequently, the firm should have the resources to successfully market its offering to the target segment and this should be financially favourable.

It is imperative for brand executives to understand the cultural dimensions of their target market. In fashion, most consumers connect with a brand first through visual identity and then through its product features. Colour is the main driver of visual identity and differentiation, the other two being logo and typography. Therefore, colour can help differentiate a luxury brand from a discount brand and position a brand as serious or fun, young or old and male or female. Consequently, executives should ensure their products, packaging and communication strategies are appropriate for their target market, as many consumers will not buy a certain colour or colour combination, no matter how great the product looks or who the brand is due to cultural and religious reasons. For example, the colour red is associated with luck and happiness in China and purple has associations of nobility in the United Kingdom and in Greece, but is the colour of suffering and death in Italy, Thailand and Brazil. White in India and China is worn to funerals, as opposed to yellow in Egypt, and black is associated with being expensive, formal and powerful across all cultures. Brands that have a strong identifiable position in the minds of consumers include Lanvin and its current house colour, a shade of cool blue that certainly is one of the most recognisable in the world and one

70 *Brand management*

that provokes a strong sense of refreshment, sophistication and friendliness. Hermès represents its brand with a burnt-orange that people can instantaneously recognise from afar. This colour communicates abundance, richness and energy. Christian Louboutin's house colour is scarlet red, also known as trademark Pantone 18–1663 TPX, which as a contrast colour on the sole of the shoe portrays a rich sense of sexiness, power and beauty.

Market segmentation and the target market drive the last step in the process, which is a firm's **product positioning** and centres on 'why should customers buy from you?' and 'what is your unique value proposition?' This step aims to use price, social mission, branding and lifestyle to position the firm's offering in the mind of the target customer and how its attributes differ from others by asking the question 'who is the direct and indirect competition?' Firms should ask this question in its broadest sense via 'what job does this product do?' from a functional, social and emotional perspective. This is necessary, as job-defined markets are typically larger than category-defined markets and, more importantly, customers will usually pay significant premiums for brands that do a job well. A valuable reflection is that decisions on positioning individual products must also be considered within the context of the firm's full product portfolio due to product, pricing and distribution inter-relationships.

By solving the positioning frame, the firm can leverage the **marketing mix** (product, place, price and promotion activities) to work out the tactical details of the statement and capture the value created by the earlier stages in the process. As brands become an integral part of the consumer's life, the 'power' of the brand has grown substantially. Many consumers are purchasing solely based on the brand proposition. With this in mind, the more powerful the brand, the higher the premium it can charge per unit for the same product compared to its competitors. Collectively, segmentation, targeting and positioning come together in the **positioning statement** in Figure 5.2 to specify the position the firm wishes to occupy in the customer's mind.

For, (target market),   (our product/brand offering), is (unique selling proposition), among all (competitive arena) because (single most important factor).

An example for Stella McCartney could look like:

For, (eco-fashion conscious adults),   (Stella McCartney clothes and accessories) are (the most ethically sourced and manufactured) among all (global fashion firms) because (they do not use leather or fur).

Figure 5.2 The positioning statement

This is a valuable task and should be conducted by everyone in the firm, regardless of their role, as it is clear that marketing in its traditional sense is no longer a guarantee of success. The exercise forces the firm to be succinct and ask itself hard questions such as 'are we positioned to survive?' and 'what is our unique selling proposition (USP) that makes us different from the competition?' It is also important to note that the same product can have multiple target markets and segments, which may result in a variety of different positionings. Over time, repositioning is usually required in order to stay competitive. Therefore, the firm must sustain the process of creating and capturing value and must refer to its brand purpose for guidance as customer tastes alter, market segment sizes change and ICT impacts the firm's capabilities and costs. Even so, this does not guarantee success as firms cannot completely trust consumer intentions, since fashion consumers are well known for their irrational and high-impulse purchasing behaviour. These actions are more normal than most people are prepared to admit. You only have to remind yourselves of the famous phrase 'I only went out to have a look, but then I had to have it' to relate to this.

As modern marketing centres on the consumer, it is important to identify that the domain of who owns the customer and the skills needed to interact with them has changed. Traditionally, it was the marketing department that focused on this. Now, it can be somebody in the human resources department who is responsible for training or somebody in research and development who creates products to meet their needs. Or perhaps it is the finance department or the analytics team that crunch the numbers to identify which consumers they should target using annual spend and lifetime value metrics, or a charismatic CEO who visits the major key accounts to pitch new products and help grow the business. Either way, the skills that the marketing executive needs are increasingly residing elsewhere within the firm and because of this, the whole concept of marketing is being deconstructed and reconstructed by the best firms.

Case study: Modanisa

Established in 2011 by Kerim Ture and Lale Tuzun, the Turkish start-up Modanisa is an e-commerce brand with a specific consumer-orientated mission. With a global market size estimated to be worth $200 billion and with a potential market of 400 million Muslim women, Modanisa aims to provide a traditionally underserved market known for a lack of variety and high prices with the latest fashion through 'choice in style', whilst following the traditional dress codes of Islam. Targeting a woman who is modern not marginal, feminine not sexy, conservative not narrow-minded and social not asocial, its website offers 300 brands, 30,000 diverse items and more than 22 designer offerings, all of which equates to plenty of stylish options on the traditional hijab. With its production base in Turkey and its proximity to other big Islamic fashion consumer markets such as Iran, Egypt, Saudi Arabia, France and the United Arab Emirates, Modanisa is able to offer express delivery as standard and to deliver goods to most European cities within 48 hours. Serving 75 countries, Modanisa's ambition to be the first global Muslim fashion brand is gaining momentum and it is considered to be the most popular conservative fashion site in the world, with six million visitors each month.[10]

Marketing strategy formulation

To make effective brand management decisions executives should understand and address the content and context of their **marketing strategy**. Aside from understanding the needs of the customer, the process should also undertake an objective analysis of the firm's strengths and weaknesses and what special competence it possesses to meet those requirements. In order to assess this, the firm should have an in-depth understanding of its capabilities and resources, such as manufacturing expertise, financial power, and design and marketing talent. Marketers should also aim to identify both their current and future competitors from a customer and product perspective. This is pertinent as brand marketers usually segment by the same product and category as the immediate competition and rarely see the competition that comes from outside their sphere. As a result, one of the biggest problems faced by brand executives is understanding consumer acceptance and knowing where the industry is heading. In order to do this, competitor objectives, strategies, and strengths and weaknesses need to be understood in order to predict and shape competitive reactions as the firm seeks to define its competitive advantage and USP. The reason for this is that product fit within the firm is just as important as its fit with the market. Too many buyers and brand executives develop products that they themselves like and therefore think there is a huge market for, without any real due diligence. This insider's view derives from lots of internal experience and time spent with the idea or product, and causes a self-selecting set of beliefs. This can develop into an irrational viewpoint and a failed marketing strategy as the consumer disappoints by not resonating with the offering. Therefore, great brand strategists are rational, creative, opportunistic and in tune with understanding and aligning their internal firm's skills and resources to the external environment. Brand strategists at the pinnacle of their profession are those who have a vision to take the industry somewhere new by having an innate understanding of the consumer, the competition and the industry dynamics. They do this by starting with no preconceived constraints about the product attributes, channel configuration or economic model of the firm. This is married to identifying customer groups that have been poorly served or overlooked in terms of improving the lives of the consumer rather than merely meeting their needs.

There are principal collaborators in the marketing network that the firm needs to enlist and motivate in order to help them achieve a competitive advantage. A key partner downstream is the retailer and upstream is the supplier. It is necessary for the firm to understand its cost structure and margin expectations, allocation abilities and requirements, and training and support requests. This is then contextualised against their relationship with the firm's competitors and customers. Suppliers have become critical collaborators in making marketing strategy work by providing a quality product in a timely manner. Retailers such as Victoria's Secret and Abercrombie & Fitch continue to meet the demands of consumers who are 'experience collectors' by applying experiential marketing techniques. They have made their stores retail destinations in their own right to pull in demand and have also created an online offering that stimulates deeper engagement between the brand and their customers. Deploying the ELIPSE framework can help the firm to spot, monitor and react to the signs of disruption that support or limit what is possible before competitors do so. Therefore, it is dangerous to design a marketing strategy for a context which is not carefully developed and aligned with the business environment and the firm's overall strategy. As a result, the importance of strategically managing a brand in helping to achieve a competitive advantage shows no signs of abating.

Review questions

Questions for debate regarding brand management are as follows:

- Should the structure for global marketing be centralised or decentralised?
- Is loyalty still relevant in a world of endless choice?
- Do omni-channel customers spend more than single-channel customers?
- Why do many global brands fail when entering emerging markets?
- What are the advantages and disadvantages of creating a new brand name when entering an emerging market?
- Which new brands will be the next stars of the future and why?

Further reading

1 Galliano, J. (2016) 'Voices: The Business of Fashion Conference', 2 December 2016, Oxford: The Business of Fashion.
2 Armstrong, G. and Kotler, P. (2015) *Principles of Marketing*, 7th edn. Harlow: Pearson Education.
3 Amed, I. (2013) 'The Business of Being Tom Ford, Part 1', *The Business of Fashion*, www.businessoffashion.com/articles/people/the-business-of-being-tom-ford-part-i (accessed 4 May 2017).

4 Butler, M. and Gravatt, S. (2005) *People Don't Buy What You Sell – They Buy What You Stand For*. Oxford: Management Books 2000 Ltd.
5 Frampton, J. (2009) 'What Makes Brands Great' in R. Clifton (ed.), *Brands and Branding*, 2nd edn. London: Profile Books.
6 Jackson, T. (2016) 'Luxury Travel's State of Play: Asia Focus', London: Stylus Media Group.
   Jackson, T. (2016) 'Walpole Luxury Summit 2016: The Americas', London: Walpole.
7 Clover, C. (2015) 'Alibaba Launches Technology to Fight Fake Goods', *Financial Times*, 18 May.
8 Gaunt, S. (2016) *Social Media 2016: A Year in Review*. London: Practicology.
9 Daneshkhu, S. and Oakley, D. (2016) 'Investors Step up Criticism of Bailey for Dual Role at Burberry', *Financial Times*, 20 May.
10 Modanisa. (2016) 'About Us', http://en.modanisa.com/about-us (accessed 4 May 2017).

6 Innovation-driven growth
The formula for success

> **Chapter goals**
>
> This chapter identifies the foundation for creating, capturing and sustaining innovation, along with four principal rules of engagement for successful innovation. The key areas covered are:
>
> - Creating and capturing value through innovation
> - Incremental and discontinuous innovation
> - Getting the innovation formula right
> - Breakthrough innovation streams

Creating and capturing value through innovation

Innovation can sometimes be like panning for gold as when you do find it, it only lasts for a very short time. Building a successful firm for sustained success requires a focus on driving growth through innovation. This involves the firm aligning its innovation strategy with its business strategy. Whether it is a product, a business model or a service, the best firms have a capacity to innovate and are continuously renewing themselves to remain competitive, as newness is considered the nutrients of the fashion industry.[1] Techniques such as lean manufacturing, rapid prototyping and risk management can be used to facilitate and encourage creativity throughout the firm. But the fashion industry is not like the pharmaceutical industry where you can patent ideas for a lengthy period. If a product, service or brand is successful, others will start to copy it immediately. Top firms have a beginner's mindset and are constantly creating the future. They have high learning curves and see failures as intelligent learning opportunities to start again without fear. In essence, they are ready to 'fail fast', 'fail cheap' and 'fail forward'. These firms relentlessly ask questions to give clarity on what the future could look like and where value can be created. Whether the firm is meeting demand or creating demand, successful innovation requires the firm to educate its potential customers on why they might need its product or service. Just producing, pricing and advertising a product or service is no longer enough. Great fashion firms educate, seduce and surprise their potential customers about why they might need and desire their proposition.

Case study: The Dandy Lab

The Dandy Lab is a pioneering interactive men's lifestyle pop-up shop that was situated in London's iconic Old Spitalfields Market from July 2015 to February 2016. Working closely with various retail technology firms and 52 independent British lifestyle brands, its aim was to create the blueprint of the future for stores operating in smart retail environments. The store was fitted with modular shelving units embedded with a plethora of digital sensors and equipment, all powered by one single Ethernet cable, which allowed easy and agile deployment. Using cloud computing, real-time data analytics and the philosophy of rapid iteration, the Dandy Lab was able to test a variety of new technologies. For example, by using footfall cameras and Wi-Fi data points, it was able to produce heat maps of where customers lingered the most and their demographic profile, to identify the most popular products viewed and to change the visual merchandising accordingly. Other technologies trialled included interactive mannequins that pushed information about the products to customers using their phone. MishiPay, a mobile payment app, was also trialled and allowed customers to scan a product barcode and pay directly through their phone rather than at the till. At the same time, RFID labels deactivated the security tags on the products, providing the customer with a quick and convenient purchasing method. Similarly, by providing their top customers with an RFID-enabled loyalty card that gave them a 10 per cent discount, staff aimed at delivering a more personalised service. A tracker installed at the shop front worked by transmitting data from the card, such as style preferences and purchase history, as the customer entered the store. This allowed a sales associate to tailor the service in a non-intrusive manner in order to increase customer engagement and boost sales. Though this technology had already been trialled and tested, this was one of the first times that it has been collectively used in a single environment. Because some of these technologies were a success and others less so, it shows that future retailers will need to continuously innovate in terms of their retail strategies to intuitively engage and adapt to the individual customer if they are to create and capture value.

Innovation-driven growth 77

Successful innovation helps the firm to capture a consumer's willingness to pay for its product over others. During the early stages of a product's life cycle, a product competes on the basis of special features or an innovative design. As the market matures, consumers then typically gravitate towards a small number of products that compete primarily on price, which can be a costly strategy. The window to capture profits is very short, as the firm's competitors will have access to the same kinds of data and general industry knowledge. Even with help from top-tier management consultants, the firm's future is limited unless it can develop new expertise and dynamic capabilities. This proficiency is based on the ability and capability to strategically leverage the firm's proprietary knowledge and unique resources. This is a high-risk, high-reward area to compete in, as shown in Figure 6.1. The business environment is moving from a world of predict, produce and sell to a world of sense and respond. Marketing is moving from being transactional in nature to a paradigm of relationship and immersive experiences, although it must be said that not all customers want a relationship, whether this is short-term or long-term. Firms that can nurture the relationship tend to be those that are leaders in their field. Analysing the bottom-left-hand-side of the quadrant, **small but easy wins** create uncomplicated and low-value opportunities for the firm. Taking a successful style and adding more colours to it for the new season or changing the fabric composition slightly would fit into this box. The top-left-hand-side of the quadrant focuses on **certain failures** due to low product changes, which require a high behavioural shift to capture the value generated. This is a risky area, as the value created is usually not meaningful enough in the minds of consumers to shift their behaviours and purchasing habits. These product changes usually result in gimmicky ideas which can be

	Low Product Change	High Product Change
High Behavioral Change	Certain Failures e.g. Velcro Closure On Shirts	Long Hauls e.g. Wearable Technology
Low Behavioral Change	Small, But Easy Wins e.g. Minimal Styling Change	Smash Hits e.g. Compression Sports Apparel

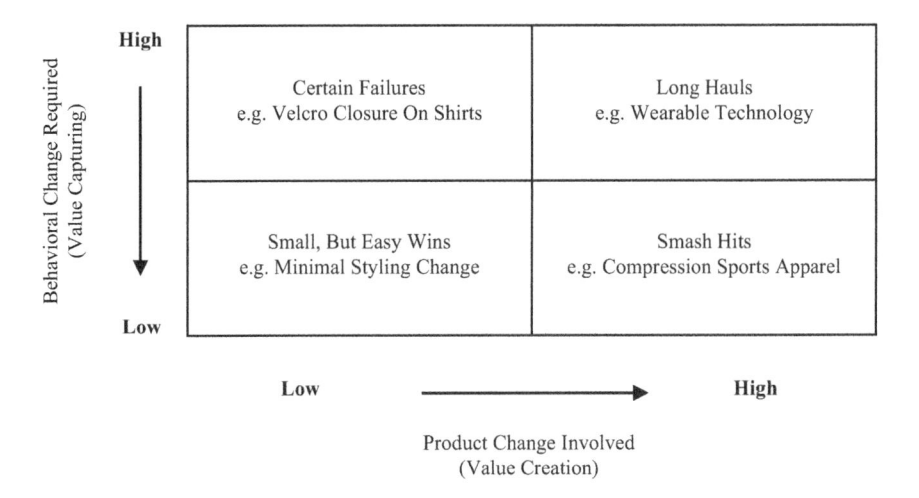

Behavioral Change Required (Value Capturing) — vertical axis (High to Low)
Product Change Involved (Value Creation) — horizontal axis (Low to High)

Figure 6.1 Innovation and value matrix

characterised as a fad or as too edgy and narrow to attract an audience for the idea to survive and become commercially meaningful. A case in point would be the slow consumer adoption of a shirt that had its buttons replaced with Velcro fastenings.

The top-right-hand-side centres on **long hauls** and requires a high amount of product amendment, with a corresponding change in consumer behaviour. An example of this would be the open innovation of wearable technology amongst a firm's competitors. By sharing propriety technology such as a colour-changing running jacket that measures the wearer's heart rate to identify the intensity level of the activity, not only does the firm pull the mainstream industry into a more innovative position, but through network effects increases the likelihood of the technology being adopted by a larger number of consumers. Crucially, as more firms offer the product, the innovation inevitably becomes the norm and a successful ecosystem is created. Yet there is a rate of advancement that customers are willing to absorb as they may love the enhanced products, but are unwilling to pay a premium price for products and services that they do not really need right now or that do not provide a quantifiable gain to them in terms of increased performance. Even with a strong brand, the type of improvement for which the customer will pay needs to be calibrated carefully to avoid overshooting and create diminishing marginal utility.

At the bottom-right-hand-side of the grid are the **smash hits**. These products require high product modifications, but little adjustment in consumer behaviour. These are often innovations that consumers do not know or recognise that they need, but when they do, they love the products and often become very loyal, helping to quickly capture market share for the firm. For example, body-mapped seamless technology used in compression sports apparel would fall into this category, as sold by Under Armour, one of the fastest-growing firms in the world. Very often innovation offers users new benefits, but also requires them to give up some existing benefits, which if not carefully considered can actually decrease the overall value created and captured by the idea.

Incremental and discontinuous innovation

Few subjects have received as much attention from social scientists, senior executives and public policy-makers as innovation. Innovations vary widely in terms of size, novelty and temporal duration, but are a key strategic driver of corporate growth and can be segmented into two different forms. **Incremental innovation** improves or maintains profit margins by exploiting or reconfiguring existing products, processes and cost structures to make use of a current competitive advantage. An example of this would be Burberry re-engineering its famous trench coat into multiple plays. **Discontinuous innovation**, also called disruptive innovation, originates in low-end or new-market footholds over a period of time rather than at one fixed point. Established products, processes and technologies are displaced or new markets are entirely created, such as a radical new wearable technology that attracts a way to turn very profitable non-consumers into consumers. During this time, the locus of disruption comes from both smaller competitors with fewer resources and also other industries as the firm cannot disrupt itself. This helps explain why established firms frequently overlook disrupters and often get caught out. Referred to as **punctuated equilibrium**, this term is applied to the process of how incremental innovation is usually interrupted by a discontinuous innovation. Both go hand in hand as incremental innovation steadily improves performance or extends a product's application before it is disturbed and the process is repeated.

Incremental innovation takes less time and involves less risk compared to discontinuous innovation, which helps explain why executives favour it and usually follow 'observe and apply' replication practices. Truly discontinuous innovations occur so intermittently that no firm has a practised process for handling them. Subsequently, successful innovation, whether it is incremental or discontinuous, is usually shaped by a highly determined leader with a great strategy who challenges the firm to solve new problems or because of a serious internal or external crisis. For these reasons, innovation as an entity can be considered a specific function of creative entrepreneurship and is at the heart of any economic model of fashion. Successful firms that demonstrate high levels of innovation are good at it as they simply try more things. Not every innovation needs to be a blockbuster, as sufficient amounts of small or incremental innovations can lead to substantial profits. In order for this to successfully take place, a number of parameters and activities are applicable, depending on the nature and stage of the firm.

Broadly speaking, if the innovation of a young firm is sustaining in nature relative to the business model of a significant incumbent, the firm is very unlikely to win, due to a lack of resources to remain profitable. Therefore, start-up or young fashion firms are most suited to creating value using ideas that fit a disruptive positioning. These types of firms can initially expect to utilise an emergent strategy to validate concepts and establish a viable profit formula before aggressively switching to a deliberate strategy. Firms like this should calibrate funding sources to be patient for growth but impatient for profitability during the early stages of their existence. They may also need a new distribution channel and a different communication strategy to support the disruptive innovation. Alternatively, for established fashion firms, the target should be on sustaining and nurturing spin-off innovations through focused exploitation of their investments so that the firm is patient for profit, but impatient for growth. These firms should aggressively scan the business environment beyond their core offering for disruptive threats and opportunities. This is critical for mature firms whose culture can also become an impediment to their own growth and success.

Case study: Adidas

Fashion is an evolving industry and the products of the future will involve enhanced customisation, increased speed to market, and greater automation and flexibility. Adidas' pilot project called the 'Speedfactory' is a highly flexible manufacturing facility based in Germany that can be placed anywhere in the world. The facility incorporates innovative processes, including 3D printing, computerised knitting and robotic cutting with new materials to produce shoes in a non-traditional but cost-effective way. The shoes feature Adidas' Boost cushioning technology, with the aim of reacting to local market nuances and focus on co-creation and customisation. Technology used in the automotive and aerospace industry is applied to collect data on feet movement, shape and stress points. So, rather than draw a design and manufacture the shoe, the new show is grown from an algorithm. By bringing production closer to the consumer, Adidas is able to dramatically reduce the time to market from as much as 18 months to a few months, weeks and even hours. As the shoe is produced locally, it significantly cuts transportation, storage and energy costs. This provides a more sustainable approach and limits the impact on the environment. Though the facility is heavily reliant on ICT, Adidas sees the project as complementary to its existing manufacturing facilities and is expected to create around 150–160 new production jobs as a result.

Getting the innovation formula right

In other industries, such as the automotive and aviation industries, innovation is labelled research and development. In the fashion industry, many firms like to talk about innovation, but there is plenty of pressure against it. New ideas or innovations that are not perceived to be useful or are not commercially successful are often labelled 'mistakes'. This is why many firms, especially mature ones, do not undertake pilot studies or testing as it causes blame and heightens internal politics and bureaucracy, which can force executives to make bad decisions and even lose their jobs. Objectively, it is only after the innovation process is completed that an innovation can be fairly assessed and judged. Consequently, 'the rules of engagement' contain four pieces of advice that can help guide executives in achieving successful innovation. As shown in Figure 6.2, a successful innovation is closely linked to the firm's overall corporate strategy, its business model and through a viable **customer proposition**. It is vital that executives focus on getting the business model and not merely the product right. Because of this, the firm should pay careful attention to how it structures itself versus the new business unit that is tasked with the innovation. A strong alignment is required to minimise conflicting agendas

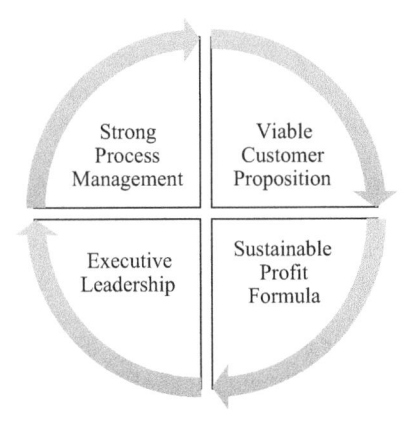

Figure 6.2 Rules of engagement for successful innovation

[Diagram: A circular arrangement with four quadrants labeled: Strong Process Management, Viable Customer Proposition, Sustainable Profit Formula, Executive Leadership]

and to avoid a clash of cultures as one group is perceived as continuing to work hard to protect the core business and generate most of the firm's revenues, whilst another group has all the fun experimenting, free of rigid rules and immediate revenue demands. As a firm's culture varies depending on its stage of growth, it is important to manage innovation correctly and in a sensitive manner.[2]

Holding the new unit to the same processes and financial requirements as the incumbent business can be detrimental to its success. This is because the **profit formula** that is required in the early stages of the innovation has different constraints from the parent business, as the established business is concerned with the needs of its biggest customers and generating significant cash flow rather than requiring significant investment in capital. Here, the resource allocation process operates within conventional control mechanisms and is typically designed to support its most established products and sustaining innovations rather than championing disruptive innovations. This issue is compounded, as most firms continue to maintain the status quo and apportion approximately the same amount of capital to their business units for research, marketing and sales promotions as they did in the previous year rather than focusing on how much is needed this year and in what form. This is magnified by having the same planning, budgeting and performance review metrics applied to the new innovation unit. This influences executive behaviour in terms of what gets prioritised and acts as a severe constraint to disruptive innovation. This is an asymmetry of motivation, which in the end becomes a competitive disability, as these customers heavily influence not only the resource allocation process but also the competition. For example, when a competitor's actions threaten a brand's territory through a price reduction of a core item, it forces a response from the firm. This diverts crucial finite resources and limits the future potential of an innovation that was in the early stages of its design phase or was close to going-to-market. This itself can be a self-fulfilling way to become uncompetitive and can eventually lead to the demise of a firm. In early-stage innovations, executives focus on profitability and numerous small opportunities in order to quickly create healthy gross profit margins. This requires the new innovation, especially if it is discontinuous in nature, to be allowed to compete with and cannibalise the parent firm's other divisions in a controlled manner.

Further problems can also arise because as the new innovation starts to gain traction and the firm becomes commercially successful, it alters the profit formula. Opportunities that were seen as lucrative and in the low thousands or millions of dollars in terms of profit and revenue when the firm was small now get filtered out as being too small when the firm becomes bigger and are denominated in millions or even billions. As the process 'crystallises', the criteria that is used to approve new projects and prioritise the resource allocation process become distorted. Innovative projects get shot down by senior management because they do not pass internal hurdle rates as they cannot get 'big enough fast enough' in the small markets of today that will become the large markets of tomorrow. Opportunities are missed, especially disruptive profit-driving innovations that can cause the next wave of growth. Executives continue to focus only on projects that produce large enough revenues and meet senior management's requirements. In doing so, this usually requires the firm to innovate in an obvious market space where consumption can already be statistically substantiated and in this way be safely presented to senior management. This implies competing against existing firms and subsequently the intensity of the rivalry increases and the opportunity becomes less lucrative. However, as growth is under pressure and time-sensitive, especially in publicly traded firms, senior executives will go ahead and allocate resources in the hope of delivering the required profit formula or at least gaining some time whilst they think of something else to come up with for their next quarterly meeting with analysts. Consequently, expenses such as sales and marketing are ramped up as the new product must perform better than the existing competition and temporary losses are tolerated. Eventually, the fabled 'vision' is a flop and the results are lacklustre. Mid-level executives hope for a sufficient change in the external environment to provide them with an 'excuse' to senior management as to why the project did not deliver the required expectations. This becomes a cyclical path as senior executives then become impatient for growth and have no choice but to keep dishing out capital in the hope of a return on investment. Unfortunately, corners are cut, capital is wasted, morale is affected, long-term brand equity is sacrificed and ultimately the survival of the firm is bought into question. This is less the case for privately held firms, as they are not subject to the external pressures that public firms face, and therefore the expectations are less intense and immediate. However, their need for innovation is just as important in order to ensure their survival.

New smaller disruptive players enter the market at the less-profitable end, which the larger firms have regarded as not interesting enough. Eventually these entrants start to gain momentum to move upmarket, where profitability is highest, and to challenge the dominance of the incumbents. Established firms are caught off-guard, especially in the digital world, where the smallest firm can be big enough to challenge anyone. One way to reduce the risk of the profit formula is to reserve pools of special funds for unexpected opportunities, which can help innovation flourish. In this way, a promising idea does not have to wait for the next budget cycle and be stifled by internal bureaucracy. In addition, leaders can divide business units in order to allow them to invest in small opportunities and take advantage of prospects that might not otherwise be chosen if they were centrally controlled under a larger business unit. Furthermore, the executive leadership team should minimise the use of profit from established revenue streams to subsidise losses in new revenue streams. By encouraging separate profit-and-loss accounts, the new innovation is under greater pressure to become independently successful. Here sporadic reviews are eliminated and the focus on key milestones that relate to tangible activities such as the completion of a product development plan or recruitment of key technical personnel are established before it can receive further funding. By using metrics for longer-term viability, it allows executives to exit their thinking to hit short-term financials and avoids premature scaling of the business. As a result, the new venture should only be fully staffed when the strategy, business model and value proposition are strong, compelling and crystal-clear. Finally, a wise executive knows that a first-mover advantage does not necessarily translate into a competitive advantage and that firms that have the expertise and can gain first-scale advantage are usually the winners.[3]

In order for innovation to be successful, the firm has to put not only its best technical, design, sales and product development people in charge, but also its most experienced general management **leaders** who have proven experience in running operations, building businesses and championing investment in employee training and development. The focus should be on the capabilities needed at each stage and, if necessary, the firm should look externally and adjust compensation schemes to recruit the most suitable and brightest people who are willing and able to innovate. There is a misguided view that innovation is conceived as a solitary act of top-down genius; it is not. Instead, it is a bottom-up, voluntary and co-creation act that is emotionally and intellectually taxing. Acting as social architects, these leaders aim to foster creative friction by harnessing individual and collective talents, experiences and perspectives to create new ideas through honest discourse and rigorous debate. Similarly, they are tasked with helping to implement a structure to provide access to innovation mentors and role models who enable individuals and teams to create the future. This requires leaders who are ambitious, strong, confident and possess excellent relationship and communication skills, as formal and informal networks need to be leveraged throughout the firm in order to form interdisciplinary groups to help with the cross-fertilisation of ideas. Conversely, to resolve conflict and bring together disparate creative and analytical teams, excellent listening and integrated problem-solving skills are required so that everyone is heard and so that dominance or compromise does not affect the end result. Strong leaders are skilled in influencing and persuading executives at all levels of the firm to ensure that they have the patience and resilience to see through the innovation, as interest and commitment quickly wane in the fast-paced fashion industry.[4] In doing so, finite resources can be correctly managed to support the established core competencies of the firm, whilst also building for the required future competencies. Capabilities are identified and leveraged in the context of nurturing and protecting the firm's culture. This is especially true in global fashion firms, where the product will target diverse customers across the world with different tastes, needs, cultures, traditions and rules of engagement. Firms are starting to realise the benefits of managing innovation in a disciplined way and are appointing chief innovation officers. Recent positions at Ralph Lauren and Nordstrom have been created to deliver an enhanced customer journey, increase brand strength and drive financial performance.

Very often, the cause of an innovation's failure is that the wrong **processes** (formal and informal) were used in managing its development and implementation. As a process is created from repetition over a period of time, pursuing a process in the wrong way can be worse than no growth at all. Frequent questions concerning the process include the following:

- Should the host business unit coming up with a new innovation be spun out from its parent firm or incorporated into it?
- Is it necessary for the firm to move its best people to the new unit?
- Does the firm try to enforce its existing values and culture upon the new unit?
- How long does the firm support the 'explore' and 'exploit' process?
- How should employees be rewarded for innovative behaviour?

Overall, there is no one answer to these questions, as it all depends on the context of the situation and the resources available. For instance, disruptive new growth initiatives normally require an independent organisational structure and support, plus sponsorship and protection from executive management. Whatever the choice, some guidelines exist to steer the process in order to ensure that it is integrated as much as possible. First, the executive team should make sure that if the best ideas are to be incorporated back into the parent firm, that reintegration does not lead to the innovation being weakened because of the process, resources and profit formula of the parent firm becoming the dominant criteria for success. This is exacerbated as the CEO often has the challenge of overseeing an existing mature business, whilst nurturing a small but rapidly growing business unit that has a new innovation to market. This requires strong leadership and new ways of working and thinking. CEOs who are deeply committed to growth devote 20–40 per cent of their time to these activities. As a dynamic capability, it requires executives to accurately sense changes to the business environment. Executives should act upon these opportunities and threats by reconfiguring both the firm's tangible and intangible assets to meet these new challenges. Because of this, it is the CEO who has the tie-breaking authority to decide when and for how long the firm keeps the 'explore' and 'exploit' process separate so that the exploit does not damage the explore phase. Similarly, it is wiser to play with innovation when times are good and the core of the firm is still healthy, as resources will be abundant and momentum in the business environment will help the firm to be patient for growth. The best firms are constantly striving to suck complexity out of the system and obtain as much data as they can in order to be congruent with the opportunity, as explore and exploit are best done in a proactive rational manner rather than a reactive and irrational way. Therefore, the execution of a successful innovation blueprint can help to distinguish those firms that are leaders or followers in the industry.[5]

Breakthrough innovation streams

Not all fashion firms are equally innovative, proactive or open to risk. Knowing when to launch an innovation becomes crucial to a firm's success as at some point, profits will start to fall as growth slows down. New growth platforms are required to fill this gap quickly. CEOs, creative directors and senior executives who refuse to play this game will be replaced by others who are willing to try and align to the demands of executive management. This is becoming more prevalent as many firms are failing to adapt to the growing complexity of the business environment and, as a result, have a shrinking lifespan. Figure 6.3 shows a hypothetical **innovation stream**. Here, innovation should be delivered with a purpose and not just for its own sake, and should be in a form that cannot easily be copied by the competition. If a firm is not successful in managing the process of diffusing a new innovation, it will

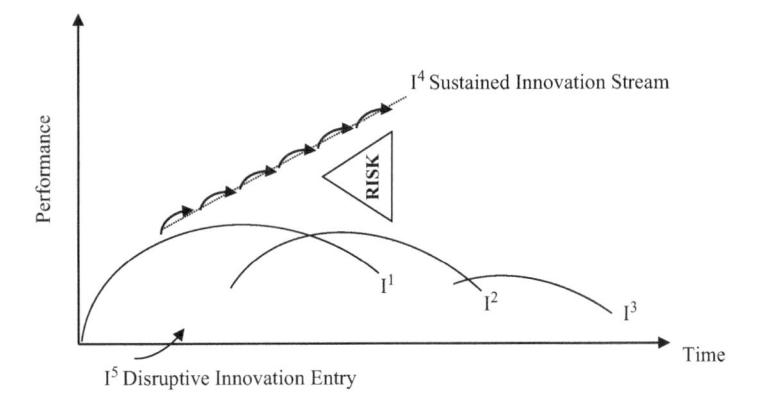

Figure 6.3 Managing innovation streams

face a sudden drop in sales and profits. Consequently, if the pipeline is not strong enough or executives harvest the current innovation for too long, then the firm's survival can become jeopardised, as shown in I^1 to I^3, as there is always tension between optimising a current innovation and creating a new innovation. This is because the current innovation is meant to fund future innovations and support the firm's survival, as it operates in an ecosystem where a new innovation works alone, the competition then catches up and then it starts all over again with a disruptive pioneer, as indicated by I^5. An experienced executive knows that it is better to cannibalise yourself in a controlled manner than to let the competition do it to you so that the initial threat quickly becomes an opportunity. A sustained innovation pipeline, as shown in I^4, is one where through effective feedback loops, insights are translated so that the innovation process is carefully planned and executed. At this point, smart executives are able to identify where in the value chain products and services are likely to become commoditised and, similarly, where they will become decommoditised and where the next growth opportunity will arise. Finding these spots is extremely challenging as the process often happens both simultaneously and continuously, but once found, they can lead to significant opportunities to rapidly capture vast profits through differentiated products and scale-based cost advantages. This normally requires allocating resources from an existing cash cow in order to set up and fund the next big innovation, whilst having an innate understanding of what the customer is looking for both now and in the future.

When taking into account the full cost of development, at the beginning of its life a new innovative product typically promises a lower profit margin per unit sold. This requires a very brave executive to divert resources away from an existing cash cow to a new innovation that is not fully proven and less profitable. This becomes a daunting ambidextrous challenge, as getting out too soon can leave substantial profits on the table and can lead to insufficient capital flows which can jeopardise the future of the firm. For many firms, the stream of innovation comes from interpreting seasonal trends. This has resulted in major consolidation or contraction in the industry as the curse of innovation sifted out the weaker players, especially in the low to middle market such as BHS, Marks & Spencer and Debenhams, whose propositions offer little in terms of brand recognition, desirable products, process or service innovation. This is because they are not agile and accessibly priced to be different enough from their fast-fashion competitors or do not have a strong enough brand to justify the price-quality ratio associated with premium and luxury brands. This has resulted in these firms resorting to low-cost sourcing, mass personnel reductions, increased promotional activity and leveraging their balance sheets to return capital to disgruntled shareholders.

By managing the innovation formula, executives are able to nurture breakthrough innovation streams and gain a sustainable competitive advantage. This advantage can be supported by analysing a firm's **attribute map**, as shown in Figure 6.4. Embedded in the map is a wealth of strategic knowledge

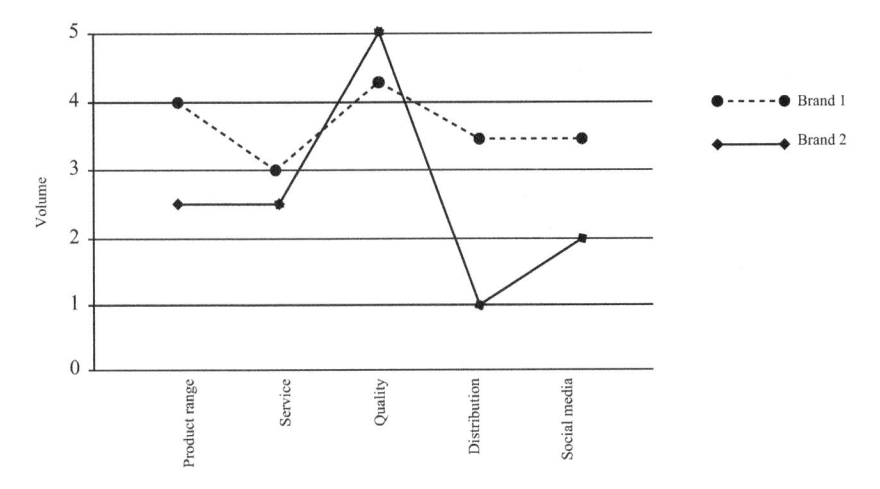

Figure 6.4 Attribute mapping

on the current status and future of the firm. A brand can evaluate itself based on dimensions such as price, quality, features and distribution, and can ask the question whether its market share and profitability reflect both its strategy and mirror its investments to create a divergent value curve. This is because the closer these attributes converge between the firm and its main competitor, the more intense the rivalry will be and the more limited its growth will be, a fundamental issue in strategy creation. By modelling future competitive responses or changes in the business environment, the firm can reflect and understand how its innovation pipeline and resources need to be adjusted and on what axis to remain competitive. This could be based on reimagining benchmarks, looking to emerging markets for new disruptive ideas, mass customisation or co-creation with other firms to create a complementary goods ecosystem. This is a fruitful exercise for any executive as it can be very costly and painful if there is a long pipeline of unwanted goods in which the firm has heavily invested and cannot liquidate quickly and profitably.

The best firms, such as H&M, have built an internal rapid prototyping facility or have found external suppliers that can turn around sample and production runs in a very short time frame. These initial designs are then put through a 'test-learn-adapt-implement' process to see how buyer behaviour affects conversion. For example, using online A/B testing such as those provided by Optimizely or evolutionary algorithms from firms like Sentient, the 'control' and 'challenger' products are rapidly tested to determine which one works best for the customer. Tag-based analytics captures information about the activity on the web page and offers rich data on user interaction. Providers including Google Analytics and Adobe Analytics are able to provide reports on acquisition, behaviour and conversion. Furthermore, providers like

Clickdensity can represent data through heat maps, which show clear areas of interest to the user in terms of what is clicked the most and least. From this process, the results are analysed and new learnings are incorporated to produce a modified final design before a larger order is placed. In firms such as Shop Direct, the United Kingdom's second-largest pure play online retailer, where the firm has a website that generates significant traffic, multivariate testing is used to analyse several criteria to reduce risk and increase conversion.

Innovation-driven growth theory will never fully explain everything about innovation and the success of the firm. There are far too many other forces and anomalies in play. However, a better understanding of the process can significantly help in getting an innovation to market and successfully predict shifts in the competitive landscape. Most fashion firms are not very innovative and merely unnervingly replicate each other's designs and ways of operating, with only a handful expressing their true creative mindset to the fullest. Firms such as Christian Dior and Fendi, with a deep culture of nurturing creative freedom and an abundance of capital and resources, are successful in innovating to constantly reinvent themselves. Along with some luck, these firms are usually design-led and have an excellent management team who can balance commerce with unlimited artistry and are adept at successful strategy implementation, making them leaders in their respective fields.[6] Moreover, to truly create breakthrough innovation-driven growth, firms will need to move from an innovation to an invention mindset.

Review questions

Questions for debate regarding innovation-driven growth are as follows:

- Is innovation more of an art or a science?
- Does product innovation generate more growth than new business model creation?
- What are the advantages and disadvantages of outsourcing innovation?
- Do individual rewards versus collective rewards increase motivation for coming up with successful innovations?
- Do emerging markets create more innovative products than mature markets?
- In the future, which job function will be the most desirable in terms of creating innovation?

Further reading

1 Buckley, C. and Vecchi, A. (eds) (2016) *Handbook of Research on Global Fashion Management and Merchandising*. Hershey, PA: IGI Global.
2 Bryant, A. (2014) *Quick and Nimble: Lessons from Leading CEOs on How to Create a Culture of Innovation*. New York: Henry Holt & Company.

3   Christensen, C.M. and Raynor, M.E. (2003) *The Innovator's Solution*. Boston: Harvard Business Review Press.
    Govindarajan, V. and Trimble, C. (2010) *The Other Side of Innovation: Solving the Execution Challenge*. Boston: Harvard Business Review Press.
4   Brandeau, G., Hill, L., Lineback, K. and Truelove, E. (2014) *Collective Genius: The Art and Practice of Leading Innovation*. Boston: Harvard Business Review Press.
5   Govindarajan, V. (2016) *Three Box Solution: A Strategy for Leading Innovation*. Boston: Harvard Business Review Press.
    O'Reilly, C.A. and Tushman, M.L. (2016) *Lead and Disrupt: How to Solve the Innovator's Dilemma*. Stanford: Stanford University Press.
    O'Reilly, C.A. and Tushman, M.L. (2002) *Winning through Innovation*. Boston: Harvard Business Review Press.
6   Basso, A. and Caro, A. (2014) *Commercialising Creativity*. London: British Fashion Council & London Business School.

7 Mergers and acquisitions
Deal strategy, execution and integration

Chapter goals

This chapter explains from a historical context the rise of mergers and acquisitions, the current forces driving it and the deal-making process from due diligence to exit options. The key areas covered are:

- The rise of mergers and acquisitions
- The deal-making process
- The bidding process
- Restructuring the business
- Exit and monetisation

The rise of mergers and acquisitions

In 1946 Harvard Business School Professor Georges Frederic Doriot, well known for his course on manufacturing, raised along with his partners $3.5 million to back start-ups run by Second World War veterans. Named the American Research and Development Corporation, it is considered the first publicly funded venture capital firm and offered entrepreneurs financial resources and managerial support.[1] In taking a long-term approach to his investments, Doriot did not believe in turning around firms quickly for an instant profit. Instead, he pooled capital from institutions such as insurers and endowments to fund emerging technologies and innovative start-ups into sustainable firms. He played a pioneering role in the emergence of the post-war entrepreneurial economy and planted the seed for what is now a $3.6 trillion venture and private equity industry.[2] The assumption was that the failure of most firms would be compensated for by the success of a handful in the portfolio. Before these institutions were created, entrepreneurs had to turn to wealthy families like the Rockefeller brothers to fund their ideas. The landscape today is much broader and includes players like sovereign wealth and hedge funds, private equity firms, social entrepreneurs and foundations. These operators provide vital access to capital that supports firms in their growth objectives, such as international expansion or greater control of their supply chains. They also provide 'smart capital', which comes with insight, counsel and networks. Such support can make the difference between being able to successfully execute or not.

Mergers and acquisitions (M&A) is a transformative option for reshaping business, accelerating growth strategies and future-proofing the firm. M&A rapidly reconfigures resources to better implement strategy by combing multiple firms and their assets and capabilities. The terms 'mergers' and 'acquisitions' are repeatedly used interchangeably, but are two distinct options. To clarify, most **mergers** can be described as a mutual alliance that pools the assets together of two relative equals to create greater value and usually involves a weakening of control for the firms involved. A merger can be considered a success if it increases shareholder value faster than if the firms had remained separate. A horizontal merger concerns direct competitors in the same product lines and markets, whilst a vertical merger combines the customer and the firm, or the supplier and the firm. **Acquisitions** involves the dilution of control as one firm takes over a controlling interest in another firm. It overcomes the constraints of organic growth and reduces the relatively long timescale of achieving sizeable scale. This option can strengthen the core business and can be used as a route towards diversification, which makes it an attractive option for firms that want to gain a quick competitive advantage whilst carefully managing costs and risks.[3] Through an acquisition, a firm can gain access to an innovation pipeline, important talent and capabilities, and pull more sales through an existing asset base to gain an established market position. For example, through its subsidiary Paraffection, which supplies top couture houses, Chanel has been acquiring specialty handcraft ateliers including Desrues (buttons), Lemarié (feathers and fabric flowers), Causse (gloves), Montex and Maison Lesage (embroidery) to preserve vital skills and artisan knowledge needed for couture work. This has been a rising theme, as industry structure and changes in consumer behaviour lie at the core of firms taking opportunistic and defensive measures in order to protect market share and keep pace with the larger conglomerates that dominate the industry, such as LVMH, VF Corporation and PVH. Overall, the fashion industry can be characterised as being heavily acquisition-focused rather than mergers-based. This is because by nurturing finite individual brands into becoming global players, the notion is that the firm's owners aim to increase long-term value rather than dilute it through a merger.

Analysing the history of M&A, three main factors have contributed to its rise and why it is considered a particularly relevant growth strategy for today's fashion firms. As shown in Figure 7.1, **globalisation** has fuelled interest from an increasingly prevalent middle-class consumer group, especially

92 Mergers and acquisitions

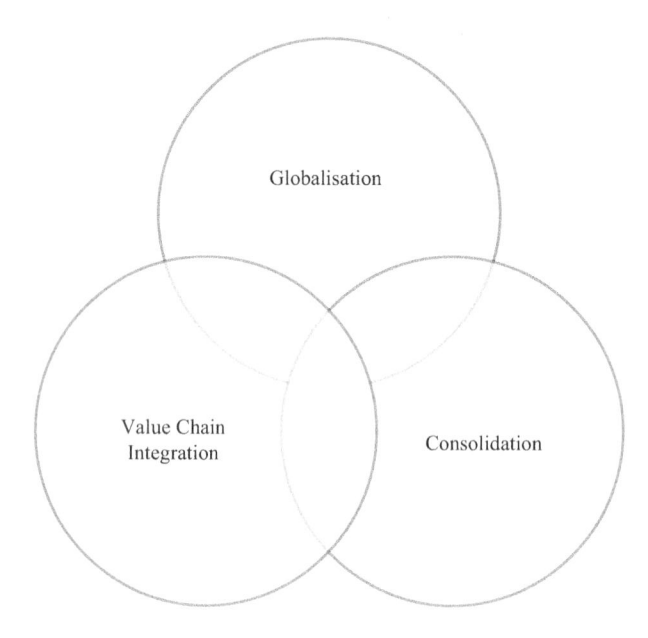

Figure 7.1 The facilitation of mergers and acquisitions

in underpenetrated and evolving markets like China. This has increased the appetite for well-known European and American brands among Asian consumers as they start to view clothes as an extension and expression of their new lifestyles. Increasing consumer buyer power has prompted many firms to expand into these territories. At the same time, many investment firms are actively seeking to acquire brands to help raise their profile in this region and for those brands already in demand but underexposed to help them to facilitate the path to growth. For example, the Blackstone Group acquired a 20 per cent stake in Versace and provided its first capital injection in 2014. This allows Versace to expand its geographical footprint, increase its retail store network in existing markets and expand its product offerings, especially its accessories line with the goal to publicly list the firm in the near future. Globalisation and the development of ICT have also meant innovative ways of matching potential firms with investors such as investment banks and private equity groups. Apps like MergersClub and DealNexus have attracted thousands of members and financial institutions such as UBS and Bank of America to facilitate transactions, in particular small to mid-size deals. This is useful for firms in remote areas where access to capital is limited, and is helping to facilitate global reach and contacts for the industry in a way that was unheard of just a few years ago.

Value chain integration is often a complex structure in the fashion industry. In the luxury goods arena, forward and backwards vertical integration has become an important factor in fuelling M&A activity. At one end, backwards vertical integration such as access to suppliers that have amassed the experience and technical know-how over many decades is a key driver in remaining competitive by safeguarding supply and brand appropriate levels of quality. For example, firms such as Hermès rely on their sources of supply to provide the finest proprietary skins in the industry. This has resulted in Hermès recently acquiring the French calf leather specialist Tannerie d'Annonay, a strategy it has been pursuing since it bought its first tannery in 1996. Kering, a competitor to Hermès, has also taken steps to consolidate control of its supply of key raw materials by taking a majority stake in France Croco, one of the largest exotic skin factories in the world, which engages in sourcing, tanning and processing of crocodile skins. This transaction enables Kering to further secure high-quality skins and specialised knowledge that its leather and footwear brands are known for. At the other end of the value chain is forward vertical integration. Here, firms are seeking to better understand patterns of consumer demand and achieve greater control at the point of sale with the aim of improving service to realise higher sales and increased margins. Consequently, directly owned retail and e-commerce operations have become the norm for firms to gain better control of their product distribution, pricing, brand image and communication strategy. This is principally the case in developing markets, where initial entry strategies such as joint ventures, franchising or licensing agreements are transitioned to directly controlled operations. Firms including Burberry, Kate Spade and Coach are examples of brands that continue to seize control of their operations.

Case study: Coach

Established in New York in 1941, Coach is a premium handbag, accessories and apparel firm. It has been acquiring ownership of its international operations worldwide since 2005, when it bought out its joint venture partner's 50 per cent interest in Coach Japan. In fiscal year 2009, this was followed by the acquisition of its domestic retail business in Hong Kong, Macau and China. In 2012, it continued this strategy and purchased its domestic retail business from its distributors in Singapore and Taiwan, and in 2013 Malaysia and South Korea. This helped Coach to implement a consistent brand image across its direct-to-consumer operations, raise brand awareness and speed up infrastructure investment in the lucrative Asia region. During the fiscal year 2014, Coach acquired full control of its joint venture in Europe by purchasing Hackett Limited's 50 per cent interest. In 2016 Coach's international operations increased by 47 stores to 522 from 475 in 2014.[4]

94 Mergers and acquisitions

Consolidation in the industry is the third factor that is also playing a key role in M&A. Each consolidator brings with it its own expertise, whether this is operational prowess, financial liquidity or management expertise. Many brands would not exist today or would have developed less rapidly if they had not become a part of another group. This is mainly the case for Italian brands, many of which have been sold to foreign firms such as the Valentino Fashion Group, which was acquired by the investment vehicle of the Qatar royal family, Mayhoola for Investments, for $889 million. Leveraging expertise in manufacturing, implementing new operating systems, opening access to key real estate and extending credit facilities have resulted in two types of deal-seeking firms. First, there are those firms that are pursuing other firms who are successful and growing, but are not very sophisticated. These brands do not have the experience, knowledge and resources to manage their existing operations. Second, firms are targeting brands that have been around for a long time and are attempting to revitalise themselves. These brands have the potential to be scaled up and are usually underperforming or in a distressed state. For instance, in 2011, First Heritage Brands acquired a majority stake in the French family-owned fashion label Sonia Rykiel, the Belgian luxury firm Delvaux Createur and the renowned French shoemaker Robert Clergerie, with the aim of leveraging its expertise and strong distribution network in the world's fastest-growing markets.

The fashion industry has seen intense activity in the last few years driven by well-known brand names and financial investors, as shown in Table 7.1.

Table 7.1 Acquisitions in the fashion industry by value

Buyer	Completion year	Acquired firm	Value (US$)*
VF Corporation	2011	Timberland	$2.90 billion
LVMH	2013	Loro Piana (80%)	$2.83 billion
PVH Corporation	2013	Warnaco Group Inc.	$2.79 billion
Hudson Bay Co	2014	Saks Fifth Avenue	$2.40 billion
Shandong Ruyi	2016	SMCP (Sandro, Maje & Claudia Pierdot)	$1.50 billion
Mayhoola for Investments	2012	Valentino Fashion Group SPA	$889 million
TowerBrook Capital Partners	2013	True Religion Apparel Inc.	$750 million
G-III Apparel Group Ltd	2016	Donna Karen International	$650 million
Mayhoola for Investments	2016	Balmain	$547 million
Coach	2015	Stuart Weitzman	$530 million
Kering	2012	Brioni SPA	$415 million
Hudson Bay Co	2016	Gilt Groupe	$250 million
G-III Apparel Group Ltd	2012	Vilebrequin International SA	$106 million

* Approximate values due to timing of foreign exchange conversion

Nevertheless, the number of disclosed deals, of which some can be classified as mega-deals, is only one measure of activity in the industry. Many deals are private transactions where the value is not reported or they involve the acquisition of minority stakes.

Before the last recession, a hallmark of the time was a business environment that used borrowed capital to fund deals, many of which were often highly leveraged. Access to this tightened during the recession, but since the downturn, debt and equity underwriting has rapidly increased along with a rebound in the capital markets. This has meant a different approach to how deals are formulated and today's transactions are being financed with a combination of capital and stock. The increased use of shares is due to the strong re-rating of the equity value that most firms are currently displaying. However, some CEOs have been sceptical of engaging in aggressive M&A activity as continued uncertainty in the economic and geopolitical environment has led to many firms to hold on to their capital, as there is little pressure to update plant, equipment and infrastructure or repurchase shares. Instead of growing via acquisitions, these firms have focused on strategy execution, operational optimisation and reducing expenses. Alternatively, some forward-looking firms are now searching for additions to their portfolio to drive strategic growth and market share as organic growth is proving insufficient in opposing global economic conditions. With boardroom confidence increasing and firms sitting on large levels of capital and with access to cheap financing, investing in M&A has become a particularly attractive option for them.

Whilst most M&A is friendly, changes in the economic climate have also given rise to the **activist investor** or 'corporate raider', whose objective is to purchase or sell a large shareholding through either a tender offer or a proxy fight in order to push senior executives to boost returns or force strategic issues with large institutional investors, ultimately voting for change at annual meetings. Through, for example, increased share buybacks, higher dividends, unlocking real estate value or even dismantling the firm, these activist investors have CEOs and boards thinking much more actively about mitigating their vulnerability because of large capital reserves or a low debt capital structure. The Jones Group and Crocs are a few examples of firms that have been affected and forced to make sweeping changes by activist investors frustrated with their financial performance and strategic direction. Similarly, when a distressed firm such as J.C. Penney received unwanted attention from the famous activist William Ackman, Ackman did the firm no favours by distracting its management from turning around the firm with his plan for an extreme makeover and eventually gave up, losing more than $650 million in the process after selling his entire 18 per cent holding.[5] This is because many fashion turnarounds have a 5–10-year horizon in terms of time and capital investment, which usually does not match the timeframe of activist investors. Making a firm private has been one way of expediting the process and avoiding the scrutiny of the stock market, a tactic from which Kenneth Cole has benefited. Firms such as Macy's are reacting to activist threats like those from Jeffrey

96 *Mergers and acquisitions*

Smith of Starboard Value by assembling their own squadron of professionals consisting of investment bankers, real estate specialists, tax experts and lawyers to garner counsel on topics such as strategy and capital structure. By understanding these issues on a regular basis through the lens of institutional investors, the firm avoids becoming complacent and exposed. Likewise, after several high-profile failures, activist investors have started to accept a lower profile and enter non-hostile engagement. Their focus is on greater collaboration with the board and other key stakeholders to unlock strategic value for the firm and its principles.

Case study: Kate Spade

Kate Spade's shares have dropped 63 per cent since their intraday high on 11 August 2014 to $18.67 at the end of 2016. Revenues is estimated to grow 11 per cent versus 2 per cent for its closest peers. EBITDA is forecast to grow 21 per cent at Kate Spade and is expected to contract at Michael Kors and grow 16 per cent at Coach. In today's climate, this would normally mean that it would not be a target for disgruntled investors as earnings and revenue growth is well ahead of its rivals. But missed sales and margin targets on three different occasions and a valuation multiple of less than eight times, which is a 50 per cent discount compared to its peer group, have led to Caerus Investors sending a letter to Kate Spade's board, requesting that it realises shareholder value by pursuing a strategic sale to an industry player such as a lifestyle firm. A deal with a 50 per cent premium to its closing share price in December 2016 would still realise a price well below its all-time high. With 80 per cent of sales coming from the United States, there is plenty of room for international expansion. Perhaps through strengthening its management team and communicating a strong growth strategy, it will be able to resist dissident shareholders, but only time will tell.[6]

The deal-making process

> The retail industry is much more visible than other sectors because it's an easier industry to understand. (Professor Suraj Srinivasan, Harvard Business School).[7]

M&A is predominantly conducted with the objective of creating economic value for all the parties involved in the transaction. Key players in the industry reiterate the dominance of American and European firms, and include the Blackstone Group, Carlyle Group, Goldman Sachs, 3i Group, TPG (Texas Pacific Group) and KKR & Co (Kohlberg Kravis Roberts).

Yet, there are numerous smaller players that are also involved, such as Bain Capital (which have a stake in the famous outerwear brand Canada Goose and shirt maker T.M. Lewin), Sciens Capital (which owns the British luxury retailer Asprey) and M1 Group (which owns Pepe Jeans, Hackett and the French premium brand Faconnable). Moreover, there are a minority of qualified M&A firms that offer fashion specific advice on strategy and operational issues as their core business model. With the exception of a few, such as Savigny Partners, Michel Dyens and Ohana & Co, most try to apply generic strategies to an industry they know very little about or have the patience to understand.

Private equity firms avoid cyclical and capital-intensive businesses. Depending on the stage of investment and the maturity of the firm, most investment firms have a pre-defined objective to exit the business in three to seven years. However, conglomerates like Richemont and Kering take a longer-term view. Brands under **target** are those that are less dependent on a star designer, especially namesake brands, and those that do not have a high degree of seasonal volatility. **Sponsor** firms look for a clear product direction, a firm that creates consistent collections and those that have a defined consumer base, along with brands that have a strong DNA. The target brand should ideally have the potential to open retail stores and have a solid digital platform with growing IP assets. They should also have a proof of concept that is scalable, especially in developing markets, and have the capacity to generate realistic revenues, all backed up by an experienced management team who complement each other.

From a sell-side perspective, the seller usually hires an investment bank with which it has a strong relationship to ascertain a comprehensive financial analysis and to understand its strategic options. This can include a complete sale or just part of the firm, recapitalisation, a management buy-out, an initial public offering (IPO) or a continuation of the business. Both the seller and the buyer are looking for speed of execution and certainty of completion as two major features of the deal. Transactions are usually conducted through an individually negotiated sale or an auction. In general, auctions tend to increase the price paid by the sponsor, especially in larger deals, and provide a transfer of value from the sponsor to the target. If value has not been created as a result of the process, then there has been leakage due to transaction costs. Most sponsors prefer to avoid auctions and focus on individual negotiations with the target firm. This provides better access to executives inside the target firm and helps to create a more informed view, but can lead to a lower sale price for the seller.

From a buy-side viewpoint, when a target firm has been identified, the first step is to understand what the seller's motivation is and ask 'why is this firm, division or business up for sale?' Once this has been identified and if it fits the buyer's objective, for example, of being a scope or scale deal, then the next step is to investigate further by conducting a thorough valuation and creating a deal thesis. Typically, full due diligence will take not less than three or four weeks to complete. To start, a **comparable analysis** is undertaken to help frame the target firm against similar-sized rivals in the same industry or sub-sector. This benchmark helps to establish a valuation at a given stage and provides a reference point using certain business parameters such as sector, geographical scope, product line and services, distribution strategy, customer profile and key financial metrics, including net income, price-to-earnings and earnings before interest, taxes, depreciation and amortisation (EBITDA). Other indicators measuring profitability, growth, returns and credit strength are also calculated at this stage. Annual reports, analyst coverage, sector reports, investor presentations and social media are scrutinised in order to gain a broader view. The outcome of this analysis helps to determine the target's relative ranking against the comparable set and provides the basis for deriving a valuation range. This usually begins by using the mean and median for the relevant metrics and helps constitute the high and low multiples to set the ceiling and floor price. The closest comparable firms are then selected to serve as the ultimate basis for producing an implied valuation range. For a target with no publicly traded comparable, the buyer seeks to attain this information from firms outside the target's core sector that provide this information on some fundamental level.

To gain a broader understanding of the potential valuation of the target firm, a **precedent transactions analysis** is conducted. This analysis is based on multiples paid for comparable firms in prior M&A transactions and helps to establish a potential range for the sale price. Transactions that have been executed in the previous one to three years are considered the most relevant as they are likely to have taken place under similar market conditions. The range of multiples generated from this analysis tends to be higher under normal market conditions than comparable analysis, as the purchaser places a buyer's premium on the target. Simultaneously, the buyer is looking to piece together vital information that helps formulate a 'story' behind each transaction and the multiples paid, whilst examining the market conditions and **deal dynamics**. Past deal dynamics represent a plethora of options, such as whether it was a strategic buyer looking to realise significant synergies or a financial investor looking for a leveraged buy-out to add to its portfolio. It is important to understand whether the target sold a core or non-core part of the business and whether it was bought through an auction process or a negotiated sale. It should also be noted if the purchase was friendly or hostile and how swiftly the deal was executed or if it was abandoned. Next, understanding how it was structured, for example, a mix of shares and capital, stock-for-stock or an outright capital purchase is vital information for the buyer. This is because using stock as a large portion of the purchase tends to result in a lower valuation than an all-capital deal, as the latter transaction means the target firm is unable to participate in value-creation opportunities as a result of combining the two firms. Conversely, the target's shareholders that receive stock envisage an increase in value due to future growth and expected synergies. During this analysis, senior banking colleagues are consulted to balance the 'science' with the 'art' against their own extensive experience in order to understand the deal's strategic logic, potential pitfalls and the ability to realise value from the transaction.

The third step in the process is to undertake a **discounted cash flow (DCF)** analysis. DCF examination is useful when there is limited or no 'pure play' public comparable firms. Initially, it is conducted over five years, which is usually enough to cover at least one business cycle and execute the firm's planned strategy. For early-stage firms experiencing rapid growth, such as digital commerce start-ups or firms experimenting with new business models, a period of 10 years may be needed. The DCF is derived from the present value of its projected unlevered free cash flow (FCF), which is the cash generated by the firm after paying all of its cash operating expenses, taxes and working capital funding. The valuation implied for the target by DCF is known as the **intrinsic value**, as opposed to the market value, as calculated in the previous two analyses. After the initial projection period, the firm's financial performance should have normalised so that a terminal value can be used to capture the remaining value of the target. The projected FCF and terminal value are discounted to the present at the target's **weighted average cost of capital (WACC)** at a discount rate corresponding to the firm's business and financial risks, and is closely related to the firm's capital structure. Next, the present value of the FCF and the terminal value are summed to provide an **enterprise value**, which is the debt-free, cash-free value of the operating firm and the basis for the DCF valuation. Small variations in the WACC and the terminal value have a considerable impact and therefore a DCF valuation range is provided rather than a single estimate. This is achieved through a sensitivity analysis based on certain assumptions, such as sales growth, profit margin and sector due diligence, which allows the financial structure to be 'stress tested'. Like any analysis, it is only as good as the assumptions that are inputted into the model, and unrealistic data like future sales growth or cost savings can dramatically skew the analysis. The derived valuation range is then compared to the previous comparable and precedent transaction valuations to get a sharper viewpoint to support or refute the initial thoughts on the target.[8] Today, ICT and the use of advanced deal risk-predictive analytics such as EY's Cyber Econ are now being employed to help firms speed up the due diligence process, flag potential integration risks and complete deals faster before competitors can pounce. By using complex algorithms based on historical data, firms can dig deeper to check indicators such as reputation, human resources records, customer sentiment, sales figures, IP portfolios and supply chain relationships to help identify and provide well-defined insights before the deal-making process is too far advanced, which if not correctly managed can be very costly for all the parties involved.

The bidding process

Once the mandate is launched and the preliminary due diligence is complete, bids are invited. The process can take anything from one month to one year, but normally takes between three and six months. Investors may also use third-party advisors if they do not have in-house expertise such as tax advisors, lawyers and accountants to help them in this process. To assist in this, virtual data rooms are often set up to provide secure online access to sensitive documentation and to minimise the need for trips to far-flung cities, whilst also expanding the pool of potential cross-border buyers. As the M&A process involves hefty financial costs and time, the buyer will not want to discover that while it is incurring this expense, the target firm accepts investment from other investors. To protect themselves, most buyers will ask for an **exclusivity period**, during which the firm is prohibited from seeking investment from any third parties. The exclusivity period is secured through a fee which is paid by the buyer. For example, Aquascutum's owner, YGM Trading, put the brand up for sale and received a non-refundable $5 million down payment for exclusive rights to the deal.[9] A breach of this obligation results in the target firm incurring a financial penalty, which depends on the complexity of the transaction, but typically will be around 5–7 per cent of the capital being raised. Next, submissions should be at least equal or above the reservation value and both parties should have a definitive best alternative to a negotiated agreement or walk-away price in their mind. These offers also contain multiple contingency clauses and involve complex negotiations as buyers and sellers become increasingly creative in how they structure deals to optimise value.

As the industry continues to consolidate, there are a limited number of good-quality fashion firms available for purchase as buyers move fast on what is a shrinking pool of targets. With this in mind, mono-brand firms tend to garner higher valuations than portfolio firms due to the latter presenting greater complexities to investors. Consequently, many mono-brand negotiations get 'deal fever' and sponsors usually overpay for what they get as any financial synergy usually goes to the target firm and not the sponsor. For example, independent firms such as Giorgio Armani and Paul Smith are privately held, with many of them having owner-designers at the helm. These firms make attractive acquisitions as they are all global 'trophy' brands and will probably not be up for sale more than once in a generation, and hence carry a substantial premium if they were to be sold. Therefore, quality fashion firms or successful entrepreneurs with the right proposition are in a strong position if they are looking to sell. It is worth noting when there is a valuation difference between what a buyer thinks the firm is worth and what the seller expects, an **earn-out** provision can bridge this gap. Earn-outs are milestone-based compensation schemes where key stakeholders are compensated for the partial sale of the firm and are also contractually obligated to remain with the firm through a transition period, which is usually three to five years. Going forward, this provides the stakeholders with an incentive to have a demonstrable effect on the firm's financial outcome. Achieving or exceeding a certain level of performance results in the seller of the firm earning the remaining amount or more from the sale in the form of stock or cash. For buyers, an earn-out can offer protection against overpaying for a firm that does not end up growing as planned and security for sellers who strongly believe that their firm will offer substantial returns. A case in point is Coach, which in 2015 initially paid $530 million for the acquisition of the designer footwear brand Stuart Weitzman, with an additional $44 million due to be paid upon the achievement of revenue targets during the three years after the acquisition closes.[10]

Once the prospective bids have been received, each initial offer can be classified as a strategic or financial buyer. At this stage, a good investment banker will be able to weed out any firm that is only interested in 'window shopping' to gain financial insights into the target firm. The next round in the process involves presentations from senior executives, typically the CEO, CFO, legal counsel and other divisional heads and allows for a sense of 'fit' between the two parties. Here, the target firm's culture must be thoroughly assessed especially if it is a cross-border deal as a firm's culture is difficult to observe and understand from the outside and cannot just be 'plugged' into a valuation model. To achieve a successful match with the target firm the sponsor must have a clear understanding of their own culture and the capabilities and disabilities it signifies.[11] This is because what made the target firm successful and attractive in the first place is now in danger of becoming very quickly vaporised. In some cases, this maybe the intent of the sponsor if they are only after physical assets or proprietary information but more than often this is not the case. Furthermore, a discreet site visit and store tours will also take place to conduct deeper due diligence and see first-hand the firm's operations and assets. This period weighs very heavily on the CEO, the CFO and the larger finance team, reducing their ability to focus on the day-to-day operational activities of running the firm. Therefore, it is crucial that a strong sub-layer of management is in place to take on this additional workload.

During the second round following the review and discussion of the business plan and negotiations on capital structure and other terms, an offer letter known as a **term sheet** is submitted. Without being legally binding on either party, the term sheet demonstrates the investor's commitment and that it is seriously considering making an investment in the target. The document outlines the key financial terms, guidelines and milestones for the bid package from the acquirer's perspective. In addition, a term sheet will usually contain certain conditions that need to be met before the investment is completed, and these are known as **conditions precedent**. For instance, it may specify that the target firm secures a contract with a major account within a certain period or secures a new supplier for the launch of a new product.

When the amount of capital required is particularly large or the investment is considered to be relatively high-risk, the sponsor may consider **syndicating** the deal. This is where several investors participate in the transaction, each contributing to the total equity package for a proportionate amount of equity. However, usually only one firm will act as the lead investor. Afterwards, negotiations are narrowed while good relationships and strong alignment are built up. In order to create and extract maximum value, the dialogue takes place with at least two interested parties. At the end of the negotiation process, the

102 *Mergers and acquisitions*

term sheet will be incorporated into the shareholders' agreement and therefore it should be as detailed and unambiguous as possible. The final draft will cover, for example:

- The amount to be invested, instruments, valuation and capital structure.
- Liquidation preferences, dividend and conversion rights, anti-dilution protection, redemption rights and lock-ups.
- Board composition, consent and information rights.
- Warranties, vesting, option pool and milestones.
- Confidentiality, exclusivity, fees and conditions precedent.

Once the due diligence process is complete and the terms of the winning bid have been agreed by all parties, an **agreement in principle**, along with the necessary legally binding documents, is drawn up by the legal counsel of the target firm. This is presented to the board of directors for their approval. Because M&A can reduce competition, it is a heavily legislated industry and often requires regulatory approval from not only majority shareholders but also anti-trust regulators, such as the Competition and Markets Authority in the United Kingdom. Consequently, the bid can be rejected or approved. Because some hedge funds search the records of newly incorporated acquisition vehicles for clues on pending deals so that they can trade ahead of an official announcement secrecy is paramount in any M&A deal. Alongside the standard time-bound non-disclosure pro-forma agreement firms often use secret monikers. Examples include 'Project Medusa' for Versace and 'Project Crocodile' for Crocs, which were both used by the Blackstone Group, and 'Project Light', which was created by the Japanese bank Normura for Net-A-Porter.[12] The names should be secret enough to be discussed in the lift or by the coffee machine, but not too complicated so that executives get confused, especially if multiple deals are being done. Bad code names and leaked information can prove fatal. They can result in non-completion or an extended time to complete a deal, as well as forcing sponsors to change their strategy or result in them overpaying for a deal, which is good for the target's shareholders, but can be very costly for the sponsor.

Case study: LVMH versus Hermès

A high-profile case of an attempted acquisition was between LVMH and Hermès, two of the greatest luxury houses in the world. In late 2010, LVMH, the largest player in the luxury goods industry, steadily amassed a 17.1 per cent stake in Hermès via equity swaps. This rapidly increased to 23.2 per cent, a move which Hermès described as an 'attack' on the family-controlled business. LVMH's strategy was to maintain a medium to long-term position in Hermès and wait for its family members to change their mind and sell their shares so that it could secure another prestigious brand to its portfolio. This promoted a strategic response from Hermès by setting up H51, a holding entity with 50.2 per cent of the share capital, in a move to protect the company against a hostile takeover. Members of H51 agreed a deal to purchase an additional 12.6 per cent of the group's shares in the event that some of the Hermès family members decided to sell. In 2012 Hermès filed a legal suit against LVMH over the manner in which it purchased its shares. This led to an €8 million fine for LVMH by the French stock market regulator in 2013. LVMH did not appeal the fine and in late 2014, both firms agreed a deal in which LVMH would liquidate its holding and would not be entitled to buy Hermès shares for another five years. Although LVMH's desire to acquire a magnificent brand did not quite materialise, it did manage to make a capital gain of approximately €3.8 billion, as the share price had increased from €106 when it first started to acquire its shares in Hermès to €253. Now that the speculation for acquiring Hermès has died down, its share price should also decline and trade more in line with its historical average, as its stock has traded at a price to forward-earnings ratio of about 29 times, almost double the sector average. This created both value in the form of an excellent investment for LVMH and for Hermès, the continuation of the family-owned business which survived the most serious attack in the firm's history.[13]

Restructuring the business

M&A is likely to involve a restructuring of the business. Like any other business initiative, **business process re-engineering (BPR)** should start by defining the benefits, costs and timeline to deliver it. In order to achieve the new stakeholder's plans, a new CEO and senior executive team are appointed to kickstart this process. Many CEOs who are new to a firm will use BPR as a way of imposing their authority. To start with, a 'quick scan' review of the firm's operations is undertaken to assess its strengths and weaknesses and where the opportunities and challenges lie. Suggestions on the overall quality of the firm will decide on the type of organisational design and here much debate can take place as to whether BPR should be driven by the numbers such as EBITDA and comparable sales or be centred around the 'brand dream' and the desired brand positioning. Either way, it usually ends up being a mixture of the two. After this point, the design of the firm should be built around a structure and not current reporting lines or key players. From this analysis, recommendations are rolled into a short-term action plan and if needed, any immediate proceedings are undertaken. A mid to long-term plan is also devised showing the strategic direction the firm intends to take, which can involve whether the entire business model needs changing. For example, such as moving from a decentralised geographical model to a centralised product and brand management operation, especially if the firm is performing very badly or faces a fundamental market shift like a move from bricks-and-mortar to online or vice versa. Similarly, if the firm is performing well, then the changes might only affect a certain part of the firm, such as replacing the leader of the marketing or design function. By utilising solid project management methodology and ensuring that the right people are available to execute the strategy, the firm can aggressively implement the post-integration plan. The transfer of knowledge, expertise and best practice across the firm is used to reduce bureaucracy and unproductive activities, especially if the firm is in distress. Management consultants are often hired to rapidly map out an ideal structure, identify roadblocks and leverage industry best practices. Undertaking internal surveys and conducting interviews with a cross-section of employees and asking a few questions such as 'what can be improved around here?' and 'what should we stop and start doing?' is usually enough to provide most of the initial answers that the leadership group is searching for. In spite of this, many firms are reluctant to undertake this assessment themselves, due to internal capability, time constraints, secrecy and office politics. Instead, external advice and validation is readily sought in the short timeframe, which is useful for the planning phase, but not so good for the execution phase. This is because external consultants struggle to fully understand the internal culture of a firm well enough and therefore underestimate the requirements to successfully execute their recommendations. Take, for example, strategic planning, brand positioning and the innovation process, which are highly inter-related, thus making it very taxing to implement re-engineering from the outside.

The end goal of BPR is to deliver a profitable value system around the customer that places increased emphasis on their needs. The aim is to have the target firm operating and contributing value to its parent within six to nine months. To aid this, reporting lines and responsibilities are redesigned, along with the sponsor firm usually placing one or two senior executives in the target firm to create a stronger executive team. These executives can be from the parent firm, a trusted consultant or an independent expert appointed as a non-executive director to the board. For example, the investment firm Eurazeo provided a €20 million capital injection to Vestiaire Collective and in turn gained one seat on its seven-member board of directors. These directors normally bring financial expertise plus proven operational proficiency and credibility, especially to the investor community if it is a public firm. These managers will have direct input into the firm's direction and are also strategically bought in to keep the executives of the sponsor firm updated with the firm's progress, which otherwise is not always as forthcoming if they are not involved in the day-to-day running of it. As executives are parachuted in to deliver rapid change, here urgency supersedes empathy and this can cause conflict in the leadership team and confusion amongst the general staff as to who really has the power and control. Consequently, conflicts of interest can arise as executives battle to balance brand and capital investment decisions based on a misaligned governance structure, office politics and executive dominance.

Fashion firms usually have inherent value, including brand, IP, royalty streams and real estate assets that can be leveraged. When the target firm is acquired, reducing corporate overheads is high on the agenda. Synergies are targeted with the parent firm through shared services such as distribution and human resources, accounting systems, client relationships and sales teams. Similarly, extending credit lines and liquidity may take place as the sponsoring firm will have a superior credit rating and access to additional working capital. This helps to lower the firm's borrowing costs and to reduce its debt, whilst providing vital funds to finance expansion, such as, increased production capacity or upgrading ICT systems. Acquired firms are scrutinised on all financial levels, from capital expenditure, staff costs and expenses to even the legal structure of the firm. In a bid to keep its principals happy, a resourceful CFO will often do some 'positive smoothing' or 'creative accounting' of financial accounts and business plans in order to win some time for the executive team to show progress in executing the firm's strategy. In a bid to reach profitability, financial engineering can result in some drastic moves to create the optimal capital structure for the firm and alleviate financial distress. It can consist of changing the financing structure of a firm's balance sheet to increase the generation of positive cash flows. For example, tax inversions, where the competitiveness of a tax regime constitutes a major factor on deciding where to operate from, play a critical part in the race to drive the firm towards breaking even and eventually profitability. Countries such as Ireland, the Netherlands and Switzerland are keen to attract large firms that will create jobs, boost infrastructure and eliminate the complexity of doing business.

The strategies employed by firms to facilitate successful BPR are shown in Figure 7.2. Most firms will undertake **horizontal diversification** as an area of focus. This involves developing the firm's current range of products and services, and reducing complexity to release managerial and financial

Horizontal Diversification   Vertical Diversification   Financial Management

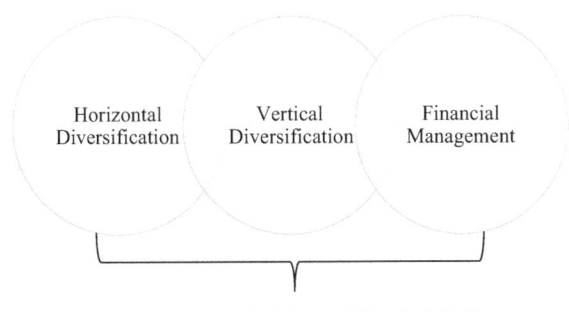

Influenced by Brand Vision and Key Stakeholders

Figure 7.2 Business process re-engineering levers

resources. Typically, by paying a premium and hiring key executives such as a new creative director or chief merchandising officer from the competition, the firm aims to enhance its value proposition and revise its market position to relaunch itself and attract new customers. In doing this, the firm signifies that its past range of products and services were outdated, uncompetitive and unsustainable. Principal areas of focus involve the firm strengthening its core brands, slimming down the product portfolio (especially unprofitable lines) and concentrating on markets or segments that are key and growing so that they can sustain revenues. For example, Sonia Rykiel closed its diffusion line Sonia by Sonia Rykiel in 2016 with a view to repositioning its mainline with lower-price points, which resulted in 79 members of its 330 staff losing their jobs as part of its restructuring efforts to return the brand to profitability by 2019.[14] ICT also plays an important role in accelerating the firm's capabilities through the radical redesign of core business processes to achieve improvements in the speed of product development, enhanced marketing and new product innovation. Finding the right balance between product innovation to attract new customers whilst not alienating old customers is not an easy task, particularly as many firms are centred around an iconic product, single category or distinct design sensibility. This involves trade-offs in resources and capital expenditure, such as investments in new marketing and adverting campaigns versus refurbishing stores and paying suppliers.

Vertical diversification focuses on expanding the points of distribution as a strategic orientation. The aim is to unlock real estate holdings (especially those in important flagship locations), remodel current selling space to increase productivity and expand direct-to-consumer footprints into new territories through new stores and e-commerce operations. These efforts aim to increase productivity, leverage ICT to support the sales and client experience, and build brand awareness in an enticing environment, thereby gaining a better position with, for example, department store buyers, customers and the press. Maintaining strategic investments requires plenty of capital and also takes time, as establishing a website and the operations that go with it or waiting for a shop front in a key location to become available can take a year or longer, and there is no guarantee that it will be successful.

Financial management is a leading issue for all firms and any cost-cutting must be done intelligently and effectively so that this has a limited impact on the quality of the firm. The signs of inadequate financial management include inaccurate sales forecasting, deteriorating margins, poor receivables and payables, unclear inventory holdings and worsening working capital. This is amplified in distressed firms that are haemorrhaging capital and therefore it is important to stop or drastically reduce any activities, operations and projects that are severely affecting liquidity. By creating a strategic segmentation of clients and suppliers, introducing new pre-payment terms and ensuring accurate inventory holdings and sharing forecasts with key accounts, firms are able to achieve rapid results. For long-term improvements, the firm may need to reorganise its financial function. This may involve upgrading ICT systems to receive accurate reporting and for firms with an international presence that use different ICT systems implementing centralised cash pooling so that there is better visibility of where the capital is and when the firm will receive it.

The ideal outcome for any acquired firm is growth in terms of scale, scope and profitability. Still, integration remains a major issue, as was the case in Kering's acquisition of Puma, which was acquired for a large premium in 2007 and has failed to generate the required hoped-for returns. Often the intended strategy fails to deliver, as a M&A requires a shift in business operations from governance and financial reporting to remuneration and culture. This invariably means hard choices and many firms do not succeed because their leaders are not courageous enough to make bold decisions swiftly enough, and therefore buy-in from stakeholders is weak or there is a conflict in relation to strategic direction with the shareholders. Consequently, it is important to keep staff morale high as they can easily become disillusioned and turnover can dramatically increase, as human beings are traditionally hard-wired to avoid change. This is intensified if changes to the firm are causing public scrutiny or negative press as was the case with American Apparel. In this case, it is important that the firm does not stay silent and instead it should have a competent communication plan in place, which should be led by the CEO and the executive management team. If integration remains challenging, then the investors will reassess all aspects of the strategy from capital expenditure to brand potential, product lines and creative direction, together with the ability of the current management team and sum up if it is worth continuing with it or offload it to another party. This was the case of Jaeger, whose owner Better Capital recently sold the brand to the Edinburgh Woollen Mill group at a loss after an unsuccessful turnaround attempt.

Case study: Roberto Cavalli

Roberto Cavalli is an Italian design house synonymous with high-octane red carpet glamour and was at its peak in the 1980s and 1990s. Famed for its signatory use of gold, bold materials, exotic prints and sand-blasted denim, the brand is inspired by the opulent and bohemian lifestyle of the rich and famous. However, business has not been so glamorous, with EBITDA losses of €2m in 2015, and as a result the brand was sold to Italian private equity house Clessidra in May 2015. In mid-2016, Clessidra appointed Gian Giacomo Ferraris, who turned around Versace, as the brand's new CEO with the remit of initiating a comprehensive restructuring plan to return Roberto Cavalli to profitability by 2018. This includes parting ways with its creative director, who was only appointed in March 2015, and cutting almost 30 per cent of its workforce. It will also close its Milan corporate and design office and transfer all functions to its headquarters near

Florence. Its supply chain function will also be rationalised and numerous stores will be closed or relocated to align its costs with its revenues, which fell to €179.7 million in 2015 compared to €209.4 million in 2014, mainly due to a drop in orders. The Roberto Cavalli, Just Cavalli and Cavalli Class collections, which cover different price and consumer segments, along with its numerous licensing agreements, will need to be revisited in order for the brand to be more productive and to ensure long-term profitability.[15]

Exit and monetisation

As with any investment, there is a risk of losing the capital invested. **Exit strategies** for private equity firms usually occur within a three to seven-year holding period and where the sponsor firm aims to monetise their investment. Ideally, the sponsor has created some value in the target firm, for example, increasing its EBITDA or reducing debt, and thereby increasing its equity value and post-capital valuation. A return refers to the annual internal rate of return and is calculated over the life of the investment. This takes into account capital redemptions, possible capital gains through an exit, and income through fees and dividends. The return required depends on the perceived risk and the stage of the investment. As a rough guide, the average return required should ideally exceed 15–20 per cent per annum for established ventures, which are those that have typically been in existence for five years or more, and 50 per cent or more for seed-stage investments where financing is required to develop a firm.

An exit strategy can include shares being sold back to the management or to another investor, receivership and liquidation, a 'strategic' or 'trade' sale to another firm or the firm achieving a stock market listing through an IPO, like in the cases of Moncler and Boohoo.com. Focusing on the latter two, a strategic sale can be a fruitful method to monetise the target firm as buyers are usually looking for a strategic fit as well as obtaining sizeable synergies, and therefore tend to pay a premium. For instance, Yoox's merger with Net-A-Porter is slated to generate annual synergies of approximately €60 million by the third full year.[16] This premium can involve key personnel such as the creative director or CEO, which apart from non-compete clauses are often incentivised by a small equity stake to remain with the firm when it is sold. This provides an ongoing strategic motivation to reduce the turnover of key talent, which is integral to the firm's long-term plan. A case in point is Kering, which took a novel approach to securing its key creative talents when it took a stake in Bottega Veneta's creative director Tomas Maier's own brand, signalling what could be a new strategic path by investing in his signature business, yet at the same time retaining and nurturing his talent for Bottega Veneta, a star brand in its portfolio. This is influential when M&A concerns namesake brands like Rebecca Minkoff or Elie Saab.

Planning for an IPO or 'floatation' should usually start one or two years beforehand, depending on a firm's financial reporting system and which stage of development it is in, as a typical IPO process takes about 6–12 months to execute. Firms should consider whether an IPO is the right option for its management, investors and other stakeholders. As the firm will be subject to higher scrutiny, senior management will need to assess the firm's readiness regarding issues such as its financial projections, capital requirements and structure, risk and compliance controls, its governance framework and investor relations team, as executives representing the sponsor will no longer be involved in the detail on a day-to-day basis and the board's outlook will shift to a much longer-term focus guided by the all-important quarterly earnings cycle. An IPO is usually a route undertaken when firms need to raise capital to either pay down debt, fund capital structure or provide working capital for expansion. For example, this could be to grow direct-to-consumer operations in order to better control brand integrity or investment in new ventures such as cosmetics, home interiors, hotels and restaurants. These activities require heavy upfront capitalisation, along with the ability to secure managerial expertise and organisational resources to run a larger, more complex enterprise. Though firms such as Dolce & Gabbana and Ermenegildo Zegna would make a successful IPO as they have strong global visibility, their founders are reluctant to do so, as it would mean a loss of creative freedom and absolute independence.

When a listing is pursued, the sponsor sells a portion of its ownership to an investment bank to price and underwrite the shares. The proportion of shares issued depends on the IPO's objectives and so the pricing is increasingly linked to how many shares are offered, along with the investment bank's secondary research. The assumption is that a full exit will come at a later date along with any potential upside and therefore only a portion of the target is monetised upfront. The sponsor will retain the largest single equity holding and will benefit from an open market for its remaining shares, whilst keeping control of the firm. The prospective share issue is then released to the public in a legally approved prospectus to financial analysts, brokers and potential institutional investors during a 'road show'. The intention of the tour is to obtain a preliminary valuation and generate interest with large investors such as pension funds before the shares are finally offered for sale on the open market on a particular stock exchange. The stock exchange used for listing will have its own specific requirements, including earnings history, shareholders' equity, market capitalisation, the number of expected shareholders and corporate governance requirements, and this should sit comfortably with the firm's future business strategy. For instance, Prada chose to float on the Hong Kong Stock Exchange in 2011 and was launching into a market where there was growing demand for its brand and luxury goods in general.

As the prospectus is circulated, feedback on the firm's strategy and subsequently demand based on investor confidence from the road show result in the underwriter adjusting both the number of shares and final share price to be sold up or down, as the discounted present value of its projected cash flows are taken into account. Nowadays, private equity groups tend to do pre-marketing activities to attract investors much earlier to ensure a successful IPO. This involves extensive media training for the CEO and the CFO as they will frequently be developing new relationships from a low base each time. The IPO has become more about decreasing debt than selling stock on the first day of trading, whereas before it was about maximising the price of an IPO. Today it is less instant and more about medium-term monetisation rather than realisation on day one. The result is less financial engineering and 'popping' or 'flipping' of shares on the first day of trading. This has partially helped some firms to avoid the noise and hype in the media that comes with being 'the next big thing' in the marketplace and instead focused efforts towards creating long-term relationships with key investors. Like any other sale, an IPO can be unsuccessful if a decent valuation cannot be achieved or due to cyclical market factors. The outdoor clothing and equipment retailer Mountain Warehouse pulled a £200 million listing in 2016, citing concerns about Brexit, and Neiman Marcus withdrew its plans to go public in early 2017 due to limited market appetite and struggling comparable sales. Therefore, the exact timing and valuation of the exit strategy depends on the performance of the target firm and the business environment. If there is no contingency plan in place, recovering from a failed IPO can be a mammoth task and an intense emotional cycle. Motivating and re-energising executives can be a tall order, especially as many of them may no longer stand to make a life-changing amount of capital for themselves and their families and subsequently attention should turn quickly to reorientating the firm so that alternative avenues are explored for an exit or refinancing.

In the United States, when firms file a Form S-1 with the Securities and Exchange Commission, which is a disclosure of a firm's IPO plans, many participants such as investment banks, public relations advisers, legal firms and insurance brokers can earn millions in lucrative transaction and advisory fees. This is a whole ecosystem in itself and is one of the principal drivers of why M&A continues to be a money-spinning business, as it is also in the interests of these third-party advisors to keep the fashion industry active and encourage buyers to always be on the lookout for the next 'star brand'. Though many M&A deals are successful, others are abandoned or simply fall through due to a lack of strategic agreement, shareholder dissidence or low valuation. It can be said that one-third of M&A transactions are abysmal failures and an additional one-third fail to live up to expectations due to overestimated synergies, and instead end up diverting capital and managerial resources from their existing businesses. Many deals of the pre-2000 era have struggled as M&A can help deliver synergies and reduce expenses, but can at the same time be a costly exercise. This is because the capital saved can easily be outweighed by the value destroyed if the integration is not correctly executed due to significant differences in customer type, competitor composition and legislation, which vary according to the country and fashion sector. This is where the long-standing Latin adage of *caveat emptor* or 'let the buyer beware' remains an important construct in the fickle and high-stakes fashion industry.

Review questions

Questions for debate regarding mergers and acquisitions are as follows:

- Should governments allow the sale of domestic firms to foreign countries?
- Can the same value be generated by creating firms rather than acquiring them?
- How do you identify and model if profits will move upstream or downstream in the value chain?
- Is borrowing large amounts of capital to acquire firms and then selling them at a large profit ethical?
- Can firms use M&A to permanently replace their own research and development process?
- Do you think fashion firms will move away from M&A in the future?

Further reading

1 Harvard Business School (2015) 'Baker Library Historical Collections: George F. Doriot', www.library.hbs.edu/hc/doriot (accessed 4 May 2017).
2 Donlon, C. (2016) 'M&A Boom Set to Continue in 2017', *Financial Times*, 29 December.
3 Argyris, C. and Cooper, L.C. (eds) (1998) *The Concise Blackwell Encyclopedia of Management*. Oxford: Blackwell.
4 Coach Inc. (2016) '2016 Form 10-K', http://uk.coach.com/financial-reports.html (accessed 4 May 2017).
5 Weiss, M. (2013) 'Ackman Sees J.C. Penney Losses Crossing $650 Million', *Bloomberg*, www.bloomberg.com/news/articles/2013-04-09/ackman-sees-j-c-penney-losses-crossing-650-million (accessed 4 May 2017).
6 Business Wire (2016) 'Caerus Sends Letter to Kate Spade Board', www.nasdaq.com/press-release/caerus-sends-letter-to-kate-spade-board-20161114-00148 (accessed 4 May 2017).
7 Srinivasan, S. (2014) 'How Activist Investors Change the Game', *Footwear News*, 12 May.
8 Pearl, J. and Rosenbaum, J. (2009) *Investment Banking: Valuation, Leveraged Buyouts, and Mergers & Acquisitions*. Hoboken: John Wiley & Sons.
9 YGM Trading Ltd. (2016) 'YGM Trading Limited 2016/17 Interim Report', www.ygmtrading.com/eng/images/pdf/eInterim%20Report%202016–17.pdf (accessed 4 May 2017).

10 Coach Inc. (2015) 'Coach Completes Acquisition of Luxury Designer Footwear Brand Stuart Weitzman', http://uk.coach.com/press-releases.html (accessed 4 May 2017).
11 Schein, E.H. (2010) *Organizational Culture and Leadership*, 4th edn. San Francisco: Jossey-Bass.
12 Hoffman, L. and Tan, G. (2014) 'Project Funway: Code Names Help Spice up the Art of the Deal, *Wall Street Journal*, 29 August, www.wsj.com/articles/bankers-lament-loss-of-code-names-for-deals-1409279749 (accessed 4 May 2017). Amed, I. (2016) 'The Secret Deal to Merge Net-A-Porter with Yoox', *The Business of Fashion*, www.businessoffashion.com/articles/bof-exclusive/richemont-net-a-porter-yoox-merger-secret-deal (accessed 4 May 2017).
13 Adams, S. (2014) 'Hermès and LVMH Make Peace', Forbes, 11 September. Jolly, D. (2014) 'LVMH Boss and Hermès Family in Pact', *New York Times*, 3 September, www.nytimes.com/2014/09/04/business/international/lvmh-and-hermes-strike-deal-to-end-shareholder-dispute.html?_r=0 (accessed 4 May 2017).
14 Conlon, S. (2016) 'Sonia Rykiel Closes Diffusion Line', *Vogue*, www.vogue.co.uk/article/sonia-rykiel-closes-sonia-by-sonia-rykiel-label (accessed 4 May 2017).
15 Berrington, K. (2016) 'Roberto Cavalli Employees Take Action', *Vogue*, www.vogue.co.uk/article/roberto-cavalli-employees-strike-following-restructure-announcement (accessed 4 May 2017).
16 Paton, E. (2015) 'Yoox Bags Net-A-Porter in Merger Plan', *Financial Times*, 31 March.

8 Management and leadership
Approaches, styles and activities

> **Chapter goals**
>
> This chapter outlines how management is distinct from leadership, but why it is equally important. The role of senior leadership teams is covered along with an overview of the key topics that gravitate to the top of their agenda. The key areas covered are:
>
> - Keeping management relevant
> - What does leadership look like?
> - What does the senior leadership team focus on?

Keeping management relevant

Take a glance online or on the shelves of your local bookstore and you will see that most business books centre on leadership, strategy, branding and finance. Little space (if any) is designated to management. Management is a fascinating topic of research and a noble profession if it is practised well. Helping others to learn and grow, take responsibility, be recognised for their achievements and contribute to team success is what most people desire. Since the industrial era overtook agrarian activity, the fundamentals of management have changed little over the decades. Essentially, **management** entails doing work as efficiently and competently as possible within the established boundaries of the firm. Advocated by classical **scientific management** theorists like Henri Fayol and Fredrick Taylor, early management traditionally centred on planning activities such as selecting corporate objectives and establishing plans to achieve them, plus the organisation of resources and how the firm would be structured. By comparing the firm's actual performance versus planned performance it could control and allocate resources. Effective staffing was used to get the best return from all employees and aimed at securing the optimum coordination of all the firm's activities. Consequently, getting work done through others meant that many large industrial firms of that time, such as the factories and mills which produced low-cost and standardised products, implemented formal structures and hierarchical frameworks of clear control and command. Amongst a homogeneous population, this model of management with its clear lines of reporting and decision-making, which focused on efficiency and process, was immensely successful and helped fuel the growth of numerous firms in the twentieth century.

This was balanced by the **Human Relations School** of thought. Theorists such as Elton Mayo, who conducted studies at the Hawthorne Works between 1927 and 1932 highlighted the importance of social relationships, motivation and employee satisfaction to boost productivity. This work was added to by motivational theory and behavioural experts like Mary Parker Follett, Abraham Maslow, Douglas McGregor and Frederick Herzberg. This way of thinking was also furthered by influential modern management writers such as Henry Mintzberg and Peter Drucker. In particular, Drucker wrote that the fundamental task of management is to 'make people capable of joint performance through common goals, common values, the right structure and the training and development they need to perform and to respond to change'.[1] Underlined by the basic laws of social interaction, this concept focused on getting people to work together to achieve the desired goals and undertake them in the correct way. Interestingly, his definition has no reference to firms, hierarchies or bureaucracy. Rather than qualifying this concept in order to make it relevant to the firms of today, executives and firms still continue to conjure up images of the industrial past and its associated behaviours. Subsequently, the term 'management' has become tainted and pigeonholed by both management writers and executives as they focus on what managers do rather than why they do it. You only have to watch the classic film *The Devil Wears Prada*, in which the actress Meryl Streep plays a frosty fashion magazine editor, watch the recent television documentary *Absolutely Fashion: Inside British Vogue*, which films the run-up to *British Vogue*'s centenary celebrations at the National Portrait Gallery in London, or *The First Monday in May*, which centres on an exhibition held at the Metropolitan Museum of Art in New York and the staging of the famous star-studded fundraising gala known as the Met Ball, to confirm the stereotypes and the poor depiction of management in the industry.

From the large industrial firms of the past to the craft guilds operating the master-and-apprentice model to the modern graduate entry programme, management has not changed drastically in the past 100 years or so and probably will not change dramatically in the next 25 years. But what is changing are the methods and context of how firms conduct business and will continue to do so, as the industry firmly enters a knowledge and digital society. For example, why should we assume that all the important decisions are made by executives at the top of the hierarchy in a society where experts and specialists can contribute to a business problem through freelancing and crowdsourcing techniques? Why should we not let these people make the decisions? Likewise, do firms need to make huge investments in terms of hiring and training when today's employees no longer intend to spend any substantial period of time with the same employer and when the skills they need can be readily bought? The fact is that this all depends on, for example, the nature of the decision being made, the firm's size, the competitive environment and its human capital capabilities. That said, the concept of management is definitely likely to still be around, but perhaps not in the way we are used to knowing it, and many firms will need to substantially change the way in which they are organised, managed and led if they are to remain relevant.[2]

Case study: Zappos

The online apparel and shoe retailer eliminated managers and fully embraced a new means of self-management known as Holacracy in 2015. Developed by Brian Robertson in 2007, Holacracy is an anti-totalitarian concept, with its main tenets centring on individual autonomy, empowerment, efficiency, entrepreneurialism and self-governance. Like past participative management efforts such as quality circles and continuous improvement efforts, highly motivated workers who thrive on creativity in flat organisational structures are best suited to working in this environment. Zappos' employees belong to voluntary business groups called 'circles' and each circle (of which there has been more than 500 formed) has a 'lead link' similar to a project manager, who has limited authority and is subject to the circle's governance process. Employees in each circle are co-dependent on each other and everyone has an equal say when tackling agenda items such as problems, projects or new ideas known as 'tensions'. Employees are evaluated and rewarded by peers instead of a manager, with a focus on keeping a small-firm and entrepreneurial culture. As employees hold multiple roles in various circles, responsibilities continually shift as the work changes. Enterprise software such as GlassFrog is used to help codify accountability and decision rights of every circle, and 'badges' are awarded to employees so that others can see what skills they have to offer. In spite of this, some employees have left the firm as they found that Holacracy led to too many meetings and vague decision-making rights, along with unclear pay and career progression. Because Holacracy takes time and a lot of trial and error, especially when prioritising and allocating resources, it is yet to be seen if it will be totally successful in terms of increased employee engagement, financial impact and, most importantly, meeting Zappos' own high customer service standards.

What does leadership look like?

The process of influencing people by providing purpose, direction and motivation while operating to accomplish the mission and improving the organization. (United States Army).[3]

Leadership has been talked about since the time of Plato. With strong roots linking leadership to the military and intertwined with economic theory, leadership has traditionally been portrayed through the lens of turning inputs into outputs for consumption. This principal-agent approach as a unit of analysis focused little on human behaviour. It was thinkers such as Max Weber and Sigmund Freud who were the first to have contributed to the influence of human behaviour in the realm of leadership through their seminal work on 'authority' and 'legitimacy', 'rationality' and the 'unconscious mind'. Over time, leadership has accumulated a gamut of views and opposing statements by blending psychology, philosophy, economics, sociology and organisational behaviour literature and to a lesser extent, history, politics and anthropology. Nowadays, a more accurate representation of how firms are run moves beyond pure economic theory to incorporate some form of managerial initiative and leadership. Research tends to focus on three data points: first, the persona of the leader such as motivation through status, wealth and power or autonomy, mastery and purpose; secondly, leadership as a process which is supported by key interventions; and third, the effects of leadership on others.

So what does leadership look like? Leadership is a concept that is too loosely defined and remains more of an 'art' than a 'science', even though there have been many efforts to bring rigour to the profession. Often leadership is portrayed as heroic or as being on a pedestal, especially in the Western world. You only have to study the biographies of great leaders and they read like they had some sort of special pre-ordained powers with an illusion of invulnerability and moral superiority. This is why leadership remains elusive to many of us and why it is deemed a racier and more dynamic part of an executive's job than purely management. Do not believe it. Certainly, many of these leaders showed great courage, skill and intellect, but many good leaders have faced adversity in their life at some point, such as being from a poor family, severe illness or lacking a full education. Therefore, everyone at any level or point in their life can show leadership, no matter how big or small the impact.

Fundamentally, leadership has moved on to creating a capacity for cumulative change in what we do and how we do it to inspire and mobilise people. By defining the challenge, making sense of it and providing insight, leaders are able to answer the question 'what is going on?' and commit to a course of action. Because we are living in a world with big, global and complex challenges that we can no longer solve in isolation, it is important to cooperate together and understand each other's perspectives. Without comprehension, executives will look at the unknown as a threat. For this reason, leadership has become increasingly more forward-looking and concerned with getting others to belong and follow through believing in a vision, setting a direction, managing change and motivating people. Key skills are about influence, persuasion, imagination, networks and intelligence compared to traditionally being focused on authority, position, hierarchies and coercion. Leadership has become less top-down and more circular, with a heavy slant towards transparency, morals and accountability. To this point, just as there is no one best way to manage, there is no one best way to lead, and that leadership is contingent on the specifics of any given situation, the resources available and the individuals involved.[4]

For many generations, except for a privileged few, work meant a form of servitude with few rights. Coming to work and toiling hard to secure a day's pay was the collective agreement. Over the past century, being entitled to just a salary has moved on to job satisfaction and now self-directed career management. Leadership plays an important part in this as it is leaders who direct, motivate and coach employees to fulfil their potential through the inextricable relationship of 'knowing', 'being' and 'doing'. Whether you are the CEO of a global firm, a sole proprietor or you have just graduated, it pays to have a sense of leadership. Most executives have arrived at their current position by virtue of their individual contributions and through being results-orientated in a team setting. Being next in line or the oldest member of the team seldom equals success, as for many executives, the stage of their career is not in sync with the leadership qualities and behaviours that the firm needs. Leading others requires having the right experience, skills and fit to set the context for others to do excellent work. Consequently, the most effective leadership approach may not be the one that suits the executive's personality and style; instead, it is often the one that best suits the firm's needs and objectives. Accordingly, being aware of your leadership abilities, limitations and requirements is a fundamental skill to develop for any executive in navigating the corporate workplace as it is difficult for the same person to be an effective leader as well as an effective manager.

Table 8.1 shows the various **leadership styles** based on the renowned work of the psychologist Daniel Goleman. These styles require time, attention and energy to master with some level of **leadership presence**, which is defined as 'the ability to connect with the thoughts and feelings of others in order to motivate and inspire them to achieve a desired outcome'.[5] This entails the main leadership qualities of collaboration, listening, authenticity, adaptability, engagement, humility and transparency, especially as executives are being judged quicker than ever before. Successful executives should balance the portrayal of self-confidence, but also develop the ability to see themselves as others see them. There are various levels of leadership for different levels and activities of the firm, and for different stages in an executive's career. A successful executive is willing and able to pivot between the various styles, depending on the context of the situation. One of the greatest misconceptions

Table 8.1 Taxonomy of leadership styles

Style	Characteristics
VISIONARY	Targets shared dreams Useful when a clear direction/vision is required Builds team commitment
COACHING	Brings together people with the firm's goals Coaches executives to improve performance Establishes long-term development goals and capabilities
DEMOCRATIC	Gains participation through input and commitment Relies on motivated staff to achieve goals Consensus can remain elusive
PACE-SETTING	Meets challenging and stimulating goals Limited to motivated and competent executives Often focuses on short-term goals
COMMANDING	Provides clear direction in an emergency Useful in a crisis and turnaround situations Based on compliance

Source: adapted from Goleman (2000).[6]

of leadership is that of the well-rounded leader. No one leader is perfect, as roles like the CEO have become too complex for any single central figure to master, since the range of skills required is increasing rapidly. Instead, executives are better off focusing on their strengths and working to sharpen them rather than trying to be great at every facet of leadership. This is why strong leaders build great teams around them. Through collaborative leadership and shared goals, they instil mutual trust and employ skills and experience that complement each other, as it is not about being the smartest person in the room and having all the answers, but about being able to ask the right questions that stimulate ideas and discourse that build on insights to guide the firm towards adding value. Therefore, the CEO needs to make tough people decisions quickly, as the firm will often need new people with new energy and attitudes to accelerate its strategy.

In the 1980s and late 1990s the leadership pendulum shifted from managerial enterprise to investor capitalism. 'Visionary', 'entrepreneurial' and 'charismatic leaders' were all buzzwords that were prevalent in the business literature, as leadership success (defined in terms of titles and money) frequently got confused or mistaken for effective leadership. The bubble soon started to deflate as the aggressive, egocentric and charismatic C-suite executives who had previously been hugely successful became reluctant to change or be questioned about their morals, ethics and competence in relation to making good decisions on behalf of the firm. Consequently, they became embroiled in major corporate frauds and bankruptcies. Legislation was tightened and incentives were scrutinised as the focus shifted to steady competent execution. For many firms, a commanding style of leadership became the norm as it provided clear direction and a shared purpose to turn around or stabilise the firm with the mandate of regaining stakeholder confidence.

With the digital era now firmly upon us, many firms have installed leaders to capture this opportunity, either through internal growth and the introduction of new products, services and platforms or through M&A activities. As a result, the war for talent from data scientist, digital merchandiser and consumer insight analyst to employing a chief information officer has meant a pace-setting style of management being used to scale up firm operations to gain a competitive advantage. Equally, the coaching and democratic style of leadership has also become very popular, especially with Millennials who prefer being managed this way, and focuses on coaching executives to improve performance. By diverting attention away from their own personal power, security and authority, managers gain participation and commitment from others. As this style carefully mutes the leader's authority, it can often exercise more authority as it fosters a sense of belonging through continuous support, new learning and growth opportunities without the constraints of a rigid hierarchy. In an increasingly knowledge society, there will be tension to ensure the correct degree of collaboration between the team and subject-matter experts, who will want to exert their authority. In this instance, in order to increase teamwork, centres of excellence may be formed and compensation metrics may be closely linked to team and individual performance. Additionally, collaboration should not be confused with consensus and careful attention should be paid by executives to ensure that the two are nurtured.

As they become experienced, many leaders progress from an individual-orientated identity focused on themselves to a collective orientated identity focused on their self and others, with the aim of sharing their experience to help drive long-term development goals and capabilities. As the human psyche is well trained to live in a defined and stable structure, most employees are happy to defer responsibility to others, since they are often constrained by either personal or organisational reasons and are not fully committed to the leadership cause. Therefore, great leaders are those who want to lead and know how to act and behave. As a result, some of the most testing situations for a leader to be in is when a leadership challenge is pushed upon them. Finally, most executives will explain that they have had to lead in a different way from their predecessors. Therefore, the next 10–15 years could see even greater transformation to what leadership looks like and means in the workplace.

What does the senior leadership team focus on?

Membership of the **senior leadership team (SLT)** is an important and a coveted position. Typically, the SLT comprises the CEO and his or her direct reports, who each have a separate individual leadership responsibility as well as a shared purpose for aligning the firm, its performance and the overall effectiveness of the strategic choices it makes. They are a self-governing team and operate in a global and virtual capacity. Success is a team effort, but some SLTs are repeatedly out of sync. For example, opposing priorities, multiple players and a lack of communication along with questionable ethics can lead to warped performance measures that reward individual accomplishments rather than collective results. Office politics and 'turf wars' can mean that much time is wasted in long and arduous meetings that centre on trivial topics, where discussions frequently end with members agreeing to disagree or with individuals saying one thing but doing another thing as they fight to keep their position. This is evident in family businesses, where the governance structure can be blurred and where cultural practices dictate that decisions are not challenged in order to keep the peace and respect elder members. This misalignment can result in shared tasks that were originally slated for collective action being reassembled and based on individual achievement and personal networks. Bad decisions are made on behalf of the firm and because of these impediments, the firm can quickly become bureaucratic and slow, causing its financial performance to suffer. Strikingly, many team members choose this path as they see the senior leadership team as the CEO's team rather than a collective team in which they are all equally responsible. Oddly, this type of sub-optimal outcome would not be tolerated in their own teams.[7]

As firm performance is often equated with the CEO's performance, if the firm is fundamentally challenged, then it will need to look for new capabilities and bring in fresh talent to transform it. This is why today's senior leaders have a short period of time in which to make an impact and why most senior leaders have rolling three-year contracts or are replaced within three to five years. Conversely, if the firm is performing well, then the firm is wise to promote from within, as this creates a sense of passion and engagement among its staff, whilst sending out a strong signal that the firm takes internal succession planning seriously.

Given that the business environment is constantly changing, there is no fixed task list for the SLT. Similarly, there is no theoretical or practical model that exists in terms of what senior leaders should do with their time. Because of this, most firms have no clear understanding of how and on what their senior leaders and employees are spending their time. However, a SLT is responsible for making good decisions on behalf of the firm in allocating finite resources whilst dealing with the unpredictability of the business environment and time limits. As the SLT does not always have the best information or the required technical ability to make every decision, executives closer to the situation and those with the appropriate skills and expertise are normally better suited to making these decisions and can have a material impact on the performance of the firm. Therefore, strong direct and indirect decision-making skills, along with the necessary allocation of responsibility, become key constructs for the SLT. For this reason, a great senior leadership team focuses on the direction, organisation, communication, selection, motivation and implementation of a handful of important activities that are considered the most pressing, but are often competing priorities. The activities that the SLT spends its time on can be broadly divided as follows:

- Governance, including risk management and fiduciary duties.
- Corporate and business unit strategy, including specific financial goals and operational matters.
- Brand management, including product and customer experience.
- Change management, including shaping culture and transformation.
- Human capital and performance management, including leadership continuity, talent management, diversity, firm structure and rewards.
- Systems and processes to support the firm's goals and strategy, including ICT investment, optimising operations and reporting requirements.
- Stakeholder engagement, including managing reputation, ethical and legal standards and external stakeholders.

Though these activities should be strategic in nature, collectively the SLT frequently focuses on operational and administrative issues rather than on strategic matters, as shown in Table 8.2. Competitive advantage strategies being discussed on the corporate agenda include a heavy focus on product innovation and marketing, increasing customer intimacy to drive firm performance, and developing and running agile global supply chains for operational excellence. Other strategies include upgrading existing systems and investing in new ICT, managing international expansion predominately through e-commerce and franchising and lastly, leveraging human capital to attract, develop and retain talent.

Top operational priorities for senior executives often focus on increasing market share, overseeing human capital and investing in ICT. This is followed by managing complexity and optimising end-to-end supply chain performance, international expansion and scouting potential M&A opportunities. Talent is the common factor that underlies all these issues, as high-calibre executives drive great performance in meeting the customer's needs and ensuring that the firm remains relevant. But interestingly, while human capital

Table 8.2 Differences between competitive advantage and operational strategies

Strategic initiatives	Operational priorities
1. Marketing/product	1. Increased market share
2. Customer service	2. Human capital
3. Supply chain management	3. ICT
4. ICT	4. Supply chain management
5. International expansion	5. International expansion
6. Human capital	6. M&A

Source: adapted from Harvey Nash (2008).[8]

comes in second place as an operational priority, it is unfortunately last in terms in being a strategic initiative for many firms.

Whether it is in an established firm, a young start-up, a for profit or a non-profit, all require their senior leadership team to have a clear plan for translating purpose into action. This necessitates the courage and skill to guide, connect and develop the firm so that it continues to matter. This is because a firm can have all the environmental advantages to leverage when utilising the ELIPSE framework, plus an abundance of resources, and yet still fail due to an absence of strong leadership. Effective leadership correlates to better firm performance, lower staff turnover and increased employee commitment and productivity. Without good leadership, any advantages just melt away.

Review questions

Questions for debate regarding management and leadership are as follows:

- Does the study of leadership deserve greater recognition than management?
- Is money and power still a relevant hallmark of success in the modern workplace?
- Is management and leadership a rational task performed by rational people?
- What is a greater motivator – hope or fear?
- What is your added value as a leader – why should anyone be led by you?
- What skills are required to manage tomorrow's talent?

Further reading

1 Drucker, P.F. (1994) *The New Realities*. Oxford: Routledge.
2 Birkinshaw, J. (2012) *Reinventing Management*. Chichester: John Wiley & Sons.
3 Department of the Army (2012) *U.S. Army Leadership Handbook*. USA: Skyhorse Publishing.
4 Khurana, R. and Nohria, N. (2010) *Handbook of Leadership Theory and Practice*. Boston: Harvard Business School Publishing.
5 Walsh, B. (2013) Ariel Group 13 PLD 16 Workshop, Boston: Harvard Business School.
6 Goleman, D. (2000) 'Leadership that Gets Results', *Harvard Business Review*, Vol. 78, No. 2, pp. 78–90.
7 Burruss, J.A., Hackman, J.R., Nunes, D.A. and Wageman, R. (2008) *Senior Leadership Teams: What it Takes to Make Them Great*. Boston: Harvard Business School Press.
Hackman, J.R. (2002) *Leading Teams: Setting the Stage for Great Performances*. Boston: Harvard Business School Press.
8 Harvey Nash (2008) *Strategic Leadership Survey: A Retail Boardroom Perspective*. London: Harvey Nash.

9 Culture and inclusion
Capabilities, diversity and action

Chapter goals

This chapter covers the different cultural contexts in which the firm operates and the importance of culture in creating a competitive advantage. Diversity and inclusion are discussed with a focus on women in the workplace. The key areas covered are:

- Climate and culture
- The cultural continuum
- Diversity and inclusion
- Women and workplace inclusion
- Closing the pay gap

Climate and culture

Individuals and groups with diverse cultural backgrounds are increasingly working together in the business world. Analysing a firm's climate and culture can help us to understand the environment in which a leader leads and how to maximise the context for employee performance. **Climate** can be defined as a short-term experience originating from how employees think and feel about the firm on a daily basis and derives from shared perceptions and attitudes. Drivers of a positive climate can be characterised by a leader's behaviour who does the right things for the right reasons. Examples include being fair, ethical, open and inclusive, whilst creating a learning environment which actively identifies opportunities for training and development to harness individual experiences and expertise in order to further the firm's growth. This can have a significant impact on employee motivation and the trust people feel for their peers, team and leaders. **Culture** can be described as a longer-lasting and more complex set of shared experiences, both tangible and intangible.[1] It is an amorphous concept, but one that can really drive the firm's competitive advantage, yet can also lead to its failure. Culture enables employees to address recurrent problems by acting autonomously but cohesively in their decision-making on a daily basis. It refers to a firm's shared attitudes, values, norms, customs and operating style. It helps employees to uphold appropriate attitudes and behaviours when implementing and executing the firm's priorities. Despite being difficult to measure or describe with acute accuracy, it is nevertheless a hugely important facet that shapes the modern firm and sets the tone for what is valued, celebrated and prioritised in the workplace. A strong culture provides consistent decision-making as the firm's size and scope expand. It can be considered perhaps one of the most vexing aspects on the management agenda of running a firm, but one that is also a powerful tool for a skilled executive to wield, as some 82 per cent of respondents to the 2016 Deloitte Global Human Capital Trends report referenced culture as a potential driver of competitive advantage. However, only 28 per cent of business leaders said they understand their culture well and 19 per cent believed they have the right culture.[2]

At one point in a firm's history, for example, during the beginning of a start-up venture, what gets done is attributable to the firm's founders and leaders as they create a culture through their occupational biases. This is a culture which is so often explicitly debated that it now comes to be adopted by assumption through prior successful work. Therefore, culture can constitute a powerful capability and enabler in addressing certain types of opportunities and problems. Conversely, culture can become a powerful disability at times when change is critical to addressing new challenges or unexpected threats. Understanding a firm's culture can be crucial for its success, as the most deeply entrenched elements of a firm's culture are often the least visible. The culture of a firm can be expressed by asking a few simple questions, such as 'why do you work here?', 'who are your firm's heroes?' and 'what stories do your employees tell about them?' Good leaders aim to establish a climate that is consistent and aligned to the culture of the enduring firm. By doing this, leaders can maximise employee performance and help optimise the daily interaction and functioning of the firm. Leaders should also use their firm's culture to let their people know they are part of something bigger than just themselves, that they have a purpose and that with this comes responsibilities not only to the people around them, but also to those who have gone before and those who will come after them. This is best done by the founders of the firm and is elaborated with insights from the different SLT perspectives and experiences. If the culture of a firm is to be documented, it is best that the founder does this rather than the human resources or public relations team, as they usually turn it into some corporate verbiage that employees do not believe in or care about, or can even remember.

Case study: Nike

Strong leaders such as Nike's founder Phil Knight embody their passion and creativity through the firm's clear mission: 'to bring inspiration and innovation to every athlete in the world. If you have a body, you are an athlete'. The use of internal maxims or 'social glue' in the workplace such as 'Simplify & Go' and 'Just Do It' exemplify the type of thinking and mindset that is needed by employees to emotionally connect with and succeed at Nike. These values are also reinforced externally through 'visual cues' and 'persona' not only by hiring former athletes but also through the high-profile sponsorship of elite athletes who are known for winning, like Serena Williams, Cristiano Ronaldo and LeBron James. Furthermore, the university campus-style layout and extensive leisure facilities along with the casual dress code, open-plan workspace and flat hierarchy amplify the type of culture Nike embodies.

The cultural continuum

Although a culture is unique to each individual firm, understanding it can help a manager predict how the firm is likely to respond to different situations. In its purest form, culture can be placed on a diametrically opposing continuum, as shown in Figure 9.1. At one end of the scale is a **control** culture, which values consistency and productivity, with an emphasis on

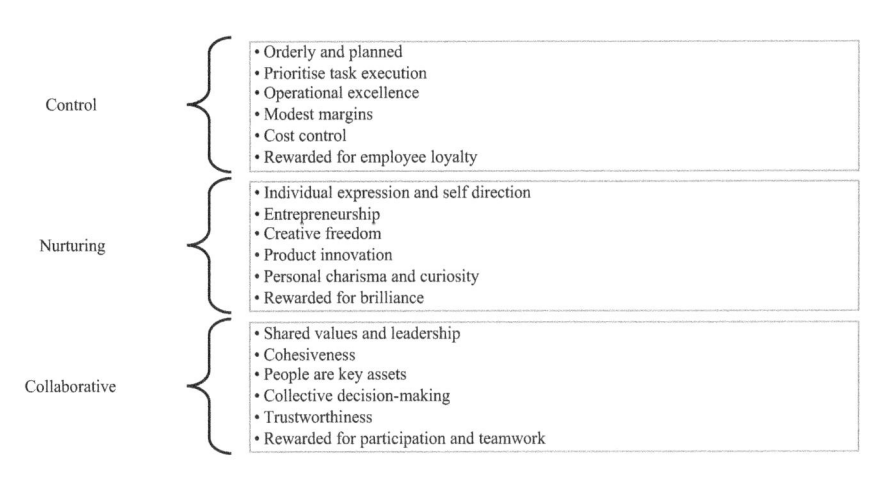

Control	• Orderly and planned • Prioritise task execution • Operational excellence • Modest margins • Cost control • Rewarded for employee loyalty
Nurturing	• Individual expression and self direction • Entrepreneurship • Creative freedom • Product innovation • Personal charisma and curiosity • Rewarded for brilliance
Collaborative	• Shared values and leadership • Cohesiveness • People are key assets • Collective decision-making • Trustworthiness • Rewarded for participation and teamwork

Figure 9.1 The cultural continuum
Source: adapted from Cameron and Quinn (2011).[3]

achieving financial results against plan as profit margins are often small in these firms. Sustained operational efficiency derives from the resource allocation of work and responsibility rather than individual flair and judgement. While fewer innovative ideas might be put forward, implementation tends to be straightforward once the authority to make a decision is given. Employees demonstrate loyalty and are interested in 'what' needs to get done, as set out by rules, policies, procedures and hierarchy. These are typically older firms that have survived due to their uniformity and structure. Senior management are the executives who have the relevant information so act as coordinators and administrators, as rules, policies and procedures bond people. A control culture is most often likely to be found in industrial firms whose strategic emphasis is on stability and predictability, for example, in a firm such as the t-shirt producer Hanes, which operates in the fashion basics segment of the market.

In the middle of the continuum lies a **nurturing** culture. This focuses on talent management and employees who are highly creative, technically astute and experts in their fields. Individual expression and self-direction are supported by an interest in 'why'. Risk taking and adaptability are key employee traits that are highly rewarded. By leveraging disruptive technologies and investing heavily in protecting their IP, these firms produce innovative products and are at the forefront of their industries. Senior executives are usually described as entrepreneurs, innovators and brand officers, with the strategic emphasis being on growth and new ideas. The outdoor brand The North Face closely displays this type of creative and knowledge culture.

At the other end of the scale, a **collaborative** culture emphasises the distinct needs of the employees and the firm's customers. Products relate closely to customer preferences and duties are organised around teamwork, 'how' and 'who' executes the task. Strong shared values act as an enabler for decentralised decision-making and empowerment as executives across all levels and locations share relevant information. Dominant attributes include cohesiveness, participation and sense of family. Successes and failures are collectively embraced and loyalty is high in relation to achieving performance and shared goals. Senior executives are usually described as mentors and facilitators, and the strategic emphasis is on developing human resources. Culture-building efforts may range from employee appreciation week to breakfast with the senior management team or a question-and-answer forum with the CEO. These are clearly aimed at creating a sense of bonding and transparency. Consequently, retention, commitment and morale are high in these firms. An example can be found in firms like the British retailer John Lewis, which operates a successful partnership structure and has attained an industry-leading position in relation to employee engagement, training and retention. Balancing collaboration with accountability and responsibility can be a key challenge, as collaborative efforts can be very time-consuming and can lead to paralysis in decision-making and goal implementation.

Every firm will exhibit a hybrid of the type of cultures identified. For example, in a new venture, executives who have left other firms to become entrepreneurs are keen to create a culture as quickly as possible, as previously they had one to help guide them. This is important because as firms grow in size, senior executives have reduced contact with staff and new formal structures, systems and processes are introduced to share information, harness creativity and innovation in order to gain efficiency and control. As systems, structure and processes are inter-linked, making changes can be challenging, costly and time-consuming to implement. This can result in a change in culture to reflect the new challenges the firm is facing, which can lead to cultural resistance as norms and values of 'how things are done around here' become sticky and deeply rooted. This challenge is further augmented on various levels. First, **national culture** heavily influences corporate culture and this varies from country to country. Whether a firm operates in the United States, the Middle East or Japan, these countries embrace different attitudes and traditions to buying patterns. For instance, the control culture is most prevalent in Chinese, Russian and French firms, whilst a nurturing culture is most likely to exist in German and American firms. A collaborative philosophy exists in, for example, Denmark and the Netherlands, where the national culture is very egalitarian. Thus, in different environments, for example, in a stable environment, culture provides an effective way of controlling and coordinating employees without the need for rigid formal control systems. In unstable environments, culture can present itself as a barrier to change for the firm.

On a more granular level, this complexity is furthered because as human beings we are biologically hard-wired from birth to form deep social bonds. From our families and friends to our work colleagues and business partners, our societies are built on a layer of multi-dimensional social interactions and hierarchy which is heavily dependent on collective activity. Surrounding us, we see relationships simultaneously formed, nurtured and broken; after all, our survival depends on the rapid assessment of who is friend and who is foe. This can lead to executives pursuing their own goals and agendas, resulting in the dominant culture being in conflict with another one. This 'herding' or 'tribe' effect is a fundamental behaviour of human groups and results in tension and silos within the firm, as the ultimate limitation on the firm is not a lack of capital, human intelligence or ICT, but the ability of people to work together effectively. This becomes a key challenge that executives are faced with and therefore the most dominant culture typically prevails. This usually derives from the CEO and their past work and life experience. However, many senior executives do not understand the DNA of their current firm and try to replicate a culture from a previous employer, which is very hard to cascade and can backfire. This is why when a swift change in culture is required, a new CEO and executive leadership team are hired. In support of this is the famously short tenure of former J.C. Penney CEO Ron Johnson, who joined the firm from Apple, where he had had a very successful career. In his new role, he attempted to make copious changes, many of which alienated the retailer's core consumer base because he tried to innovate too fast in a culture where the firm did not have the desire or character to change. Subsequently, his tenure only lasted 17 months, as he was fired after sales fell 25 per cent in his first year.[4] Conversely, Nordstrom has sustained its relentless customer-centric ethos to deliver the best possible shopping experience, which has enabled its customer-driven culture to be its main competitive advantage for over 115 years.

In sum, many executives think the firm's problems reside in functions such as marketing or production. In fact, it is the firm's culture that is commonly the main problem and a huge destroyer in creating value. If it is tackled quickly, turning a negative culture into a positive culture can lead to rapid results. Firms that advocate and decode their customers' and suppliers' needs and desires through their culture are well positioned to reap the rewards, as the real test of leadership is devising a successful firm culture in today's increasingly complicated, diverse and global network.

Diversity and inclusion

Society has rapidly increased in diversity, yet it has been slow to fully filter through the fashion system. Discrimination and stereotyping continue all around us, even though laws against discrimination exist in most countries. This can be considered a strange phenomenon as the fashion industry is considered to be global, creative, diverse and open to all. A diverse population forms a large proportion not only of the potential workforce but also of the consumer market. Their engagement in various social relationships, cultural practices and economic activities bring different experiences and perspectives to the value chain. Nonetheless, many firms still do not have a good and fair representation of ethnic minorities, lesbian, gay, bisexual and transgender executives in their workforce, especially in the senior ranks. This is amplified as the industry is criticised for being ageist and also biased towards the most discriminated group in the workforce, which is those labelled as disabled and covers individuals with mental health conditions or physical challenges. Furthermore, the Creative Diversity Report commissioned by the UK Creative Industries Federation found that only 11 per cent of all creative jobs are held by Black, Asian and minority ethnic workers (BAME), despite the fact that 32 per cent of jobs are in London, which is 40 per cent BAME.[5] With a diverse workforce leading to greater engagement and variety in thinking, which can lead to higher returns, the industry has been slow to tap into this overt competitive advantage. Particularly as in the fashion industry, there is a lack of role models who people can look up to and identify with. Therefore, a good CEO and SLT recognise their responsibility to cascade diversity and inclusion through the firm, and see it as a fundamental plank of their leadership and corporate goals.

Influenced by the world around us and a reflection of popular culture, international fashion magazines exercise considerable influence over fashion trends and the way consumers think, behave and act. Using the United States as an example, as shown in Table 9.1, only 35.4 per cent or 52 out of 147 front covers from 10 leading fashion publications, including *Nylon* and *Elle*, featured people of colour in 2016. This was a 15.5 percentage point improvement on 2015, which had 27 covers out of 136 or 19.9 per cent. *Teen Vogue* featured the most diversity, with seven of its 11 issues or 63.6 per cent of its covers showing a woman of colour, such as Willow Smith, Zoe Kravitz or Simone Biles. This was a 54.5 percentage point increase compared to 2014. *InStyle* showed a woman of colour on seven out of 12 covers or 58.3 per cent, including the likes of Jennifer Lopez, Michelle Obama and Priyanka Chopra. This was a 50 percentage point increase compared to 2014. *Glamour* magazine showed a person of colour on three out of 14 covers or 21.4 per cent and *Harper's Bazaar* featured a person of colour on one out of 11 or 9.1 per cent of its covers, both showing no change compared to 2015. Disappointingly, *Glamour* decreased by 3.6 percentage points in 2015 and 2016 compared to 2014.

Table 9.1 Models of colour on the front cover of American fashion magazines

Magazine	2016		2015		2014		2016 vs. 2015	2016 vs. 2014
Allure	5/13	38.5%	3/12	25.0%	2/12	16.7%	+13.5%	+21.8%
Cosmopolitan	4/12	33.3%	2/12	16.7%	1/12	8.3%	+16.6%	+25.0%
Elle	9/26	34.6%	3/19	15.8%	5/22	22.7%	+18.8%	+11.9%
Glamour	3/14	21.4%	3/14	21.4%	3/12	25.0%	0.0%	−3.6%
Harper's Bazaar	1/11	9.1%	1/11	9.1%	0/13	0.0%	0.0%	+9.1%
InStyle	7/12	58.3%	5/12	41.7%	1/12	8.3%	+16.6%	+50.0%
Nylon	5/11	45.5%	1/11	9.1%	4/11	36.4%	+36.4%	+9.1%
Teen Vogue	7/11	63.6%	4/11	36.4%	1/11	9.1%	+27.2%	+54.5%
Vogue	4/11	36.4%	3/12	25.0%	4/12	33.3%	+11.4%	+3.1%
W	7/26	26.9%	2/22	9.1%	4/20	20.0%	+17.8%	+6.9%
Total	**52/147**	**35.4%**	**27/136**	**19.9%**	**25/137**	**18.2%**	**+15.5%**	**+17.2%**

Source: adapted from Brannigan (2016).[6]

On a global scale, international publications such as *Vogue, Paper* and *Dazed* were analysed by the Fashion Spot in 2016 and the criteria broadened to cover race, gender, body type and age. The findings showed that out of the 679 front covers, 482 or 71 per cent featured white models, whilst 197 front covers or 29 per cent of models were women of colour, the latter being up 6.2 percentage points from 2015 (22.8 per cent) and up 11.6 percentage points from 2014 (17.4 per cent). Magazines which had no women of colour on their front covers included *Love, Jalouse, Marie Claire UK, Porter, Vogue Paris, Vogue Germany, Vogue Netherlands* and *Vogue Russia*. Analysing body type, only six out of 679 or 0.9 per cent belonged to women who were size 12 and above. Notable 'plus-size' covers included size 16 lingerie model Ashley Graham for *Cosmopolitan* and the singer Adele for *Vanity Fair*. Caitlyn Jenner's cover for *Vanity Fair* in July 2015 created much welcomed media attention on the issue of broadening awareness on accepting transgender persons. With transgender models on the catwalks and small screen increasing, the focus is at an all-time high. However, in 2016 transgender models were the least featured and accounted for only five front covers or 0.7 per cent. Four of the five covers showcased the model and actress Hari Nef and of these, three out of the four were shared with other celebrities. In terms of age diversity, magazines such as *W*, *InStyle* and *Elle* showcased women like Barbara Streisand (aged 74), Michelle Obama (aged 52) and Helen Mirren (aged 71) on their covers. In total, women aged 50 and above appeared 34 times on the front covers in 2016, accounting for a total of 5 per cent, and as with transgender models, there is a trend for magazines to shoot the cover campaigns with younger models.[7] Overall, 2016 was the most diverse year that the fashion industry has ever seen, but differences in colour, gender and age continue to be central issues and highlight how far the industry still has to go in terms of diversity and inclusion if it is to be truly representative of the world in which we work, live, play and create.

Women and workplace inclusion

In reality we all have some level of unconscious bias and most of us lack the self-awareness to combat it. Consequently, discrimination and stereotyping still continues as executives appoint the default manager who mirrors their own image. In senior management roles, this usually translates to being white, male and from an elite educational background. Concentrating on gender imbalance, the lack of senior women executives in the industry remains a pressing issue. This can be considered a strange phenomenon, as in the fashion industry women frequently make up a large proportion of the workforce and are often the target user or a major influencer in the purchase-making process. Their engagement in different social relationships and economic activities brings distinct experiences and perspectives to the workplace. Therefore, having a minority of women in senior executive positions can potentially increase the firm's propensity for being out of touch with the market and its workforce. Aside from those who have created their own brand or firm, only a few examples exist of women who have made it to the highest echelons of senior management, such as Alannah Weston (Deputy Chairwoman of Selfridges), Christine Beauchamp (President of Amazon Fashion), Francesca Bellettini (Chief Executive of Saint Laurent) and Stacey Cartwright (Chief Executive of Harvey Nichols).

Much ink has been spilled on this topic. However, it is easy to forget that the presence and transformation of woman in the workplace has been a relatively recent phenomenon. Progress occurred in Europe and the United States in the twentieth century after many countries granted woman the right to vote. This was also amplified by the First World War (1914–1918), which bought woman into the factories, and the Second World War (1939–1945), which saw women being employed in unprecedented numbers. Yet, the United Kingdom and the United States still adhered to 'marriage bars' and this required woman to leave their jobs once they were married. The United Kingdom started to lift the bar from 1944 onwards and paved the way towards a platform for equality. Since 2007, McKinsey & Company has tracked the role of women in the global workforce and in particular their representation on corporate boards and executive committees. The findings from its 2016 Women Matter report show that in Western Europe, women make up 17 per cent of executive committees and 22 per cent of the corporate boards of firms listed on the main stock exchange of their country, an increase of four percentage points for boards and seven percentage points for executive committees over the last four years. In the United States, women occupy 18.7 per cent of board seats, a 1.7 percentage point increase since 2012, and 17 per cent of executive committee seats, the same proportion as in 2012. In Asia, woman equated to just 6 per cent of the seats on Asian boards in 10 Asian markets, the same ratio as in 2012.[8] This can be contextualised more deeply, as according to Catalyst, a non-profit organisation that champions workplace inclusion for women, there were 23 female chief executives or 4.6 per cent of CEOs in charge of a Fortune 500 firm in 2016, of which only one, Barbara Rentler of Ross Stores in the United States, was leading a fashion firm.[9] Furthermore, Japan has called for corporate boards to have at least one female member, whilst Norway introduced a 40 per cent female quota in 2006 and countries like Malaysia, Kenya, Iceland, Germany and the United Kingdom have legislated for them. Conversely, countries such as Saudi Arabia, Qatar and Indonesia, along with China, India and North Africa have some of the lowest participation rates in the world. The data is slightly more encouraging in Latin America, where the vast number of family-owned firms provides a path for women to succeed. This is because there is a strong culture of family support for the main provider, regardless of gender.

Whilst most agree on the need for gender balance and diversity, the best way of executing this strategy remains a subject of debate. No woman wants to be in a senior executive position, only to be seen by her peers to be in the role as a token gesture and not based on competency. Conversely, some male executives see it as a zero-sum game and fear that they could be purposely hit by job losses because of their gender. The idea of introducing quotas to help break through the 'glass ceiling' has also led to some disturbing discourse surrounding the 'glass floor', in that some women who reach senior positions of management will make it intentionally difficult or slow for other aspiring women to rise through the ranks. This inward thinking identifies that only a select few women who have worked arduously should enjoy the perks of executive management, and this glass floor helps reduce the competitiveness between their female peers and reiterates their hard-earned executive status.

There is much written about how woman perform better than men at every stage of academic life. Still, as women get older, motherhood and a lack of relevant part-time work, the absence of affordable childcare and caring for extended family members become evident barriers to corporate advancement. You only have to observe the frequent after-work ritual where men are discussing business, building relationships and getting tips from mentors on professional development over drinks or whilst watching sports in a bar, whereas women are picking up the kids, doing the laundry and preparing the dinner because they shoulder the burden of household responsibilities. The journey in the fashion industry is a prime example and can be split into two parts. First, there are a disproportionate number of women enrolled on fashion courses compared to men – approximately 85 per cent of those at university are women. This is probably due to the ill-informed perception of the industry and the careers advice given at school and college. After graduation, there are many more woman than men entering junior to middle-management functions, including buying, product merchandising or public relations. There tends not to be a difference in terms of career priorities between men and women at university and early on in their careers. Both aspire to the same job titles, family happiness and work-life balance. Cracks in the system appear around the core childbearing years of 27–34, when most women are likely to be at manager level and decide to start a family. In doing so, the higher levels of management, such as a buying or creative director, are often sacrificed as many women have left the workplace to raise families or take a career break. When they return, it is to similar pre-maternity level roles, where they work excessive hours to prove they are still in the 'game' or they down-skill and take on unfulfilling work as they are no longer considered 'strong players' in the field. This is communicated in salient but subtle ways, such as being passed over for high-profile assignments, reduced international opportunities, difficulties in finding mentors and sponsors plus being removed from project teams they once led. This is exacerbated as colleagues assume they are unwilling to travel, work late hours or handle difficult clients. Taking on part-time work can also take women out of the structured review process and promotion ladder. This leads many women to search for work in a different industry and one that better fits their lifestyle in terms of convenience and location. These are unreasonably high punishments associated with taking a career break, penalties that are out of proportion with the deterioration of human capital and an issue that is primarily considered to be a women's problem to solve.

The work-family conflict in the professional-managerial context varies by social class. This is particularly true for low-wage jobs that do not require a college education, such as retail sales associates, which have shifted away from a steady job with benefits towards part-time roles without benefits. The consequences are not having too many hours to work, but too few. Often ring-fenced by employer exclusivity clauses, firms such as Sports Direct and Urban Outfitters use open availability or zero-hour schedules that vary from week to week to keep costs low and service flexible. This makes it a challenge for low-income families, many of which are headed by single parents, to find and afford the appropriate childcare. For mothers of disabled children, this makes it virtually impossible for them to find work. From an academic perspective, young executives deciding to pursue postgraduate management education such as a Master of Business Administration (MBA) are more likely to be men than woman. The even holds true in the lecture theatre, as the majority of the case studies taught are noticeably based on male executives, with few featuring female protagonists. For example, the number of cases featuring a woman at Harvard Business School is about 9 per cent. Recognising this, Harvard has set itself a goal of having at least 20 per cent of the cases used in its MBA program featuring a woman by 2018. Given that Harvard Business School is responsible for about 80 per cent of all graduate-level business school case studies worldwide and sold 13.2 million cases in fiscal year 2015 for use at other business schools and in firm training programmes, this initiative could positively help shape not only management education worldwide but also the workplace.[10]

Many women in the workplace are presented with limited opportunities. The only probable exception is the senior role of finance or seemingly 'soft positions' like human resources and communications, where it is more likely to be a woman in charge. Even then, it is rare that executives, whether male or female, can move from a support function to an operational function. Strategies to promote the role of women in the workplace include going further than the basic endeavours of 'body counts' to firms examining why women do not get hired, why they do not get promoted and why they leave, the latter being notable as when high-ranking women leave or opt out of the workplace, their departure attracts particular notice and reinforces stereotypes about women's lesser capabilities and commitment. Strategies include targeting college recruitment and females, especially women of colour, which helps recruiting managers become diversity champions and starts the process from an early stage. Senior executives can help by emphasising the development of a female talent pipeline, especially in the middle management-ranks, and encouraging them to take positions with profit and loss responsibility and accountability for core operations. For senior hires, a prerequisite can be to have at least one female from a minority background on the candidate shortlist, as recently advocated in the United Kingdom by the Parker Review, an industry-led consultation conducted by Sir John Parker. Next, having more mentors and sponsors who are not only women but also men to help expose the issues that exist in their own firms can help ensure that firms do not create a silo effect by leaving the issue for only women to resolve.

With the increase in online media, efforts should be made by executives to gain different perspectives from a variety of 'influencers', such as bloggers or celebrities who go beyond the mostly white and male stereotype. Additionally, firms that offer flexibility are more likely to be rewarded with enhanced loyalty. In an age where talent is extremely mobile, this is a key message for firms.

134 *Culture and inclusion*

Another course of action is to encourage more men to take paternity leave, like in Canada and the Nordic countries, where both parents are more likely to actively share the upbringing of their children. Because this encourages more women to go back into full-time roles with the same seniority as they held pre-maternity, it releases the pressure on men and women and helps create a new gender-conforming mindset for employees and their firms. Finally, external investors such as pension funds can also pressure the SLT to be more transparent on disclosing gender targets, as poor results can determine whether they will invest in these firms or not.

Even though it is acknowledged that greater representation of women in senior management positions helps provide a broader perspective on the problem and the potential solutions, it does not conclusively guarantee improved firm performance. Particularly as in the boardroom, an intentionally diverse range of executives are more frequently required to conform to a single style of leadership. Though inherent diversity like gender and ethnicity is important to improve firm performance and inclusion, executives should focus on acquired diversity, in that global experience, being multi-lingual and having a true understanding of cross-cultural skills is the real competitive advantage needed in today's workplace. Firms without a proper managerial or cultural understanding of diversity in all its forms can end up with heightened conflict and reduced productivity, as firms need to have schemes and protocols in place to get the best out of a diverse workforce. These are pertinent points for all firms, especially global entities, as today's younger generation whose personal values support a diverse workplace view a non-diverse and exclusive labour force as being incredibly negative and unrealistic of their life and surroundings.

Closing the pay gap

Along with the gender imbalance, a **pay differential** also exists, as there is no country in the world where women are paid as much as men. The economic gap is caused by a number of factors, such as women being paid much less in comparable senior roles, working on average 50 minutes a day longer and having much lower chances of reaching senior positions. According to the WEF 2016 Global Gender Gap Report, women's economic participation and opportunity is at 59 per cent as shown in Figure 9.2; in other words, women earn €0.59 for every €1.00 men earn. Out of the 144 countries researched, Iceland came top for wage parity at 87 per cent, followed by Finland at 85 per cent, Norway at 84 per cent and Sweden at 82 per cent, but this is only true when analysing woman who are young and without children. At the other end of the index, Saudi Arabia was at 59 per cent, Syria at 57 per cent, Pakistan at 56 per cent and Yemen at 52 per cent.[11]

Some of the biggest gender differences are to be found in Asia. For example, South Korea is the world's thirteenth-largest economy and has both the longest working hours in all OECD countries and also the biggest pay gap

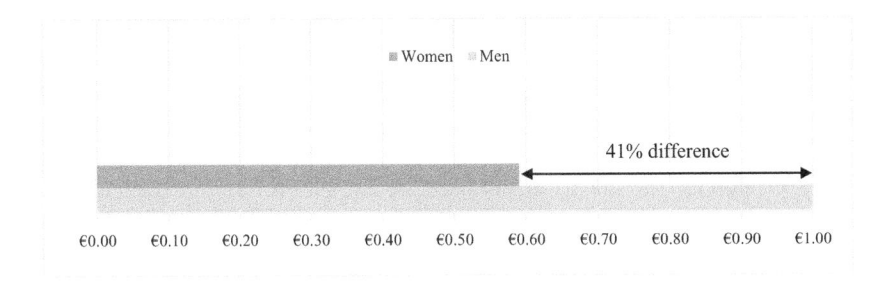

Figure 9.2 The global pay differential between men and women

of approximately 40 per cent between men and women.[12] The Seoul government is trying to decrease this parity through increased spending to promote gender equality and the introduction of legislation such as the 2011 Equal Employment and Support for Work-Family Reconciliation Act. Similarly, despite the Equal Pay Act of 1963, the United States introduced the White House Equal Pay Pledge in 2016 to further encourage firms to close the pay gap. This was signed by Amazon, Gap and Rebecca Minkoff.

At the current rate, without targeted action, pay equity between women and men will not be achieved before 2186 and has reverted back to where it stood in 2008 after a peak in 2013. Moreover, the United States is not expected to close the gap for another 158 years, the Middle East and North Africa for 129 years, East Asia and the Pacific for 146 years and Eastern Europe and Central Asia for 149 years. The regions with the shortest timeline are South Asia with 46 years, Western Europe with 61 years, Latin America with 72 years and Sub-Saharan Africa with 79 years.[13]

The reasons why there is a pay differential in gender varies according to the country in question, but the main challenges are structural issues, such as minimum wage rates, limited access to bank accounts, a lack of education, unequal numbers of men and women and in many countries women having less political power.[14] Inside the firm, reasons vary from women 'not asking' or using the correct linguistics to negotiate higher pay, both at the start of their career and throughout, to there being a deeply embedded culture that determines what is expected from men and women. This is because from an early age, girls are taught not to be pushy and dominant as they walk a fine line in order to avoid the negative cultural rhetoric surrounding assertive behaviour and being stereotyped as an Alpha female. Because of this, there is often a trade-off between competence and likeability, especially for women of colour, who encounter lower expectations of competence. Many junior women have difficulty identifying with senior women who are respected but not liked and seeing them as credible role models. For example, Asian women are particularly likely to be stereotyped as passive, reserved and lacking in ambition, whilst Latino women are seen as over-emotional and

African-American women are viewed as domineering, strident and cold.[15] The key is for women to blend assertiveness and competence with warmth and strong interpersonal skills.

Strategies to promote pay equality include pressing firms to publish data on the pay gap difference at each level to internal pay audits and compulsory training on equality and diversity. Economic Dividends for Gender Equality (EDGE) certification, as used by Stella McCartney, can also be used to create an optimal workplace for women and men by assessing policies and practices across five areas: equal pay for equivalent work, recruitment and promotion, leadership development training and mentoring, flexible working and company culture. Many women are also encouraged to develop a 'centre stage' mindset in which they feel deserving of the spotlight and frequently seize the opportunity to excel. This includes not playing down their accomplishments, not deflecting praise and challenging negative feedback. By developing strong, clear verbal and non-verbal communication skills from how they should stand to what they should wear and the type of verbs, tone and pace used in their communication, women can solidify their presence. Finally, best-in-class firms have proven that equality, diversity and inclusion programmes require persistence and CEO-level commitment. These initiatives can take three to five years to filter through, but once established will help all executives rightfully advance their careers in a fair and rewarding way.

Case study: Patagonia

There are a few firms that are changing the way the industry operates and behaves. Ever since it was created more than 40 years ago by its founders Yvon and Malinda Chouinard, Patagonia has worked hard to build a culture where women and families thrive by providing its working women with equal pay and opportunities. Thanks to its quality on-site childcare, nursing mothers and fathers are only a few feet away from their babies as opposed to being miles apart. With an equal number of women and men at every level of the firm, including executive positions and the boardroom, who are paid the same for comparable work, Patagonia is a leader in its field and is one where 100 per cent of women return to work from paid maternity leave along with 100 per cent of fathers taking paid paternity time off. This provides a family-supportive work environment which allows working mothers and fathers to continue to grow their family, career and income with equal opportunity and community support. This positive ecosystem ensures productive and happy employees and a business that continues to thrive and be an employer of choice.

Review questions

Questions for debate regarding culture and inclusion are as follows:

- How does understanding firm and national culture affect your go-to-market strategy?
- Does a diverse workforce contribute to higher financial performance for the firm?
- Should a firm's culture be documented or left undocumented?
- Should the firm accept a substantial temporary loss in profit and productivity in order to build a new culture?
- What can be done to get more disabled people to work in the fashion industry?
- What else can be done to get more women into senior management positions?

Further reading

1. Schein, E.H. (2010) *Organizational Culture and Leadership*, 4th edn. San Francisco: Jossey-Bass.
2. Deloitte (2016) 'Global Human Capital Trends 2016', https://documents.dupress.deloitte.com/HCTrends2016 (accessed 4 May 2017).
3. Cameron, K.S. and Quinn, R.E. (2011) *Diagnosing and Changing Organizational Culture: Based on the Competing Values Framework*, 3rd edn. San Francisco: Jossey-Bass.
4. Reingold, J. (2014) 'How to Fail in Business While Really, Really Trying', *Fortune*, 20 March.
5. Creative Industries Federation (2015) 'Creative Diversity', www.creativeindustriesfederation.com/assets/userfiles/files/30183-CIF%20Access%20%26%20Diversity%20Booklet_A4_Web%20(1).pdf (accessed 4 May 2017).
6. Brannigan, M. (2016) 'Diversity on Magazine Covers Widely Improved in 2016', *Fashionista*, 14 December, http://fashionista.com/2016/12/fashion-diversity-magazine-covers-2016 (accessed 4 May 2017).
7. Tai, C. (2016) 'Here's One Good Thing about 2016: Magazine Covers were More Diverse than Ever', *The Fashion Spot*, www.thefashionspot.com/runway-news/726447-diversity-report-magazine-covers-2016 (accessed 4 May 2017).
8. McKinsey & Company (2016) 'Women Matter 2016 Reinventing the Workplace to Unlock the Potential of Gender Diversity', www.mckinsey.com/search?q=women%20matter%20reinventing (accessed 4 May 2017).
9. Catalyst (2016) *Women CEOs of the S&P 500*. New York: Catalyst.
10. Harvard Business School (2016) 'Statistics Overview', www.hbs.edu/about/facts-and-figures/Pages/statistics.aspx (accessed 4 May 2017). Byrne, J.A. (2014) 'Harvard B-School Dean Offers Unusual Apology', *Fortune*, 29 January.
11. World Economic Forum (2016) 'The Global Gender Gap Report 2016', www.weforum.org/reports/the-global-gender-gap-report-2016 (accessed 4 May 2017).
12. Moore, E. (2014) 'Gender Pay Gap Shows Little Sign of Closing', *Financial Times*, 26 February.

13 World Economic Forum (2016) 'The Global Gender Gap Report 2016', www.weforum.org/reports/the-global-gender-gap-report-2016 (accessed 4 May 2017).
14 International Labour Organization (2015) 'Women and the Future of Work', www.ilo.org/gender/Informationresources/Publications/WCMS_348087/lang–en/index.htm (accessed 4 May 2017).
15 Catalyst (2004) *Advancing African-American Women in the Workplace: What Managers Need to Know*. New York: Catalyst.

10 Work-life harmony

Strategies for successful assimilation

> **Chapter goals**
>
> This chapter explores why work is important and strategies to identify, integrate and maintain a healthy work-life balance. The key areas covered are:
>
> - The joys and perils of work
> - Living a fulfilling life
> - Strategies for successful work-life assimilation

The joys and perils of work

There are many good things about work. It provides a sense of fulfilment, achievement, satisfaction and belonging, as well as financial rewards. If these factors are aligned, work provides a deep sense of motivation, passion and purpose, and hopefully you are able to earn a good living from it. For many executives, balancing work with their personal life remains an elusive concept in today's increasingly high-pressured environment. This is compounded as there has been a cultural shift over the past 40 years for both parents to work compared to only one in the past. This has had a tangible impact on their professional and personal lives. As busy executives operating in a dynamic industry, there is a constant strive to juggle competing priorities and perform as the 'ideal employee'. If we consider our typical work routine, most of us are delivering 100 per cent on the current operational demands of our jobs. Amongst the barrage of urgent emails and onerous meetings, there is little time to think strategically, sense new trends to spark creativity and develop our teams and ourselves further, let alone carve out time for ourselves on leisure activities or to spend quality time with family and friends. Talk to your high-flyer friends and they too are all executing to the maximum, which further adds pressure to not fall behind and work even harder. The consequences can be dire and have been well documented. Marc Jacobs ended up in rehab twice, Tom Ford suffered a bout of depression after departing Gucci and John

140 *Work-life harmony*

Galliano relied on alcohol and drugs whilst at Christian Dior to deal with the pressures of overseeing 32 annual collections. Furthermore, designers like Jean Paul Gaultier and Viktor & Rolf have abandoned ready-to-wear to focus on their couture line, which provides them with the creative freedom and necessary time to innovate. In some Asian countries and the United States, it is normal practice to work long hours and it is even affirmation of social status. However, in Asia the situation has become so bad that occupational mortality has become a national issue. For example, in Japan it is called 'karōshi' or death by overwork, in South Korea 'gwarosa' and in China 'guolaosi'. This has resulted in many young people choosing part-time work and opting for hourly wages to combat the overload, stress and effects of working long hours that come with traditional salaried jobs.

Case study: Lee Alexander McQueen

Having graduated in 1992 with an MA in Fashion Design from Central Saint Martins College of Art and Design, the talented and often controversial Lee Alexander McQueen became an award-winning British designer and couturier. His talents were spotted and he became the chief designer of Parisian label Givenchy from 1996 to 2001, where he designed four collections a year along with two for his own namesake brand. He left Givenchy to expand his own label in partnership with the Kering Group. As the business grew, he worked tirelessly and expected the same from his staff. Often seen as the 'enfant terrible' within the industry, his avant-garde shows heightened his reputation as a star designer and catapulted him into the limelight. His achievements were recognised by the industry, where he won the British Designer of the Year award four times and the International Designer of the Year award. He was also made a Commander of the British Empire in 2003. However, all of this success, fame and fortune played heavily on his life and his wildly unpredictable behaviour led him to become a regular user of alcohol and drugs, the latter of which he reportedly regularly paid £600 a day for. In early May 2007, Isabella Blow, a famous English fashion magazine editor and close friend of McQueen, succumbed to her depression and disillusionment with the fashion industry by drinking a lethal dose of weedkiller. Having failed in her previous attempts to commit suicide, she died aged just 48. McQueen twice tried to take his own life in 2009, but failed. Instead, on 11th February 2010, feeling overwhelmed with his life and with the recent loss of his mother, who died from cancer aged 75, he committed suicide by asphyxiation, just nine days after her death. Aged just 40, the post-mortem revealed that he had taken a cocktail of drugs, including cocaine, sleeping pills and tranquilisers, and slashed his wrists with a ceremonial dagger and meat cleaver. For a man who came from a working-class background and climbed to the top of his profession to commit suicide sadly reinforces the immense vulnerability and responsibility executives face in managing the pressure attached to their work and personal lives.

Living a fulfilling life

Being a senior executive is a stressful role and can feel like an ultra-marathon that never ends due to long hours, endless meetings, numerous presentations, frequent global travel and irregular eating. As the fashion cycle continues to accelerate, the sacrifice, commitment, motivation and resilience needed to manage your own energy as well as the energy of the firm and your team rapidly intensifies as you climb the corporate ladder. Typically, as executives gain experience and insights over the course of their lives, they acquire a sense of changing priorities and personal identity. When they are young, their early experiences, sacrifices and formative moments play a major role in shaping who they are. When they enter the workplace, their identity is situated around their work, performance and career progression. Achieving tangible incentives like a house, car and an impressive job title plays a large role in motivating them. The thinking here is that even if you are successful but the role is not fulfilling, by deferring job gratification, at least you will have a home, money and food. Therefore, most of us will work very hard and do whatever it takes to get ahead and create this foundation. As employees get a bit older and more experienced, in their middle years they probably still define themselves to a large extent in terms of their professional responsibilities and achievements, but many of them are now fulfilling roles outside of work as spouses, parents or carers. They reassess previously satisfying behaviours that are no longer aligned to their current lifestyle along with a re-evaluation of their personal goals and rethink their future with the emphasis on solidifying previously held plans which were at best distant and vague. In their mature years, their attitude to intrinsic incentives changes and wider reflections on life and career take place. Leaving a lasting legacy takes centre stage for many, maybe through mentoring high-potential executives at work or extensive volunteering in the community. This is coupled with a focus on supporting and spending time with extended family. Historically, this route makes sense as life maps look great on paper, but there is a good chance that you would not have lived a fulfilling voyage in what is a long career path in a very dynamic environment.

On reflection, though defining success is a very personal subject, many of us would have made several sacrifices which we will probably regret, especially the impact of these sacrifices on those closest to us. This is because most fast-track executives who have spare time unconsciously devote it to their careers or an immediate activity that provides tangible evidence, such as reading a management book like this one, visiting a retail shopping centre where they subconsciously analyse what consumers are wearing or going to an exhibition like the hugely popular Manus X Machina: Fashion in an Age of Technology at the Metropolitan Museum of Art in New York. They over-invest in their careers, as devoting time and energy to their family or health does not offer that same immediate sense of achievement. Even though they aim to 'switch off' from work, they still end up feeding their minds with information and activities that are directly associated with their jobs. The question is then whether it is possible to have a great career and a great personal life all at the same time? There is no clear answer to this, as you will have to make continuous trade-offs, since you will not be able to achieve a perfect balance between all the aspects of your life: your career, family, friends, personal life or involvement in the community. The key here is to pursue success such as social status and money in a fulfilling role that you are passionate and emotional about. This may seem like a false dichotomy, but it is very achievable as today's life is less of a linear path from A to Z where we defer fulfilment until we are older. For this reason, it is important to establish boundaries. For example, if you promise yourself to consciously do an activity that is different from your work, then you must make no exceptions, or if you promise to have dinner with the family every evening when you are not travelling or agree not to answer emails after a certain time, then this needs to be pursued relentlessly, as ultimately your life is an expression of the choices you have made. This is because once you bend the rules, even once, you open up the door and will have set a precedent. Your life then becomes a stream of toxic extenuating circumstances of which you can eventually lose control of as only you are accountable for your actions and behaviours.[1]

Strategies for successful work-life assimilation

There is much literature available on why executives derail in an increasingly multi-directional environment. Finding the time for self-renewal is a prominent challenge for today's executives in a **VUCA** world – a military acronym for volatility, uncertainty, complexity and ambiguity that has entered the management lexicon. Successful executives understand that optimum performance is not the result of intellectual horsepower or longer hours in the office, as everyone is very smart and working hard. Instead, balancing 'results' versus 'effort' is about being in the best possible mental, emotional and physical condition to maximise focus to support effective decision-making and strengthen interpersonal interactions. Eustress such as challenging work, strength or endurance training is good for the body in reaching peak performance, as several hormones are released into the bloodstream, the most important of which are epinephrine (adrenaline) and cortisol, which helps to increase focus and creativity and heightens efficiency. This is positive as long as you push yourself incrementally in the desired direction and understand that recovering energy is as important as expending it. Conversely, chronic physical, cognitive or emotional distress which is persistent and unresolved depletes energy reserves, which leads to burnout syndromes, including exhaustion, cynicism, anxiety, withdrawal and depression. As our bodies like to be aligned as closely as possible to a state of homeostasis, those who can control their stress to be managed incrementally are the most successful and resilient leaders. Therefore, executives should understand the need for self-reflection and self-management, whether this is through sport, mediation or simply spending quality time with family and friends.[2] Described as the **fit executive**, they have short-term and long-term goals. They have a deep understanding of their technical and behavioural competencies and through years of experience, they have crafted mechanisms to help create focus and gain perspective for the physical, emotional, intellectual and environmental demands of the job and life in general.[3] With situational factors being the biggest contributors to burnout, the following 18 interventions are offered (in no particular order) to help everyone become a fit executive:

1. Schedule meetings at times in the day when your physical energy is at its highest:
    - ✔ Keep a diary for two weeks to see how you spend your time
    - ✔ Re-allocate meetings to when you are at your sharpest
    - ✔ Cut back unnecessary talking and aim to learn, listen and ask the right questions
    - ✔ Ensure that an agenda is given before the meeting, the number of attendees is limited and action points are distributed afterwards
    - ✔ Be relentless on start and finish times
2. Eat a balanced and healthy diet:
    - ✔ Never miss breakfast as this is your most important meal of the day
    - ✔ Eat three to five small meals throughout the day rather than two to three large ones
    - ✔ Reduce your intake of coffee and sugary drinks; substitute them for water
    - ✔ Avoid excessive smoking and drinking
3. Frequently exercise and undertake sport as part of your overall wellness regime:
    - ✔ Aim to exercise for 30–45 minutes three to four times a week
    - ✔ Join a class to boost motivation, discipline and social interaction
    - ✔ Switch between high-impact and low-impact workouts, such as a boxing class with yoga
4. Ensure rich and ample social connection with family and friends:
    - ✔ Be disciplined in spending time with your immediate family
    - ✔ Regularly catch up with friends and extended family
    - ✔ Join clubs and associations to meet new people

144 *Work-life harmony*

5. Manage technology to help you rather than hinder you:
   - ✔ Leverage the cloud, mobile working, Wi-Fi connectivity and online shopping
   - ✔ Maximise dead time like commuting to review your day, complete tasks or simply rest
   - ✔ Build in boundaries to shut yourself off from technology
6. Buy-in domestic help to make your life easier:
   - ✔ Utilise cleaning, ironing and dog-walking services
   - ✔ Enlist trusted and reliable childcare
7. Hire a professional life/executive coach to provide a fresh perspective:
   - ✔ Gain unbiased and real feedback
   - ✔ Use life coaching to live a more fulfilling life
   - ✔ Leverage executive coaching to become a better manager at work
8. Enlist a mentor/sponsor at work as a soundboard to activate positive learning opportunities:
   - ✔ Gain constructive feedback to round out your skills
   - ✔ Confidentially discuss work challenges
   - ✔ Maximise the opportunity to be part of cross-functional projects
9. Build a great team around yourself and be generous to them with your time:
   - ✔ Balance team composition using skills, experience, behaviour and aptitude
   - ✔ Provide real and actionable feedback and continuous coaching
   - ✔ Offer developmental opportunities to everyone
10. Agree a shared vision of success with your partner and family:
    - ✔ Discuss and set your work-life priorities with your spouse
    - ✔ Regularly review work-life goals
    - ✔ Build support networks inside and outside of the firm
11. Establish a higher purpose through values based leadership:
    - ✔ Look outwards versus inwards
    - ✔ Focus on what you can give rather than what you can gain
12. Undertake non-profit work to help keep an emotional balance:
    - ✔ Stay in touch with the world around you and those less fortunate than you
    - ✔ Get out of your comfort zone to help others
    - ✔ Try volunteering in another country to broaden your horizons
13. Integrate journaling, meditation and mindfulness into your leadership style:
    - ✔ Make time to clear your thoughts and keep your focus and energy high
    - ✔ Practise breathing and visualisation techniques to heighten awareness and relaxation
    - ✔ Avoid daily distractions such as office gossip in order to remain focused
14. Stay humble, authentic and grounded:
    - ✔ Do not lose sight of the world around you
    - ✔ If appropriate, engage in spirituality and faith-based traditions

✔ Practise empathy on a regular basis
15. Continue self-development and professional learning:
    ✔ Aim to learn one or two new things a year
    ✔ Unconditionally share your knowledge with others
    ✔ Attend networking events and conferences
16. Take regular holidays and get plenty of rest:
    ✔ Aim for a minimum of seven hours sleep a night
    ✔ Avoid trying to catch up on sleep at the weekends
    ✔ Carve out time to do nothing except enjoy that particular moment
17. Do not live beyond your means:
    ✔ Aim to have at sufficient savings to cover six months of living expenses
    ✔ Regularly review your financial situation with an expert
    ✔ Avoid excessive amounts of credit
18. Positively engage in new experiences like food, travel and culture:
    ✔ Take advantage of low-cost travel to visit new places
    ✔ Remain curious, meet new people and respect different cultures
    ✔ Aim to read a variety of newspapers, magazines and websites to get a fuller perspective of the world

In designing your ideal job, factors including having time for family responsibilities, ensuring time for health and wellness, time away from work to take holidays and support for volunteering efforts form a large part for most well-rounded executives. By taking a moment to reflect and writing down what your week looked like and how you felt, you can assess exactly how you are spending the 168 hours that exist and what activities you need to reduce or increase in order to manage the expectations of friends, family and colleagues to ultimately feel better. This takes courage and conviction, and you must not feel guilty for the choices you make in order to sustain your career and live a happier and healthier life. If you find that situational factors provide little opportunity for positive direction, then you might need to think about a complete or bigger change to your lifestyle and seek targeted advice through professional lifestyle and career coaching. By doing this, you will be a better leader and person as you will be living a more fulfilling and integrated life.

For employers, having healthy employees is essential as they are expensive to employ, train and retain. Their efficiency, loyalty, attitude, enthusiasm and capacity to innovate and lead can make the difference between a firm making a profit or a loss. As the cost of health insurance has increased significantly over the past decade, employers must recognise that not having a productive workforce due to sickness and absenteeism can severely increase costs such as recruitment and training, which can be as much as one-and-a-half times a person's annual salary. This can affect customer satisfaction and impact the ability of the firm to effectively recruit and retain top talent if turnover rates are notably above the industry average. Furthermore, unproductive firms are bad for the economy and can erode a country's competitiveness. Therefore, though well-being programmes have many merits, employers, industry bodies and governments have a strong duty of care to ensure that employees are not taking on too much work. Overall, it remains to be seen whether a work-life balance can be maintained in today's hyperactive world in which fashion seems to be overheating because of a constant demand for new products and a feeling that there is too much of everything and where everything goes too quickly.

Case study: Soma Analytics

Soma Analytics is an app that uses sensors in your smartphone to identify behavioural changes that signal increasing stress levels and is a part of a growing band of firms trying to leverage the market for corporate wellness. By tracking subtle shifts in the tone of your voice, how long it takes to read and absorb some text to how much deep sleep you get, Soma lets employees know whether they are slowly becoming stressed. Exercises and challenges are used to focus attention, manage stress and increase positive thinking. Anonymised employee data on stress levels by department or geographical area, but not by individual employee is passed on to employers via an interactive dashboard to assess the stress levels and working culture in order to create the right workplace atmosphere to help improve creativity and productivity and ultimately employee engagement. This is particularly useful in virtual working environments, where managers and employees may not actually spend a lot of physical time with each other and thus see the build-up of stress first-hand. Results show that after just three weeks of use, users show a 15 per cent decrease in stress levels and an 11 per cent increase in mental resilience.[4]

Review questions

Questions for debate regarding work-life harmony are as follows:

- Are we more stressed in today's world than previously?
- Is working in the fashion industry more stressful than other industries?
- Should there be more regulation in the workplace to achieve a better work-life balance?
- Is technology helping us to manage stress better or is it causing it?
- Can stress be considered as the twenty-first-century plague?
- Why do some countries have a better work-life balance than others?

Further reading

1   Allworth, J., Christensen, C.M. and Dillon, K. (2012) *How Will You Measure Your Life?* London: HarperCollins.

2 Bailey, S. and Black, O. (2016) *Mind Gym: Achieve More by Thinking Differently*. New York: HarperCollins.
  Langer, E.J. (2014) *Mindfulness*, 25th anniversary edn. Cambridge, MA: Da Capo Press.
  Mumford, G. (2015) *The Mindful Athlete: Secrets to Pure Performance*. Berkeley: Parallax Press.
3 Abrahams, R. and Groysberg, B. (2014) 'Manage Your Work, Manage Your Life', *Harvard Business Review*, Vol. 92, No. 3, pp. 58–66.
4 Soma Analytics (2016) 'The Smart Way to Beat Stress at Work', http://soma-analytics.de (accessed 4 May 2017).

11 The future of fashion
A new reality

> **Chapter goals**
>
> This chapter offers a glimpse into the future and presents a selection of key trends in the industry that have the potential to significantly change the way we work, live and interact. It also identifies four main skills employers will need in order to be successful in tomorrow's workplace. The key areas covered are:
>
> - New emerging technology themes
> - Workplace skills challenges

New emerging technology themes

If the last 10 years are any indication, the next 10 years will bring about enormous changes in how we operate in the workplace, the manner in which we conduct business and the way in which we live. Focusing on the next three to five years, one of the main drivers of change will be the application of **Newly Emerging Technologies (NET)**, including image recognition, smart sensors, cloud computing, 5G bandwidth and low-power Wi-Fi, which have all been classified as the invisible revolution. With **Moore's Law** stating that ICT doubles in power every two years, many firms have successfully kept pace with their ICT efforts. However, in the future this looks like being surpassed as ICT becomes even more quicker and powerful. One NET that is generating immense discourse is **Artificial Intelligence (AI)**, a term coined in 1955 by John McCarthy, an American computer scientist. With investment in AI at an all-time high, society is firmly transitioning towards an era where human beings share the planet with cognitively enhanced non-biological intelligence such as robots and a world where today's AI capabilities complement those of a human. Take, for example, Stitch Fix, a young online fee-based styling service which uses AI to partner with its employees to create effective customer solutions. Stitch Fix does not have an online store; instead, customers fill out a style, size and price survey, snapshot Pinterest boards and send in personal notes on what they like and do not like. Employing over 70 data scientists, AI-embedded visual search technology helps quickly find suitable items and personalise recommendations for customers. Stylists then select five hand-picked items from a variety of brands to send to the customer. Clients keep what they like and return anything that does not suit them within three days. This is slowly shifting the view of AI being perceived as a stiff, detached and unfriendly technology to one that it is a powerful facilitator for enhancing the consumer experience. Stitch Fix is also testing natural language processing for reading and categorising notes from clients. For instance, whether a customer wants a new outfit for a party occasion or for an important business meeting, stylists help to identify and summarise textual information received from clients and catch mistakes in AI categorisation when putting a collection together for them. Stitch Fix has over 2,800 stylists, all working from home and setting their own hours. They are measured by a variety of metrics, including client spend, satisfaction per delivery and the rate of general suitability of the collection. With Stitch Fix tripling its workforce over the past two years and 70 per cent of customers returning for a second 'fix' within 90 days, the firm's approach to blending AI with the human touch is clearly working and producing better results, at a greater scale and speed than either could do alone.[1]

It is still to be seen whether scalable machine learning-based systems are able not only to emulate human intelligence but also to exceed it, but this is a feat which could be achieved within the next 100 years. The potential consequences are profound as ultra-intelligent machines could design other machines better than human beings at an incomprehensible rate. Known as **technical singularity**, this could lead to a runway reaction of self-improvement cycles through an 'intelligence explosion' and ultimately threaten millions of jobs or, even worse, eliminate the need for human beings. For instance, with AI machines increasingly being able to take on functions previously performed by humans such as customer service, fraud and credit risk analysis, it is entirely feasible that AI will move from solving specific and limited problems to replacing other functions in the industry, including buyers, journalists and sales associates. As these functions become increasingly trend-related, data-driven and risk-based, it is very possible that in the next decade machines like IBM's Watson or Google's DeepMind will be able to predict and react to trends faster than humans can in a more accurate and non-emotive way, which will be good for some firms and products, but less so for others. The effects will be faster replenishment, better sell-through and enhanced personalised product assortments in a 24/7 environment.[2]

For firms with a global footprint, the emergence of AI-enhanced technology and its impact will be more susceptible in emerging economies where the current infrastructure is less established to inhibit the roll-out of AI-led activities such as automated robots. This implies that many emerging markets are likely to skip the current generation of ICT and jump straight to NET, with the International Labour Organization estimating that within a few decades, more than half of all salaried workers in emerging markets could be displaced by automation and advanced technology in the fashion industry.[3] In the first instance, this will most likely affect low-skilled roles. Though AI is expensive to develop and adopt, it also presents many social, technological, legal and ethical hurdles which need to be addressed if it is to be successfully embraced by the industry.

Case study: Sewbo

In late 2016, Seattle-based start-up Sewbo had a major breakthrough by using an off-the-shelf industrial robot to manufacture an entire t-shirt, a feat which was previously not possible due to the difficulties that robots face when trying to manipulate limp and flexible fabrics. The technology works by dipping the fabric in a thermo plastic water-soluble solution to temporarily stiffen it. This allows the robot to handle the fabric as if it were a sheet of metal and the fabric panels can then be easily moulded and welded before being permanently sewn together. At the end of the manufacturing process, the procedure is reversed and the completed garment is rinsed in hot water to remove the stiffener solution, leaving a soft and fully assembled piece of clothing. The stiffener solution can then be recovered for reuse. The process can be seen at www.sewbo.com. By achieving the long-sought-after goal of automated sewing, Sewbo creates another step in shortening lead times, increases opportunities for personalisation and reduces the cost of labour.

AI has many potential uses to disrupt the industry, one being **voice-activated services (VAS)**. In the past five years, Apple, Amazon, Google, Facebook and Microsoft have bought over 30 deep-tech category firms.[4] Apple's Siri launched in 2011 and handles two billion interactions a week, whilst Microsoft's Cortana is used by 100 million people a day and has been asked over eight billon questions.[5] Currently limited in terms of what they can offer, digital assistants such as Amazon's Echo and Google's Allo's capability include creating and amending shopping lists, tracking a package, setting alarms, playing music, controlling a smart home or sending text messages and making restaurant and taxi bookings. These AI contextual-driven assistants have the potential to embrace frictionless human-like conversations with human parity in speech and multi-lingual recognition between multiple parties. Using machines with deep neural networks, also known as **deep learning**, allows voice-activated conversations to provide accurate and informative interactions, but also to create predictive and intelligent contextual dialogue. Digital agents will be able to understand our world and our goals by being able to think, remember, learn, speak and collaborate with humans. Imagine digital assistants being able to break down barriers in the workplace and allow instant communication around the world with colleagues in multiple languages, or being able to see your conversation converted into real-time text in your home language whilst continuing to speak a different language to your colleagues. The potential to conduct meetings with colleagues from around the world who do not speak the same language as you will provide the firm with access to new labour sources and prospective customers to enhance productivity and sales. Consumers will be able to order goods and services using their digital assistants, whether this be using a free-standing piece of hardware or via an in-app user interface such as Facebook, Snapchat or Instagram, in whichever language they wish, direct from retailers, brands and manufacturers.

The introduction of everyday **voice-activated commerce (VAC)** will be a game changer, especially for small firms and entrepreneurs who first do not have the capacity to build a global website and second cannot access distribution either locally or internationally through another channel, such as a department store or multi-brand retailer. Brands will be able to eliminate any intermediaries and conduct commerce directly with consumers, who will be able to self-service their own needs. This direct approach can help firms to create brand awareness, increase their margins and offer a higher degree of personalisation at scale. However, VAC will still need a high experience level and storytelling ability if it is truly to gain traction with premium-priced products or services and become the new way of conducting commerce. For example, a pair of luxury shoes from Maison Pierre Corthay is produced by skilled craftsmen in a small Parisian workshop near Place Vendôme. The process for bespoke shoes takes up to six months. Artisans select, prepare, cut, sew and colour the leather by hand using time-honoured techniques, which take over 50 hours to achieve. In-depth know-how and complete control of production has meant that Pierre Corthay has been rewarded with the distinction of Maître d'Art (Master of Art), the only men's bootmaker to have been given this honour by the French Ministry of Culture. How to get this message across using VAC remains a huge challenge for the finest brands, which are traditionally sold in selective distribution and for those customers seeking more than just speed and efficiency.

The trajectory for VAS and VAC seems to be heading towards being married with image recognition technology such as facial identification. This will enable users to be matched in real time with their accounts and to securely order goods and services, whilst tackling any account enquiries they may have at their leisure. The combination of fashion, science and technology makes it possible for an app embedded with AI linked to a smart mirror to act as an informative and predictive personal stylist; one that, by using image recognition technology and RFID, knows exactly what items you have in your wardrobe or in the washing basket and can suggest items based on your calendar appointments, planned activities, the weather or your mood, all without you having to try them on. This is enhanced by recommending complementary items from your favourite brands and stores to fill any gaps and keep you on trend. To satisfy the need for instant gratification, the products are swiftly delivered by a drone at your convenience. The question for firms then moves from 'should we do it?' to 'what should we do?'

Blockchain was introduced in 2008 and is a digital data-based payment technology which is behind Bitcoin, a currency that allows a peer-to-peer network to exchange value without the need for intermediaries. Leveraging cryptology and anonymity, Blockchain aims to make the industry more efficient and secure through sharing a sequential encrypted ledger that is grouped into blocks and open to the public. Once created, these blocks are immutable and allow users to securely and permanently record details of transactions called 'contracts'. Blockchain's main advantage is its ability to trace the origin of a product through a transparent ecosystem.[6] This has the potential to rewrite a firm's supply chain from manufacturing to finance. Firms are able to identify the different suppliers involved in the transaction as well as the price paid, date, location, quality and state of the goods, plus any other information that would be applicable. Because it is possible to trace every product back to its inception, a term called the 'genesis block', Blockchain allows the firm to avoid counterfeits, for instance, in the purchase of raw materials, and so increases transparency and enables verification across supply chains whilst reducing transaction costs.

Blockchain's adoption has been high in countries like Africa, where security, speed and trust are frail due to weak legislation and large-scale corruption. Using platforms such as BlockVerify and VeChain, firms can easily view changes in ownership through NFC or QR codes which can help in verifying sustainability and ethical endeavours by the firm and its partners. The traceability aspect allows the firm to create a strong story around the origin, provenance and manufacturing process, which can help in its marketing and branding efforts. For example, during Shanghai Fashion Week, the brand Babyghost used Blockchain technology in 20 of its 2017 S/S looks. With a chip embedded inside the clothing, users where able to scan the item to find out more about it and its journey, who originally modelled it and receive a personalised experience on the 'soul' of the garment.[7] Other uses for Blockchain include the handling of 'smart contracts' such as instant payment to a supplier once a shipment of goods has reached its location. This has the potential to rewrite the buyer–supplier relationship and reduce the need for time-consuming administration.

Still in its infancy, **virtual reality (VR)** is another NET that presents a huge opportunity in its application to the fashion industry. This was seen during New York Fashion Week in September 2016, where 13 shows, including collections from Prabal Gurung and Erin Fetherston, were broadcast in 360-degree VR.[8] VR can be described as emulating the reality of near-human experiences of people, environment and objects through the use of sensory information, which can include sight, touch, hearing and smell, to create a dynamic and even hedonistic three-dimensional computer-generated environment. Using mainly gesture-based head and hand movements, a virtual environment can be explored and interacted in as close as possible to real time. Sophisticated software and hardware such as opaque head-mounted displays and 3D sound, along with specialised projectors, omni-directional treadmills, data gloves and body suits all contribute to the immersive experience. The technology ensures that users are cut off from outside stimuli and absorbed into an environment that is able to manipulate objects or perform a series of actions to stimulate the senses together to create the illusion of presence and reality. This is a difficult task to emulate, but is one that is becoming increasingly real-life as our senses and brains are conditioned to provide us with a finely synchronised and mediated experience. Currently, VR is still very much a novelty and has its drawbacks, including the following:

- Mass-adoption is prohibited because of high costs.
- A lack of fully featured and meaningful content due to visual display and computing power restrictions limits the length of experience.
- It takes an excessive amount of time to map an environment which replicates the real thing.
- Concerns such as motion sickness restrict the user experience.
- Staff training costs are high.

In spite of the challenges, the best VR platforms such as Facebook's Oculus and Sony's PlayStation are developing their offerings so that they can leverage smartphone and tablet technology to increase the availability of applications and content to form a complete and accessibly priced ecosystem. The potential benefits are immense, especially where real-life activities are expensive or impractical to undertake. VR's use in the industry has many prospective applications, including the following:

- Using software to build, tour and experience virtual store models and planogram layouts to aid designers, architects and consumers.
- Consumers can experience entering stores in major cities around the world, which would reduce the need for in-store inventory.
- Customers can create virtual representations of themselves to try on clothes in different settings, including their workplace, home or gym, without physically trying them on.
- Brands are able to use intelligent chatbots to help consumers navigate store environments.

154 *The future of fashion*

- Retailers and brands are able to integrate 3D images into a live catwalk show as part of the 360-degree show experience.
- VR will allow customers to purchase items with a simple nod of the head or click of a finger.
- The streaming of live events such as a catwalk or store opening provides users with the best seat in the house and will solve the problem of limited seating, making content available to a wider audience in any location.
- Designers are able to utilise VR to create a 3D fashion portfolio.
- Product developers and designers are able to use VR and computer-aided design software to work on prototype product designs in 2D on their screens whilst viewing them in 3D, enabling them to understand the product's drape and resistance to the elements from any angle prior to the availability of any physical prototypes.
- Using ultrasound haptic technology, users are able to feel various elements such as different fabric textures and their weight without actually touching the items.
- VR allows for varied states of perceptions such as out-of-body experiences via body and gender swapping.
- VR creates learning environments to allow employees to virtually meet, interact and conduct training sessions without the real-world consequences of failing.
- VR makes it possible to share the same virtual space to create learning environments that allow students to meet, network and interact with each other in lectures or for group work.
- Applying VR in marketing campaigns makes it possible to create interactive forms of media and reach a completely immersed and engaged audience.

VR shares some elements with its cousin **augmented reality (AR)**. Rather than creating a complete virtual world, AR overlays what users see in their real-life surroundings with digital content generated by computer software. These images create a semi-virtual landscape which typically enhances the user's environment. Most AR systems utilise a clear headset with a camera, such as Microsoft's HoloLens, Google Glass or Magic Leap, to capture the user's surroundings or some type of display screen which the user looks at. AR currently has more traction than VR in the fashion industry due to lower costs, the ease of creating exciting content and the availability of high-quality image recognition technology. Brands like Hugo Boss, Topshop and Converse are increasingly turning to AR as a part of their brand building and client experience strategy by assisting customers with alternative versions of what they are currently wearing without the need to try on the items. The main challenge with AR and VR is for it to not come across as gimmicky and to ensure that products do not appear flat and layered so that the experience is instead natural, immersive and exciting.

Case study: Hearst Magazines and Blippar

For Christmas 2016, the Covent Garden shopping district in Central London partnered with Hearst Magazines and the visual discovery app Blippar to create the world's first bespoke augmented reality district. More than 140 stores such as Hackett, Paul Smith and Ted Baker provided customers with a digitally enhanced immersive experience where swing tags on selected in-store items enabled shoppers to unlock exclusive rewards and offers. Families could also meet Santa in an interactive neighbourhood grotto and embark on an augmented reality treasure hunt to catch eight reindeer hidden around Covent Garden. Top style editors from *Esquire*, *Elle* and *Cosmopolitan* worked with over 35 retailers to deliver exclusive content through the app, such as competitions, offers and recommendations on their favourite gift selections. The United Kingdom's first AR Christmas tree, a towering 50-foot spectacle at the heart of the piazza, enabled app users to discover presents hidden in the tree and further unlock a series of retail and restaurant offers in the area.

Workplace skills challenges

All over the world, society is increasingly changing the way people work and live. With 7.5 billion people on the planet and 4.3 billion people or nearly 60 per cent of the population not currently connected or participating in the digital world, the workplace of the future is certain to look very different from that of today.[9] This is especially true for countries such as India, China, Indonesia, Bangladesh and Brazil, where connection to the digital world is currently limited primarily due to poor infrastructure and high illiteracy rates. Millennials are expected to become the largest generation with the greatest purchasing power of any demographic for many countries, including the United States and China, and are redefining the rules of content creation and messaging. This brings challenges in terms of preparing and training the workforce to have the right knowledge, competencies and required behaviours to succeed. This is compounded as teaching and learning methods are rapidly changing, whilst the expectations of how to do the job and the anticipated rewards differ greatly by generation.

Firms investing in NET are under pressure to ensure that their workforce keeps pace with technology. To prepare and facilitate this change requires firms to embrace a cultural and skills shift if they are to sustain a competitive advantage. Accordingly, four factors, as depicted in Figure 11.1, are seen as increasingly important for those currently in the workplace and those still to enter it.

156 *The future of fashion*

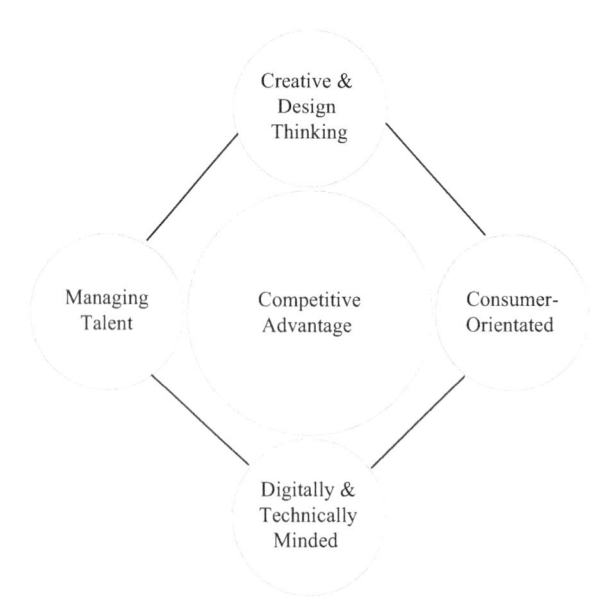

```
        Creative &
        Design
        Thinking

Managing    Competitive    Consumer-
Talent      Advantage      Orientated

        Digitally &
        Technically
        Minded
```

Figure 11.1 Workplace skills for the future

In 2016 Accenture identified being **digitally and technically minded (DTM)** as the most important skill needed to succeed over the next few years.[10] In the past, successful executives were experienced and focused on product knowledge, store operations and international expansion. Today's leaders go further and build on this through being digitally and technically savvy. They use ICT and NET to tap into the knowledge and judgement of partners, consumers and communities. Subsequently, the customer journey and the way in which brands express themselves is changing dramatically. The most obvious reason for this is the evolution of the Internet and the rise of smartphones. There are now more mobile devices on the planet than humans, with young people having more than 85 interactions a day on their mobile phone.[11] People no longer go online; instead, they live online. For instance, the Brazilian consumer is online for an average 9.8 hours per day and is the number one user in the world for Facebook and second for Instagram.[12] The result is a digitally and technically native workforce and consumer. Therefore, the DTM labour force of the future can be segmented into several camps. The first is the infrastructure architects who drive the digital engine. This includes developers, programmers, support and cyber-security engineers, network and user interface specialists. These roles require an understanding of database and automation technologies, scripting and programming, along with experience of workflow methodologies such as Agile and Scrum. Second, website performance, testing and search engine optimisation skills are progressively becoming important, along with an increasing demand for customer relationship management specialists and data-mining experts. Third, copy writers, brand creatives, media buyers and digital merchandisers are required to bring the product to life in a way that computers cannot. Lastly, consumer insight and experience marketing analysts paired with product and business analysts who can examine, interpret and visualise data into meaningful and actionable insights will be in high demand. The good news is that some countries have already recognised the need to develop a DTM workforce, such as Britain, which was the first country in the G20 to put coding on the curriculum in secondary schools. Furthermore, to increase the talent pool, there has been a noticeable increase in the sources of information available where people can learn these skills, such as using scalable massive open online courses like Coursera and in person at college or university.

In 2015 creativity was listed last by the WEF as a top 10 skill, but it is predicted that it will be in the top three by 2020.[13] **Creative and design thinking (CDT)** has been around for many decades and has had its failures, mostly due to it being misunderstood as a pure creative discipline. What began as a strategy-making process for sparking product innovation is now becoming recognised as a powerful tool through centering product, service and business model development around the end-user experience. Useful as a tool for reframing a strategic challenge or delivering an innovative solution that builds a competitive advantage, CDT is not a personality trait or general ability, but rather a behaviour and set of skills resulting from personal characteristics, cognitive abilities and environmental factors. Creative and design reasoning taps right-brain thinking, which emphasises creativity, imagination, emotion and holistic thought with left-brain critical thinking, logic and analytical reasoning. CDT works by analysing what customers want but do not have from a functional, social and emotional perspective. By immersing yourself into their lives and observing their behaviour, solutions to their needs and preferences are generated without any boundaries or restrictions. Creative thinking requires skills such as open-mindedness, flexibility and adaptability to ensure that the task remains heuristic rather than algorithmic.

As shown in Figure 11.2, the CDT process first makes use of ideation techniques such as brainstorming and divergent thinking.[14] From this, prototypes are devised and these should only command as much time, effort and investment as is needed to generate useful feedback to evolve an idea, as the goal is to learn about the strengths and weaknesses of the idea and to identify multiple new directions that further rapid prototypes might take. Utilising iterative practices such as rapid-cycle prototyping and video observation, feedback, for instance, on pricing and branding ideas, is then tested and refined into the design process before the final product or service is implemented. By incorporating user feedback early on in the design process, the likelihood of user acceptance rates and in turn market success increases. This also raises the

158 *The future of fashion*

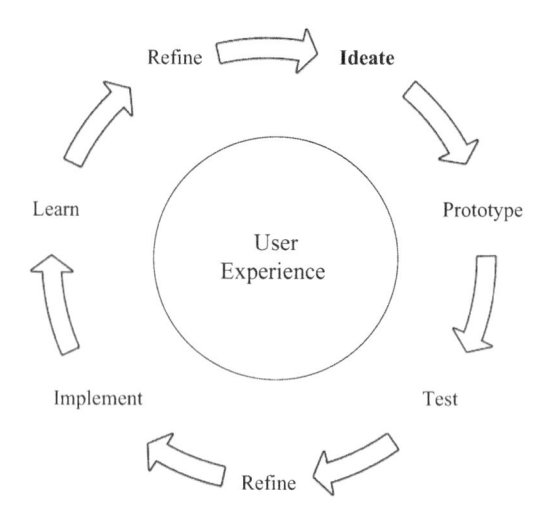

Figure 11.2 The creative and design thinking process

chances of gaining sponsorship and funding from the senior leadership team, which can create a catalyst for cultural change in previously sceptical firms.

The creative and design thinking process requires executives who are able to bring together diverse ideas to form appealing, integrated and actionable proposals. There is a need for leaders whose own creative abilities are strong, but more importantly, those with a capacity to exploit other people's creativity to layer ideas on ideas will be in demand. This obliges senior executives to provide an environment and culture that stimulates and supports CDT, like in the athletic firm Lululemon.[15] This makes creative and design thinking a natural partner to Lean and Six Sigma programmes, where the emphasis is on the removal of waste to optimise productivity. As AI increasingly proves to be cheaper, more efficient and progressively takes over some of the work of human beings, CDT will become paramount as employees will need to showcase inherently human capabilities, including managing and developing people, innovative thinking plus social and emotional reasoning if they are to retain their jobs and add value to the firm in ways that AI cannot.

It is likely that the consumer experience will overtake price and product as the key brand differentiator in the future. Being **consumer-orientated** will move to the forefront for many firms in terms of strategy and business model operations. As supply chains shorten, firms will be better placed to conduct one-to-one marketing and offer self-service, personalisation and mass-customisation platforms in a 24/7 environment. This in turn will build and deepen consumer engagement. To facilitate this, an advanced understanding of consumer behaviour and product knowledge will be key competencies to master. Successful executives will have both the technical skills to understand the consumer and an innate understanding not only of which trends are commercially viable but also the various product sensibilities that are significant brand drivers. This is balanced with an appreciation and respect for the creative process. Because we live in an increasingly globalised and diverse world, the best executives will be those who are well travelled, multi-lingual and embrace cross-cultural communication skills to bring fresh insights and experiences to the consumer journey. This interaction is likely to increasingly take place virtually, so an understanding of the digital environment will be essential. As Generations Y and Z progressively enter the workforce, many firms will need to ensure that the older executives at the top of the firm who are predominantly men in their fifties and sixties, a generation defined as Baby Boomers, remain in touch with the changing world. This is an issue for many large and medium-sized firms that do not have a sizeable and regular intake of younger workers and find themselves with a more stable but ageing workforce. With four or five generations soon set to be in the workplace simultaneously, firms such as New Look are already making this transition by having a junior board in place ranging in age from 20 to 28 to help avoid a siloed workforce and keep older executives in touch with workplace needs, fashion trends and the digital world.

In **managing talent**, the best talent will always be in demand and have options on where they wish to work. The qualities of future successful employees can be described as having a high capacity to learn new things. They are able and curious, which is the result of having high intelligence levels. Educational and technical expertise is leveraged to obtain hard skills. These employees encompass strong emotional quotation abilities, which makes them likeable, and they are able to successfully navigate the firm through their political and cultural awareness. Good with people and able to operate in an increasingly virtual workplace, they focus on collaborative leadership and are proficient at coping with the expectations of their line managers and other key stakeholders. They are self-driven and motivated, are always searching for stimulating and rewarding challenges, and want to work in a firm that has a strong mission and purpose. All these factors contribute to talent being mobile and short tenured, as gaining a portfolio of skills and experience to build upon is at the top of their agenda.

Meaningful work with a strong purpose where learning opportunities and exposure to new thinking in a rewarding and stimulating environment is where talent will reside. Coaching, mentoring and continuous personal development with a work-life balance are key requirements for the Millennial generation, which is expected to account for 76 per cent of the global labour force by 2025.[16] This group expects open-plan layouts with plenty of natural light and greenery, showers, bicycle storage and healthy eating options. Furthermore, fitness facilities, remote working, flexible hours and open spaces are seen as standard for workplace design and connectivity. Employees want the office to have a buzz and to be a destination which provides a collaborative, fun and responsive environment where work and home blend rather than just a place of work. High-potential executives are nomadic and will look for work that involves international assignments, cross-functional opportunities and projects that expose them to senior leaders. They will not necessarily want a linear path of promotion and will avoid being siloed into a single function or represented by job titles and organisational charts.[17]

Firms are responding by increasingly taking advantage of the 'gig economy', which, for example, in the United States is predicted to rise from 15.5 million people in 2015 to 60 million by 2020.[18] These types of firms envisage a smaller pool of core full-time employees for fixed functions and buy in on-demand freelancers from a global talent pool of individuals and micro-businesses for their short to medium-term needs. Former employees who leave the firm will become active members of the firm's alumni network and will become a mutual source of contacts and future potential assignments that feed into the new economy. Aside from the concerns of data security, reliability and cultural fit, the gig economy allows firms to scale up or down as needed and offers flexibility on budgets, space and time. Therefore, a 'people first' approach which embodies honesty, empathy, optimism, collaboration and flexibility will be needed to imagine a world from multiple perspectives and those of colleagues, clients and customers, both current and prospective. For internal employees, development-focused conversations will be continuous and although hidden employee ratings will still exist for internal talent mapping purposes, the end-of-year review process with scale-based gradings will firmly become a thing of the past. No longer will employees use the traditional end-of-year appraisal which was designed in the 1970s and be told they 'achieve', 'need improvement' or 'exceed expectations'.[19] Learning will be focused on competencies and behaviours set around developing soft and technical skills, and will mainly be learnt on the job, supplemented by online self-development courses and boot camps delivered by industry professionals such as the General Assembly. Managing talent will become even harder in the future as young people continue to define their own destiny. Given that men represent a larger share of the overall job market, women are set to lose out unless they can increase their participation in areas that are targeted for growth, like technology, engineering and computer science. This is amplified as the pace of ICT an NET creates new ways of working and managing employees, which firms will have to keep pace with.

Overall, the fashion industry is notoriously slow compared to other industries such as the consumer goods industry in adapting new skills, ways of working and leadership development. If firms are to succeed, they will need to quickly adopt new technologies and invest in training, hiring and developing their employees to 'future proof' the firm or risk being left behind. Governments, industry bodies, colleges and workplace training schemes can help in facilitating the most popular workforce strategy, which is to invest in reskilling and retraining current employees whilst simultaneously preparing the younger cohorts of tomorrow through comprehensive leadership development and targeted succession planning. This could take a generation to do if action is not taken immediately, as demand for quality executives already outstrips supply. Because of this, the new generation of talent will vote for themselves where they decide to go and hopefully this does not mean not choosing the fashion industry as a rewarding and lasting career.

Review questions

Questions for debate regarding the future of fashion are as follows:

- What are the advantages and disadvantages of being a technology-driven firm versus a product-driven firm?
- Will we eventually see robots in the boardroom?
- How can privacy be protected in an era of newly emerging technologies?
- Will machines be able to predict fashion trends better than humans?
- Will artificial intelligence eliminate the need for positons like creative directors and human resource professionals?
- What future skills do you think will be crucial to succeed in the fashion industry?

Further reading

1 Mac, R. (2016) 'Stitch Fix: The $250 Million Startup Playing Fashionista Moneyball', *Forbes*, 1 June.
2 IBM (2016) 'Watson', www.ibm.com/watson (accessed 4 May 2017).
3 Chang, J.H. and Huynh, P. (2016) 'ASEAN in Transformation: The Future of Jobs at Risk of Automation', International Labour Organization, www.ilo.org/public/english/dialogue/actemp/downloads/publications/2016/asean_in_transf_2016_r2_future.pdf (accessed 4 May 2017).
4 Murgia, M. (2016) 'Deep Tech Ascent: Europe's Emerging Digital Industries', *Financial Times*, 29 November.
5 Apple Inc. (2016) 'Apple Previews Major Update with MacOS Sierra', www.apple.com/newsroom/2016/06/apple-previews-major-update-with-macos-sierra.html (accessed 4 May 2017).
Microsoft (2016) 'FY16 Q4 MSFT Earnings Conference Call', https://view.officeapps.live.com/op/view.aspx?src=https://c.s-microsoft.com/en-us/CMSFiles/TranscriptFY16Q4.docx?version=2df07fcf-5291-8785-bd4c-1301bae7e555 (accessed 4 May 2017).
6 Iansiti, M. and Lakhani, K.R. (2017) 'The Truth about Blockchain', *Harvard Business Review*, Vol. 95, No. 1, pp. 118–27.
7 Campbell, R. (2016) 'Babyghost and VeChain: Fashion on the Blockchain', *Bitcoin Magazine*, https://bitcoinmagazine.com/articles/babyghost-and-vechain-fashion-on-the-blockchain-1476807653 (accessed 4 May 2017).
8 Intel Corporation (2016) 'Intel Transforms New York Fashion Week with Immersive Tech Experiences', https://newsroom.intel.com/chip-shots/intel-transforms-new-york-fashion-week-immersive-tech-experiences (accessed 4 May 2017).

162 *The future of fashion*

9 World Economic Forum (2016) 'Internet for All: A Framework for Accelerating Internet Access and Adoption', www3.weforum.org/docs/WEF_Internet_for_All_Framework_Accelerating_Internet_Access_Adoption_report_2016.pdf (accessed 4 May 2017).
10 Accenture (2016) 'Accenture Technology Vision 2016 People First: The Primacy of People in a Digital Age', www.accenture.com/us-en/insight-technology-trends-2016 (accessed 4 May 2017).
11 Nottingham Trent University (2015) 'People Check Their Smartphones 85 Times a Day (and They Don't Even Know They're Doing it)', www4.ntu.ac.uk/apps/news/180892-15/People_check_their_smartphones_85_times_a_day_(and_they_dont_even_know_the.aspx (accessed 4 May 2017).
12 Jackson, T. (2016) 'Walpole Luxury Summit 2016: The Americas', London: Walpole.
13 Gray, A. (2016) 'The 10 Skills You Need to Thrive in the Fourth Industrial Revolution', *World Economic Forum*, www.weforum.org/agenda/2016/01/the-10-skills-you-need-to-thrive-in-the-fourth-industrial-revolution (accessed 4 May 2017).
14 Istook. C.L., Little, T.J. and Pechoux, B.L. (2001) 'Innovation Management In Creating New Fashions' in Bruce, M. and Hines. T (eds), *Fashion Marketing: Contemporary Issues*. Oxford: Butterworth-Heinemann.
Bailey, S. and Black, O. (2016) *Mind Gym: Achieve More by Thinking Differently*. New York: HarperCollins.
15 Cooper, R. and Press, M. (1995) *The Design Agenda: A Guide to Successful Design Management*. Chichester: John Wiley & Sons.
Gryskiewicz, S. and Taylor, S. (2007) *Making Creativity Practical: Innovation that Gets Results*. Greensboro: CCL Press.
Jones, C. (1981) *Design Methods: Seeds of Human Futures*. New York: John Wiley.
16 Accenture (2016) 'Accenture Technology Vision 2016 People First: The Primacy of People in a Digital Age', www.accenture.com/us-en/insight-technology-trends-2016 (accessed 4 May 2017).
17 Coats, K. and Codrington, G. (2015) *Leading in a Changing World: Lessons for Future Focused Leaders*. London: TomorrowToday Global Publishing.
18 Accenture (2016) 'Accenture Technology Vision 2016 People First: The Primacy of People in a Digital Age', www.accenture.com/us-en/insight-technology-trends-2016 (accessed 4 May 2017).
19 Deloitte (2017) '2017 Global Human Capital Trends', https://documents.dupress.deloitte.com/HCTrends2017 (accessed 4 May 2017).

Final thoughts

The achievements we have seen today pale in comparison to what the coming decades will bring as we firmly enter a fourth industrial revolution. As fashion continually reflects the world we live in and is in vogue one day and out the next, complex, uncertain and changing environments are the only constant that we can comfortably say are ever more present as there are no rules anymore. With uncertainty comes cautiousness, which can act as a disabler for the firm unless it can act strategically. This book creates a much-needed link in advancing and understanding the practice of strategically analysing the international fashion industry and the firm. In this new context, the focus is on several important topics that are relevant to both students and executives.

The application of theoretical models, analysis of frameworks and real-life examples provides a compelling understanding into the complexity of the workplace and the strategic challenges facing executives in navigating the uniqueness of the industry. Subsequently, I hope it has led you to applying new business ideas, questioning issues that you never thought about before and leads to fruitful debate with smarter choices in the context of your own particular research or career. Moreover, I hope it removes some of the mystery regarding the fashion industry and provides the credit and respect the industry deserves. To conclude, I trust that you have enjoyed reading *Strategic Fashion Management: Concepts, Models and Strategies for Competitive Advantage* as much as I have enjoyed writing it.

Index

10 Corso Como 46
3D Printing 44, 80

A/B testing 87
Abercrombie & Fitch 73
Accenture 156
activist investor 95–96
Adidas 33, 52, 80
Alexander McQueen 12, 140–41
algorithm 9, 31, 52, 80, 87, 99
Alibaba 64
Amazon 9, 33, 48, 130, 135, 150
American Apparel 107
Apple 128, 150
Aquascutum 100
Artificial Intelligence 148–49
Asda 48
ASOS 66
Asprey 97
attribute map 86–87
auction 44, 46, 49, 59, 97–98
augmented reality 154–55

baby boomers 159
Babyghost 152
Balanced Scorecard 38–40
Balenciaga 64
Balmain 94
barriers to entry 48–49
Belstaff 46
Benetton 60
Better Cotton Initiative 7
BHS 86
big data 9
Billionaire Boys Club 21
biomimicry 8
Black Friday 65
Blippar 155
Blockchain 152

blogging 65–66, 133
Bolt Threads 8
Boo.com 45
Boohoo.com 108
Boston Boot Company 57
Bottega Veneta 108
Boyner 32
brainstorming 157
brand: advocacy 59, 68–69; authenticity 64; definition 63; management 62; positioning 70–71; purpose 63–67; value 30, 67
Brazil 22–24
Brexit 10, 110
BRIC countries 19–25
Brioni 15, 94
Brooks Brothers 16
Brunello Cucinelli 55
Burberry 10, 60, 67, 78, 93
business environment 6–13
business model: definition 43; efficiency-centred 48; ephemeral 56–57; networked firm 56; novelty-centred 52; subscription 52; taxonomy 46
business process re-engineering 103–07
buyer power 50

C&A 48
Canada Goose 67, 97
Catalyst 131
Causse 91
Chanel 91
China 9, 14, 20–22
Christian Dior 88, 140
Christian Lacroix 65
Christian Louboutin 70
Christopher Kane 12
Click Frenzy 65
Coach 93–94, 96, 101

Cocosa 45
Collaborative Planning Forecasting and Replenishment 30, 48
Comme Des Garcons 52
comparable analysis 98
comparative advantage 15
competitive advantage 29–30
competitive rivalry 6, 13, 51
competitive strategy 29, 36
concept store 52
conditions precedent 101
Cone Denim 16
consumer: attitudes 68; behaviour 68, 77–78, 87; focus 68; orientated 158–59
Converse 154
copycat 36
core strategic choices 36–37
corporate social responsibility 12–13, 53–54
cost leadership 30, 48–52
creative and design thinking 157–58
Creative Industries Federation 128
Crocs 95
crowdfunding 57
culture: climate 123; definition 123–24; national 127; types 125–28
customer: intimacy 31–32; proposition 80–81
Cyber Monday 65

Debenhams 86
deep learning 150–51
Deloitte 124
Delvaux Createur 94
Designs By Marc 33
despachante 23
Desrues 91
DHL Logistics 46
Diane Von Furstenberg 23
digital and technically minded 156–57
discounted cash flow 99
Disney 67
Dolce & Gabbana 69, 109
Donna Karen 94
Dover Street Market 68
Dow Jones Sustainability Index 13
due diligence 97–101

earnings before interest taxes depreciation and amortisation 98
earn-out provision 100–01
eBay 46, 49
Economic Dividends For Gender Equality 136

economic factors 7
economies of scale 30, 48
economies of scope 30, 48
Edinburgh Woollen Mill 107
El Buen Fin 65
electronic wallets 8
Elie Saab 109
ELIPSE framework 6–13
emerging markets 19–25
enterprise value 99
entrepreneurial activities 15
equal pay 134–36
Erin Fetherston 152
Ermenegildo Zegna 109
Esprit 16
ethical factors 12–13
European Union 10–11
exclusivity period 100

Facebook 65–66, 150–51, 153, 156
facial recognition 8, 151
Faconnable 97
Fair Wear Foundation 7
Farfetch 45
fashion: definition 4; future 148–61; industry characteristics 5; magazines 129–30
fast follower 36
Fendi 88
Ferrari 69
financial management 106–07
First Heritage Brands 94
first-mover 26, 55, 83
Five Forces 48–51
Forever 21 15
France Croco 93
free trade zones 8, 11
French Connection 60

Gap 13, 16, 135
Generation Y 8, 159
Generation Z 8, 66, 159
Gianfranco Ferre 65
gig economy 160
G-III Apparel Group 94
Gilt Groupe 45, 94
Giorgio Armani 100
Givenchy 140
globalisation 10–11, 25–26, 65, 91–92
Gore-Tex 40
government and public policy 9–10
Goyard 68
gross domestic product 10, 19–20, 23–24
Gucci 36, 63–64, 139

166 Index

H&M 87
Hackett 93, 97, 155
Hanes 126
Harrods 31
Harvard Business School 47, 90, 96, 133
Harvey Nichols 130
Hearst Magazines 155
Hermès 68, 70, 93, 102–03
Holacracy 115
Hopi 32
horizontal diversification 105–06
Hudson Bay Company 94
Hugo Boss 23, 154

India 11, 24
Industrial Revolution 6, 162
Information Communications
   Technology 8
initial public offering 97, 108–10
innovation: discontinuous 78–79;
   disruptive 78–79; factors 8–9;
   incremental 78; matrix 77–78; rules
   of engagement 80–85; streams 85–86
Instagram 8, 64, 66, 151, 156
intellectual property 7, 38, 40
International Finance Corporation 12
International Labour Organization 150
Internet 8, 46, 51, 156
intrinsic value 99
Isetan 31

J Crew 65
J.C Penney 95, 127
Jaeger 107
JDA software 46
Jean Paul Gaultier 140
JK Iguatemi 23
John Galliano 62, 139
John Lewis 48, 126
Jumia 45
Just-in-Time 30, 50

Kate Spade 93, 96
Kenneth Cole 95
Kenzo 21
Kering 12, 64, 93–94, 97, 107–08, 140
Key Performance Indicators 35, 39, 58

La Rinascente 31
labour costs 16, 21
Lacoste 52
Lanvin 69
leadership: definition 116–17; presence
   117; qualities 117; styles 117–19

learning curve 37, 75
legal factors 7–8
Lemarié 91
lesbian gay bisexual transgender 128
Levi Strauss & Co 12, 34, 52
Lewis Turning Point 21
Li & Fung 30
Li Ning 60
Loro Piana 94
Lululemon 158

Macy's 10, 95
Made in America 16
Made in England 15
Made in Italy 15
Maison Lesage 91
Maison Margiela 38
management: objectives 113–14; schools
   of thought 113–14
Marc Jacobs 52, 139
marketing: cultural 69–70; experiential
   73; mix 70; positioning 70–71;
   segmentation 68; strategy formulation
   72–73; target market 69–70
Marks & Spencer 86
marriage bars 131
Matahari 31
Mayhoola for Investments 94
McKinsey & Company 5, 131
mega cities 25
mergers and acquisitions: agreement
   in principle 102; bidding process
   99–102; deal dynamics 98–99;
   definition 91; exclusivity period 100;
   exit strategies 108–10; key players 94;
   regulators 102; secrecy 102; sponsor
   firm 97; syndicating 101; synergy
   100, 105, 108, 110–11; target firm 97;
   transactions 94–95
Michael Kors 65, 96
Millennials 8, 64, 66, 119, 155, 159
minimum wage 15
Ministry of Defence 46
mission statement 34
Miu Miu 23
mobile commerce 8, 48
Modanisa 71–72
Modern Meadow 8
Moët Hennessy Louis Vuitton 68, 91,
   94, 102–03
Moncler 108
Montex 91
Moore's Law 148
Moschino 69

Mountain Warehouse 110
Moynat 67–68
MTailor 52
Myntra 32

N.Peal 64
Nasty Gal 45
nearshoring 16
Neiman Marcus 110
Net Promoter Score 69
Net-A-Porter 33, 102, 108
network effects 49, 78
New Look 159
Newly Emerging Technologies 148
Next Directory 46
Next Eleven countries 25–26
Nike 31, 33, 62–63, 125
non-governmental organisations 7
Nordstrom 84, 128
North American Free Trade Agreement 11

office politics 80, 104–105, 120
omni-channel retailing 47
operational excellence 30–31
Organisation For Economic Co-Operation And Development 23, 134

Paraffection 91
parallel trade 7
Patagonia 55, 136
Paul Smith 100, 155
pay gap 135–36
People For The Ethical Treatment of Animals 12
Pepe Jeans 97
personalisation 57, 150–51, 158
philanthropy 12–13, 53–54
Pierre Corthay 151
Pinterest 8, 66, 149
political factors 9–10
pop-up retailing 46, 52, 76
Porsche Design 69
Prabal Gurung 152
Prada 9, 50, 109, 114
precedent transaction analysis 98
predictive analytics 99
Primark 39
product leadership 31
productivity 14–15
prospectus 109–10
Puma 107
punctuated equilibrium 79

PVH 13, 91, 94
PwC 19

Quality Function Deployment 68
quick response code 8, 152

Radio Frequency Identification 48, 76, 151
Rag & Bone 16
Ralph Lauren 9, 13, 84
rapid prototyping 75, 87, 157
Rebecca Minkoff 109, 135
regional drift 21
Rent The Runway 47
resource allocation 81–82
Richard James 52
Richemont 97
Rick Owens 67
risk management 9
Robert Clergerie 94
Roberto Cavalli 107–08
robots 148–150
Ross Stores 131
Russia 10, 22

Saint Laurent 4, 64, 130
Saks Fifth Avenue 94
Sarbanes-Oxley Act 8
Savile Row 10, 52
Selfridges 130
senior leadership teams: activities 121; conflict 120; purpose 119–22
Sewbo 150
Shandong Ruyi 94
shared value 53–55
ShoeBuy 57
Shop Direct 88
showrooming 47
Singles Day 65
small and medium sized enterprises 15
SMCP 94
Snapchat 8, 66, 151
snowflake theory 69
social factors 10–12
social media 8, 65–66, 98
Soma Analytics 146
Sonia Rykiel 94, 106
Sports Direct 132
Stella McCartney 12, 70, 136
Stitch Fix 148–49
Stone Island 67
strategic alignment 58–60
strategic choices 36

168 *Index*

strategic congruence 58–60
strategic gateways 26
strategic learning process 36
strategic planning 33–35, 104
strategic vision 34
strategists 29–30, 34–35, 62, 72
strategy: definition 28; development 32–34; emergent 35; implementation 36–38; prescriptive 34; types 29
Stuart Weitzman 94, 101
substitutes 50–51
supplier power 50
supply and demand 5
supply chain 7, 10–13, 16, 48, 50, 91, 121, 152, 158
Supreme 52
sustainability 12–13, 16, 54, 152

T.M. Lewin 97
talent management 159–61
Tannerie d'Annonay 93
Tannerie Limoges 50
Tannerie Mégisserie Hervy 50
Taobao 32
technical singularity 149
Ted Baker 155
term sheet 101–02
Tesco 48
The American Research And Development Corporation 90
The Blonde Salad 66
The Dandy Lab 76
The Jones Group 95
The North Face 126
The Warnaco Group 94
Timberland 94
Tmall 46
Tod's 12
Tom Ford 63, 139
Tomas Maier 108
Tommy Hilfiger 60
TOMS 56
Topshop 33, 154
Tory Burch 69
transaction cost economics 48
Transparency International Corruption Index 22
True Religion Apparel 94
Trunk Club 46
Twitter 65–66

Under Armour 78
Uniqlo 15

United States 9, 14, 16, 19–20
Urban Outfitters 132

Valentino Fashion Group 94
value: definition 30; drivers 13–17, 58–60; proposition 30–32
value chain 29–30, 46, 52–53, 56–57, 92–93
value linkage model 58–60
value net 30–32
Vendor Managed Inventory 48
Vente-Privée 46
Versace 92, 102, 107
vertical diversification 106
vertical integration 48, 92–93
Vestiaire Collective 104
VF Corporation 30, 91, 94
Victoria's Secret 73
Viktor & Rolf 140
Vilebrequin 94
virtual reality 152–54
visual identity 69–70
Vogue 65, 114, 129
voice activated commerce 151–52
voice activated services 150–51
Voice of The Consumer 68
VUCA 142

W.L Gore & Associates 40
Walmart 16
Warnaco Group 94
wearable technology 50, 77–79
WeChat 8
weighted average cost of capital 99
WGSN 46
work-life: strategies 141–46; stress 139–40
workplace: diversity 128–30; inclusion 130–34; pay differential 134–36
workplace skills 155–61
World Bank 13
World Economic Forum 6, 134, 157
World Trade Organisation 11, 22

YGM Trading 100
YKM 32
Yoox 13, 108

Zalando 45
Zappos 115
Zara 56